All About Lawns

Created and designed by the
editorial staff of ORTHO Books

Project Editor
Alice E. Mace

Writer
Michael MacCaskey

Designers
Craig Bergquist
Christine Dunham

Illustrators
Ebet Dudley
Ron Hildebrand
Ronda Hildebrand

Ortho Books

Publisher
Robert L. Iacopi

Editorial Director
Min S. Yee

Managing Editors
Jim Beley
Anne Coolman
Susan Lammers
Michael D. Smith
Sally W. Smith

Production Director
Ernie S. Tasaki

Editors
Richard H. Bond
Alice E. Mace

System Manager
Christopher Banks

System Consultant
Mark Zielinski

Asst. System Managers
Linda Bouchard
William F. Yusavage

Photographic Director
Alan Copeland

Photographers
Laurie A. Black
Richard A. Christman

Asst. Production Manager
Darcie S. Furlan

Associate Editor
Jill Fox

Production Editors
Don Mosley
Anne Pederson

Chief Copy Editor
Rebecca Pepper

Photo Editors
Kate O'Keeffe
Pam Peirce

National Sales Manager
Charles H. Aydelotte

Sales Associate
Susan B. Boyle

Operations Assistant
Gail L. Davis

Administrative Assistant
Georgiann Wright

Address all inquiries to
Ortho Books
Chevron Chemical Company
Consumer Products Division
575 Market Street
San Francisco, CA 94105

Copyright © 1985
Chevron Chemical Company
All rights reserved under
international and Pan-American
copyright conventions.

First Printing in July, 1985

    4 5 6 7 8 9
   87 88 89 90

ISBN 0-89721-063-8

Library of Congress Catalog Card
Number 85-070880

Contributing Editors
Scott R. Millard
Lance Walheim

Major Photographers
William Aplin
Michael Landis

Additional Photographers
*Listed by page numbers and
positions (T = top, C = cen-
ter, B = bottom, L = left,
R = right)*
Laurie Black: 21, 33B, 34TL,
    34TR, 45, 47
Robert J. Black: 33T
Bartow H. Bridges, Jr.: 58B
Dick Christman: back cover BR
Josephine Coatsworth: 48
Al Crozier: 60BL
Clyde Elmore: 59BL
Barbara H. Emerson: 58T
M. Ali Harivandi: 61TL
Michael McKinley: 23, 97
Pam Peirce: 9C, 10T, 12T
James Lee Sikkema: 54, 81B
Richard W. Smiley: 73
Arvil R. Stark: 65, 81T
Wolf von dem Bussche: 96
Ortho Photo Library: front cover,
    50, 88, 89, 90, 92, 93, 94, 95,
    98, 99, 100, 101, 105

Consultants
Dr. James B. Beard
Department of Soil & Crop
    Science
Texas A&M University
College Station, TX

Dr. E.O. Burt
University of Florida
Fort Lauderdale, FL

Dr. Jack Butler
Colorado State University
Fort Collins, CO

Dr. J.A. Crozier
Chevron Chemical Company
San Francisco, CA

Dr. M. Ali Harivandi
Cooperative Extension
University of California,
    Berkeley

Dr. Henry Indyk
Soils and Crops Department
Cook College, Rutgers
    University
New Brunswick, NJ

Dr. Jeff Krans
Mississippi State University
Mississippi State, MS

Prof. Kent Kurtz
California State Polytechnic
    University
Pomona, CA

Patricia Kurtz
Pomona, CA

Dr. William Meyer
Turf-Seed Inc.
Hubbard, OR

Robert C. O'Knefski
Cooperative Extension Agent
Nassau County
Garden City, NY

J.F. Shoulders
Extension Specialist, Turf
Department of Agronomy
Virginia Polytechnic Institute
    and State University
Blacksburg, VA

Mr. Ralph White
Southern Turf Nurseries
Tifton, GA

Dr. V.B. Youngner
Botany and Plant Sciences
    Department
University of California
Riverside, CA

Special Thanks to
Big Four Rents
Santa Rosa, CA

Boething Treeland Nursery
Woodland Hills, CA

Robyn Brode

Dr. Glenn Burton

Cal Turf
Camarillo, CA

City College of San Francisco
Department of Ornamental
    Horticulture

Cornell University
Department of Ornamental
    Horticulture
Ithaca, NY

Bob Cowden

The DeGeorgio's
Rutherford, CA

Ed Fack

Ferry-Morse Seed Co.
Mountain View, CA

Four Seasons Landscaping
St. Helena, CA

The Grass Farm
Morgan Hill, CA

Irv Jacobs
JDM Landscaping
Lodi, CA

Howard Kaerwer

Melinda Levine

Elinor Lindheimer

Frank Mackaness

Jean T. Michels

James F. Miller

Mr. Miller

Ken Vander Molen

Pat Montandon

John S. Nakanishi

Matthew Narog

Ellie and Lem Osborne

Pacific Weather Center
Richmond, B.C., Canada

Jim Patterson

Dr. Charles H. Peacock

Ralph Pinkus

Richard Post

Pursley Grass Sod Farms
Palmetto, FL

Rutgers University
New Brunswick, NJ

Suzanne Sherman

Silverado Country Club
Napa, CA

Dr. C. Richard Skogley

Southern Turf Nurseries, Inc.
Tifton, GA

Chester Spiering

Dr. Arvil L. Stark

Dr. K.D. Taylor

Bill Titus

Mr. and Mrs. C.J. Traverse

Dr. A.J. Turgeon

Van Winden Landscaping
Napa, CA

Warren's Turf
Fairfield, CA

F. Wiebel

Alfred Wilsey

Dr. Frank Wooding

Chevron Chemical Company
575 Market Street, San Francisco, CA 94105

All About Lawns

Choosing the Right Grass   5

The Practical Landscape ■ Development of Lawn Grasses ■ Anatomy of a Grass Plant ■ Climate and Grass Growth ■ A Gallery of Grasses ■ The Cultivar Charts ■ Lawn Grass Comparisons

Installing a Lawn   21

Preparing for a New Lawn ■ How to Take a Soil Test ■ Soil Amendments ■ Seed Lawns ■ A Sample Seed Label ■ Seed Facts ■ Germination to Establishment ■ Sprig and Plug Lawns ■ The Paving-Block Lawn ■ Sod Lawns

Lawn Care   41

Watering ■ About Hoses ■ Portable Sprinklers ■ Underground Sprinkler Systems ■ Mowing ■ Lawn Mowers ■ Fertilizing ■ A Sample Fertilizer Label ■ Fertilizer Worksheet ■ Sprayers and Spreaders ■ Weeds ■ Insects and Other Pests ■ Diseases and Cultural Problems ■ Trees in the Lawn ■ Renovating

Lawns in Your Area   87

Specific Recommendations for the United States and Canada ■ Soil and Climate ■ Recommended Grasses ■ Where to Get Your Soil Tested ■ Where to Get More Information on Lawns ■ Regional Lawn Calendars

Appendix 108 ■ Index 110

Choosing the Right Grass

Lawns are the nation's most popular ground cover. There are many types from which to choose. Look for the one that best suits your climate, needs, and ideas of what a lawn should be.

Lawns are different things to different people. To some, a lawn is a pleasant backdrop for a home landscape. It ties together the surrounding flowers, trees, and shrubs. Flower colors seem more vivid when they border a complementary green lawn. The lush, meadowlike carpet lightens and softens spacious areas between trees and shrubs in a yard.

Others think of a lawn as an outdoor living room during warm weather. Lawns bring memories of children running through sprinklers, family barbecues and picnics, suntanning, reading, or just dozing on a soft bed of grass. Maybe it is the soothing color or the uniform texture that induces the special appeal of a lawn. Whatever the attraction, a well-kept lawn possesses a certain mystique.

The Practical Landscape
Many homeowners are unabashedly proud of being able to grow a handsome lawn. You have seen them in their yards every weekend, carefully mowing, watering, and watching for weeds. As they know, growing a lawn can be a rewarding venture in gardening, even in the early stages. Lawns are relatively fast growing and give you the pleasure of a new landscape in a matter of weeks. And with proper care, your lawn will last for years.

Lawns, like trees and shrubs, can be an investment in a home. Any realtor knows the value of a landscaped yard. The lawn is often the "calm" area in a landscape, the picture frame that

◄ *There is nothing quite like an expanse of fresh green lawn—it's the perfect backdrop for summer daydreams.*

displays the house and other outdoor features. Neighbors also enjoy living next to a home with an attractive lawn.

Lawns benefit home landscapes in many environmental ways as well. When it is hot, a lawn reduces glare from the sun and keeps the surrounding area cooler. When it is windy, the blades of grass trap particles of dust. When it is rainy, a lawn stabilizes soil and prevents erosion problems.

The Successful Lawn
The first step toward a successful lawn is knowing what you want. Do you need durability for children's games or softness for that perfect display look?

Once you know how you want to use your lawn, it is easier to choose the type of grass that is just right for you.

Also think about how much time you want to spend taking care of a lawn. Check descriptive and cultural information about different grasses in the gallery section beginning on page 8. The regionalized chapter, "Lawns in Your Area," beginning on page 87, may be especially helpful to you. Divided by states and regions of the country, it guides you to those grasses that are recommended for your area.

By doing a little homework, and a little outdoor work, too, you can have the lawn that you have always wanted.

You don't have to tell kids about the pleasures of going barefoot, especially when it comes to playing lawn games.

Development of Lawn Grasses

Grasses have been around for centuries. In fact, the grasses that we use today for lawns evolved in sun-filled prairies and meadows, where they were grazed by large animals. The densely formed grasses that survived in these ecosystems were those that had growing points so low that grazers did not eat them.

Today, the descendants of these grasses exist as dense, low-growing plants that, collectively, we call lawns. Present lawn grasses tolerate the lawn mower as if it were a grazing animal.

During the Middle Ages, shortened grasses became popular for gardens, picnic areas, and sporting events. At first, the grasses were pounded with mallets and trampled by foot to keep them ''mowed.'' Later, scythes were employed for a more even cut.

Today's lawn grasses are a far cry from those of medieval times. They are dense and even textured, resist insects and diseases, tolerate high and low temperatures, and compete vigorously with weeds.

Anatomy and Growth

A lawn is made up of thousands of individual grass plants. Like any other plant, specific conditions must be met for proper growth to occur. When each plant is completely healthy, the lawn has the look of a rolled-out carpet.

Lawn grasses grow from the *crown*, which lies next to the ground. As long as the crown is not injured, the plant tolerates having its blades cut without pausing in its growth.

Below the crown is an underground system of fibrous *roots*. The roots absorb water and nutrients and anchor the plant.

Extending upward from the crown is the *primary shoot*. This is the first stem that develops from a seedling. The primary shoot consists of the blades, collar, sheath, nodes, and internodes.

The *blade* and *sheath* together make up the leaf. As the plant grows, the sheath remains wrapped around the stem while the blade flattens out and points upward. A narrow band called the *collar* marks the spot where the sheath and blade meet.

Blades and sheaths originate from bulbous joints called *nodes*. The portions of stem between nodes are the *internodes*. Several blades, sheaths, nodes, and internodes can exist on a primary shoot; nodes and internodes are also present on spreading stems.

Tillers, shoots that grow from the crown beside the primary shoot, make a lawn thick and full. While tiller growth is apparent in all grasses, bunch grasses have especially heavy tiller activity. Bunch grasses—such as the ryegrasses and the chewings, hard, and tall fescues—form clumps that expand to fill a lawn. Creeping grasses spread by stems that extend from the parent plant. These creeping stems are known as *rhizomes* if they travel below the ground and *stolons* (or *runners*) if they travel above the ground. Some creeping grasses, such as Kentucky bluegrass and red fescue, spread by rhizomes; some, such as St. Augustine grass and centipedegrass, spread by stolons; others, such as Bermudagrass and zoysiagrass, spread by rhizomes *and* stolons.

Both rhizomes and stolons produce new plants when they travel along or under the ground. A *secondary shoot*, similar to the primary shoot, develops when a node roots and sprouts along a rhizome or stolon.

Anatomy of a Grass Plant

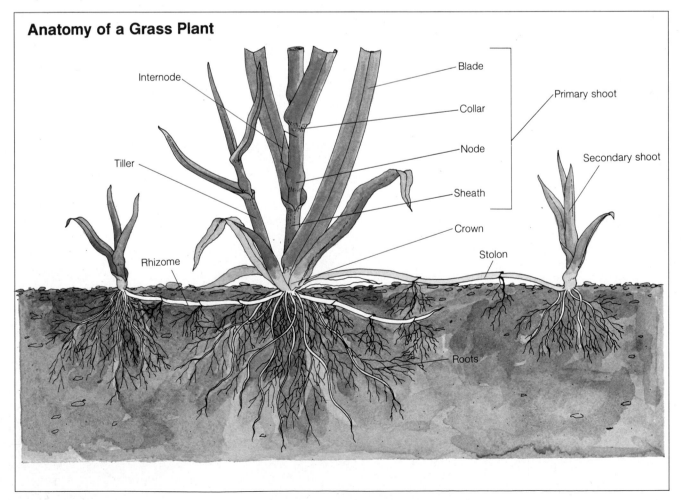

Internode · Blade · Collar · Primary shoot · Node · Tiller · Secondary shoot · Sheath · Crown · Rhizome · Stolon · Roots

Climate and Grass Growth

To the right is a turfgrass climate map. At best, all climate maps reflect generalities. Local conditions vary in precipitation, temperature extremes, altitude, land slope, and soil types. These local characteristics, as well as maintenance practices, play an important role in selecting a grass.

Grasses are categorized either as cool season or warm season. *Warm-season* grasses are best adapted to the southern part of the United States. They grow vigorously in the warm summer months, then become dormant, turning brown in cold weather. Warm-season grasses do not thrive in cold climates. Common warm-season grasses are Bermudagrass, bahia-grass, centipedegrass, St. Augustine grass, and zoysiagrass. Buffalograss and blue grama are warm-season grasses that tolerate cold climates.

Cool-season grasses grow well in the North, at high elevations in the South, and in those parts of the country that have winter snow cover. They grow actively in the cool weather of spring and fall, and slowly in summer heat. With ample water they will remain green the year around. In warm climates a cool-season grass is often seeded over a dormant warm-season grass lawn as a temporary grass during the winter months; it does not survive intense summer heat. Kentucky bluegrass, fescue, bentgrass, and ryegrass are cool-season grasses.

If you are in a location that borders two or more zones, you may have questions about which zone applies to your area. Check with your local nursery or county extension service.

Zone 1—Cold and Humid: This zone includes the northeastern United States and southeastern Canada. It is an area of abundant rainfall and acid soil. Summers are hot and humid; winters are cold and snowy. Cool-season grasses, such as Kentucky bluegrass, bentgrass, and fine fescue, predominate. Zoysiagrass lawns are occasionally found in southern portions of the Atlantic Coast.

Zone 2—Cold Winters and Summer Rains: The midwestern United States and central Canada make up this zone. Soil is not as acid, and there is less rainfall than in zone 1. The soil in zone 2 is more acid than in zone

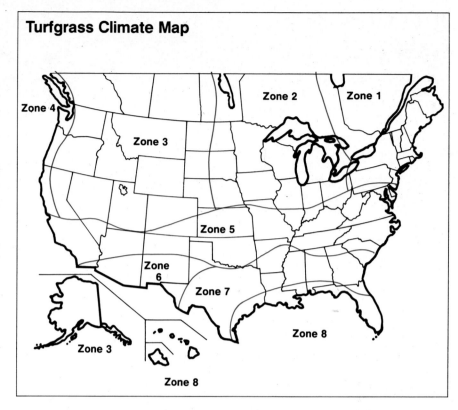

Turfgrass Climate Map

3, but the winters are less cold. Summers are warm and humid. With the exception of a few zoysiagrass lawns in the southern portion of this zone, cool-season grasses, such as those grown in zone 1, predominate.

Zone 3—Cold and Arid: This zone comprises the Great Plains States, including parts of Colorado. This area is subject to drying winds and has relatively little rain. Here grasses are subject to the widest temperature fluctuations in the country. Cool-season grasses are used where they can be watered. Native grasses, such as buffalograss and wheatgrass, are preferred on non-irrigated sites because of their drought tolerance and tenacity. The intermountain area supports fine fescues.

Zone 4—Cool and Humid: This is the Pacific Northwest, west of the Cascade Range. Rain is plentiful and soil is typically acid. Lawns seeded from cool-season grasses—bentgrass, bluegrass, fine fescue, and ryegrass—stay a beautiful green all year long. Compared with the Northeast, both summers and winters are milder.

Zone 5—Variable: In this transition zone, which runs across the entire United States, the major grass climates overlap, depending on many local factors. Both warm-season and cool-season grasses are common. It is

critical to select the appropriate grass type, since neither cool-season nor warm-season grasses adapt ideally in many areas. Tall fescue and zoysiagrass make good lawns in many areas of this zone.

Zone 6—Hot and Dry Summers: This zone comprises the arid Southwest, where rainfall is low and temperatures are high. All lawns here need some supplemental irrigation. Soil is usually alkaline. Lawns are primarily Bermudagrass with some St. Augustine grass and zoysiagrass. Buffalograss is sometimes used in northern low-maintenance areas.

Zone 7—Hot and Humid: Most lawns in this zone are made up of warm-season grasses, such as Bermudagrass, St. Augustine grass, centipedegrass, and zoysiagrass. Rainfall is high and summers are warm and humid.

Zone 8—Tropical: This zone includes the Gulf Coast states, southern Florida, and much of Hawaii. It is essentially a tropical climate; rainfall can be as high as 70 to 80 inches annually. Too much water is as much a problem here as too little water in the Southwest. In especially wet soil, carpetgrass is a good choice. Centipedegrass, Bermudagrass, bahiagrass, and St. Augustine grass make good lawns throughout this region. Zoysiagrass grows well in most parts of this zone.

A Gallery of Grasses

The 16 major grasses described in the following pages are found throughout the United States. While the gallery describes which grasses are best adapted to particular areas, it is only intended as a guide. Note the different recommendations for mowing and fertilization rates. These two differences are tip-offs to whether grasses require high or low maintenance: Those requiring short mowing and frequent, heavy fertilization are for dedicated lawn owners only.

Recent Breakthroughs

With advances in turfgrass breeding, new and improved *cultivars*—or cultivated varieties—are continually being made available. Improved cultivars, with resistance to diseases and insects and tolerance to adverse conditions, replace older cultivars each year. 'Merion' Kentucky bluegrass, for example, used to be the best Kentucky bluegrass cultivar. Now other Kentucky bluegrass cultivars surpass the qualities of 'Merion'. Cultivars are listed under each grass type or in the cultivar charts beginning on page 14.

The best of the improved Kentucky bluegrasses have dramatically increased their disease resistance compared with common bluegrass types. Some tolerate low mowing (to ¾ inch), compared to the 2 to 3 inches required for the older types. The chart beginning on page 14 describes the best Kentucky bluegrass cultivars.

Turf-type perennial ryegrasses are now a common component in seed mixtures. Improved cultivars are more persistent, are more compatible with Kentucky bluegrass and fine fescue in both color and texture, and are cleaner mowing than earlier cultivars. (Common perennial ryegrass has frayed tips that brown after mowing.) Because the most recent cultivars have retained the ability to start fast like common perennial ryegrass, they have been dubbed "crisis grass" by lawn professionals. Many turf-type perennial ryegrass cultivars are described on pages 17 and 18.

Tall fescue cultivars have also been improved recently. Many are darker green than earlier cultivars, have finer blades, and have a better tolerance of cold and disease. In many areas that use cool-season grasses, tall fescue is becoming more popular than Kentucky bluegrass and turf-type perennial ryegrass. Some of the tall fescue cultivars are described on pages 16 and 17.

The lawn grass you choose will have a great effect on the success of your lawn. Select a grass that is adapted to your area and that will match the type of use you expect it will receive. (Above: Turfgrass researchers compare different grasses.)

Index to Lawn Grasses

Check the turfgrass climate map on page 7 and the regional chapter beginning on page 87 for recommendations for your area.

Cool-Season Grasses	Page
Bentgrass, Creeping	8
Bluegrass, Kentucky	9
Bluegrass, Rough	9
Fescue, Chewings	9
Fescue, Hard	10
Fescue, Red or Creeping Red	10
Fescue, Tall	10
Ryegrass, Annual or Italian	11
Ryegrass, Turf-Type Perennial	11

Warm-Season Grasses	Page
Bahiagrass	11
Bermudagrass, Common	12
Bermudagrass, Improved	12
Centipedegrass	12
Dichondra	13
St. Augustine Grass	13
Zoysiagrass	13

Creeping Bentgrass

COOL-SEASON GRASS

Scientific Name: *Agrostis palustris*

Strengths: The grass of choice in cool climates for golf-course putting greens, lawn bowling, and similar uses. Should be mowed quite low.

Weaknesses: Requires low mowing or else it quickly builds an extensive thatch layer. Like all bentgrasses, creeping bentgrass is susceptible to several diseases.

Shade Tolerance: Somewhat tolerant, but best in full sun.

Water Needs: High. Poor drought tolerance.

Fertilizer Needs: Medium to high. For highest quality, needs 0.5 to 1.0 pound of actual nitrogen per 1,000 square feet per growing month for highest quality.

Wearability: Fair.

Mowing Height: Keep low, between ¼ and 1 inch.

Best Adapted: Grows without special care in the moist soils of the northern United States and Canada. Extensively used in the Pacific Northwest and the Northeast.

Cultivars: 'Penncross' is quick to establish and repairs itself quickly. Start 'Penncross', 'Emerald', 'Seaside', 'Prominent', and 'Penneagle' from seed. Start 'Cohansey' and 'Congressional' from sprigs.

Kentucky Bluegrass

COOL-SEASON GRASS

Scientific Name: *Poa pratensis*

Strengths: Easy to grow where adapted. Improved type has better resistance to such diseases as leaf spot, stripe smut, and summer patch. Many improved cultivars available. Seed is inexpensive.

Weaknesses: Common type suffers from summer heat or if mowed too short. Also disease prone. Improved type usually requires higher maintenance: more fertilizer and more dethatching.

Shade Tolerance: Varies. Improved in some cultivars.

Water Needs: Medium to high. Common type recovers from drought, but most improved cultivars are drought sensitive.

Fertilizer Needs: Medium to high. Needs 0.4 to 0.8 pound of actual nitrogen per 1,000 square feet per growing month. Some improved cultivars do well on as little as 0.25 pound if established in good soil.

Wearability: Varies. Improved in some cultivars.

Mowing Height: Between 1½ to 3 inches or more in summer.

Best Adapted: East of the Cascade Range, the Sierra Nevada, and the Rocky Mountains; the North Central and northeastern states; the mountains and piedmont of the upper South.

Cultivars: See pages 14 and 15.

Rough Bluegrass

COOL-SEASON GRASS

Scientific Name: *Poa trivialis*

Strengths: Likes wet, shady areas. Excellent component of shady lawn mixtures due to excellent shade tolerance.

Weaknesses: Shallow root system that does not tolerate drought. Contaminates Kentucky bluegrass and perennial ryegrass in sunny areas.

Shade Tolerance: Excellent, provided moisture is adequate.

Water Needs: High; watering necessary during drought.

Fertilizer Needs: Low to medium. Between 0.3 to 0.5 pound of actual nitrogen per 1,000 square feet per growing month.

Wearability: Poor.

Mowing Height: 1 to 2 inches.

Best Adapted: Wet, shaded sites in the northern states.

Cultivars: 'Sabre', 'Colt'.

Chewings Fescue

COOL-SEASON GRASS

Scientific Name: *Festuca rubra* var. *commutata*

Strengths: Tolerates close mowing in cool climates. Usually persistent in mixtures or blends with Kentucky bluegrass.

Weaknesses: Same as red fescue. Competitiveness can be a disadvantage in mixtures with Kentucky bluegrass.

Shade Tolerance: Same as red fescue.

Water Needs: Low.

Fertilizer Needs: Low to medium. About 0.1 to 0.5 pound of actual nitrogen per 1,000 square feet per growing month.

Wearability: Same as red fescue. May also form clumps.

Mowing Height: About 1 to 2½ inches.

Best Adapted: Same as red fescue.

Cultivars: See pages 15 and 16.

Hard Fescue

COOL-SEASON GRASS

Scientific Name: *Festuca ovina* var. *duriuscula*

Strengths: Improved performance compared to other fine fescues. Better tolerance to heat, drought, leaf spot, anthracnose, red thread, and dollar spot. Good shade adaptation.

Weaknesses: Slower to establish compared with chewings and red fescue.

Shade Tolerance: Excellent for well-drained soils.

Water Needs: Good drought tolerance.

Fertilizer Needs: Low. Needs 0.1 to 0.3 pound of actual nitrogen per 1,000 square feet per growing month.

Wearability: Fair.

Mowing Height: About 1 to 2½ inches.

Best Adapted: Where summer nighttime temperatures are moderate.

Cultivars: See pages 15 and 16.

Red Fescue, Creeping Red Fescue

COOL-SEASON GRASS

Scientific Name: *Festuca rubra rubra*

Strengths: Frequent component of bluegrass mixture. Blends well and does what some bluegrasses cannot do—grows well in shade or drought-dry soil. Fine texture, deep green color. Tolerates acid soil. Preferable to chewings fescue in a mix.

Weaknesses: Very susceptible to summer diseases in hot climates, especially in moist, fertile soil.

Shade Tolerance: Usually the best cool-season grass for dry, shady lawns.

Water Needs: Good drought tolerance.

Fertilizer Needs: Low to medium. Needs 0.1 to 0.5 pound of actual nitrogen per 1,000 square feet per growing month.

Wearability: Poor. Fine fescues are slow to recover if damaged.

Mowing Height: Normally, mow 1½ to 2½ inches. After establishment it can be left unmowed for a "meadow look."

Best Adapted: Where summers are cool, such as in the coastal northwest or at high elevations. Good in the Great Lakes region.

Cultivars: See pages 15 and 16.

Tall Fescue

COOL-SEASON GRASS

Scientific Name: *Festuca arundinacea*

Strengths: A good, tough play lawn. Some disease and insect resistance. Green all year. Good transition-zone grass..

Weaknesses: Medium to coarse textured, tends to clump. If used in mixtures, must predominate.

Shade Tolerance: Good.

Water Needs: Good drought tolerance if infrequent waterings are 10 to 12 inches deep.

Fertilizer Needs: Low to medium. Needs 0.1 to 0.5 pound of actual nitrogen per 1,000 square feet per growing month.

Wearability: Good in spring and fall when growth is fast. Less acceptable in summer.

Mowing Height: High—about 2 to 3 inches.

Best Adapted: The best cool-season grass for transition areas. Tolerates heat.

Cultivars: Many new turf-types are available. See pages 16 and 17.

Annual Ryegrass, Italian Ryegrass

COOL-SEASON GRASS

Scientific Name: *Lolium multiflorum*

Strengths: Fast germinating, quick to establish. Use as a temporary planting.

Weaknesses: Poor cold and heat tolerance. Does not mow clean. Some perennial ryegrass seed is usually mixed with annual rye, which grows in weedy clumps. Not recommended for permanent lawns; lasts for one year only.

Shade Tolerance: Poor to medium.

Water Needs: High.

Fertilizer Needs: Low to medium. Needs 0.3 to 0.5 pound of actual nitrogen per 1,000 square feet per growing month.

Wearability: Medium.

Mowing Height: Around 1½ to 2 inches.

Best Adapted: Same as perennial ryegrass. Use for overseeding dormant Bermudagrass.

Cultivars: No turf-types.

Turf-Type Perennial Ryegrass

COOL-SEASON GRASS

Scientific Name: *Lolium perenne*

Strengths: Fast seed germination and establishment. Compatible in mixtures with Kentucky bluegrass and fine fescues. Greater persistence than common perennial ryegrass. Cleaner mowing. Improved heat and cold tolerance. Tough play lawn.

Weaknesses: Suffers from winterkill in coldest climates. If it equals more than 20 percent of a seed mix, it impairs establishment of the other grasses.

Shade Tolerance: Medium.

Water Needs: High.

Fertilizer Needs: Low to medium. Apply between 0.3 to 0.5 pound of actual nitrogen per 1,000 square feet per growing month.

Wearability: Very good.

Mowing Height: 1 to 2 inches.

Best Adapted: Coastal regions with mild winters and cool, moist summers. Excellent for overseeding dormant Bermudagrass in the South below the adaptation line.

Cultivars: See pages 17 and 18.

Bahiagrass

WARM-SEASON GRASS

Scientific Name: *Paspalum notatum*

Strengths: Low maintenance. Extensive root system valued for erosion control and drought tolerance. Moderately aggressive.

Weaknesses: Forms a coarse, open lawn. Tall, fast-growing seed stalks need frequent mowing to remain attractive. Considered a weed if it occurs in another warm-season grass lawn. May turn yellow from chlorosis. Dollar spot and especially mole crickets may be problems.

Shade Tolerance: Fair to good.

Water Needs: Good drought resistance, but performs best where rain is plentiful and evenly distributed over the season.

Fertilizer Needs: Medium. Needs 0.5 pound of actual nitrogen per 1,000 square feet per growing month.

Wearability: Good.

Mowing Height: High, between 2 and 3 inches.

Best Adapted: Infertile, sandy soils. Central coast of North Carolina to eastern Texas. Popular in Florida.

Cultivars: 'Argentine', 'Pensacola'.

Common Bermudagrass

WARM-SEASON GRASS

Scientific Name: *Cynodon dactylon*

Strengths: Likes heat, easy to grow in most soils, and takes considerable abuse. The most widely adapted warm-season grass. Requires little maintenance. Makes a good lawn when given extra care.

Weaknesses: Invasive, has poor shade tolerance, often browns in fall until spring.

Shade Tolerance: Poor.

Water Needs: Drought tolerant.

Fertilizer Needs: Medium to high. Needs 0.5 to 1.0 pound of actual nitrogen per 1,000 square feet per growing month.

Wearability: Outstanding.

Mowing Height: From ¾ to 1½ inches.

Best Adapted: Lower elevations of the Southwest, Maryland to Florida in the East, then west to Kansas, Oklahoma, and Texas.

Cultivars: Common, sometimes called Arizona common.

Improved Bermudagrass

WARM-SEASON GRASS

Scientific Name: *Cynodon* species

Strengths: Most of the same virtues of common Bermudagrass, but softer, more dense, and finer textured. Generally shorter dormant season.

Weaknesses: More water, fertilizer, and mowing needed compared with common Bermudagrass. May require regular thatch control.

Shade Tolerance: Extremely intolerant of shade.

Water Needs: Relatively drought tolerant, but needs somewhat more water than common Bermudagrass.

Fertilizer Needs: Medium to high. Needs 0.7 to 1.0 pound or more of actual nitrogen per 1,000 square feet per growing month.

Wearability: Excellent.

Mowing Height: ½ to 1 inch.

Best Adapted: Popular in the South and Southwest, on the East Coast from around Long Island south to Raleigh, then northwest to mid-Kansas.

Cultivars: See chart on page 14.

Centipedegrass

WARM-SEASON GRASS

Scientific Name: *Eremochloa ophiuroides*

Strengths: Makes a good low-maintenance, general-purpose lawn. Adapts to poor soil. Aggressive enough to crowd out weeds. Needs less mowing than most grasses. Resistance to chinch bugs and *rhizoctonia;* provides an alternative to St. Augustine grass.

Weaknesses: Coarse textured. Has light green color. Tends to yellow from chlorosis. Sensitive to low temperatures. Builds thatch if too much nitrogen is used.

Shade Tolerance: Fair.

Water Needs: Shallow root system is sensitive to drought.

Fertilizer Needs: Low. Needs 0.1 to 0.3 pounds of actual nitrogen per 1,000 square feet per year.

Wearability: Not too good. Recovers slowly from damage.

Mowing Height: From 1 to 2 inches.

Best Adapted: Southern U.S. The northern limit could be shown by drawing a line between northern Alabama and Raleigh, North Carolina.

Cultivars: 'Centiseed' is a trade name for common centipedegrass that can be grown from seed. 'Oklawn' and 'Centennial' can be established by sprigs. 'Raleigh' is the most cold-hardy.

Dichondra

WARM-SEASON GROUND COVER

Scientific Name: *Dichondra micrantha*

Strengths: Dichondra is not a grass, but a broadleaf plant. It makes a lush, dense, bright green carpet when well maintained. Needs less mowing than most grasses. Attacked by few diseases in the dry Southwest.

Weaknesses: Cutworms, flea beetles, snails, and slugs prefer it to grass lawns. Hard to get weeds out once they invade. Susceptible to alternaria in Texas and eastward.

Shade Tolerance: Fairly good, better than Kentucky bluegrass.

Water Needs: High.

Fertilizer Needs: Medium to high. Needs 0.5 to 1.0 pound of actual nitrogen per 1,000 square feet per growing month.

Wearability: Poor.

Mowing Height: Depends on use. In shade where traffic is rare, mow a few inches high. A lower height from ½ to 1½ inches is best for most other lawn areas and helps keep out weeds.

Best Adapted: Dichondra likes heat. Not adapted to humid climates or where temperatures drop below 25° F.

Cultivars: None.

St. Augustine Grass

WARM-SEASON GRASS

Scientific Name: *Stenotaphrum secundatum*

Strengths: Robust and fast growing. Good shade grass. Tolerates salty soil.

Weaknesses: Chinch bugs can do considerable damage. Susceptible to St. Augustine grass decline (SAD) virus. Tends to thatch badly.

Shade Tolerance: One of the best.

Water Needs: High.

Fertilizer Needs: Medium to high. Needs about 0.4 to 0.8 pound of actual nitrogen per 1,000 square feet per growing month.

Wearabilty: Poor.

Mowing Height: 2 to 3 inches. If mowed too low, weeds are more likely to gain a foothold; there is also the danger of sunburn. If mowed too high, thatch builds rapidly.

Best Adapted: Southern California, Hawaii, mild areas of the Southwest, and Gulf Coast states. Likes neutral to alkaline soils. Check for lime needs.

Cultivars: 'Bitter Blue' has bluish color and does not tolerate wear. 'Floratam' is resistant to SAD virus and chinch bugs, but does not do well in shade.

Zoysiagrass

WARM-SEASON GRASS

Scientific Name: *Zoysia* species

Strengths: Forms dense, fine-textured lawn that is resistant to weeds. Good heat and drought tolerance. Relatively free of disease and insect pests, though billbugs may bother it.

Weaknesses: Very slow to establish. Does not thrive where summers are short or cool. The wiry blades are tough to mow if left too long. Tends to build thatch if too much nitrogen is used.

Shade Tolerance: Slow growth in shade, but much better than Bermudagrass.

Water Needs: Low to medium.

Fertilizer Needs: Low to medium. Needs 0.3 to 0.5 pound of actual nitrogen per 1,000 square feet per growing month.

Wearability: Good.

Mowing Height: 1 to 2 inches.

Best Adapted: Throughout the South.

Cultivars: *Zoysia japonica* cultivars include 'Meyer' or 'Z-52', 'El Toro', and 'Belair'. *Z. tenuifolia* is least cold tolerant but the finest textured. 'Emerald' (*Z. japonica* × *Z. tenuifolia*) is an attractive hybrid. Manilagrass (*Z. matrella*), though technically not a cultivar, is widely adapted.

The Cultivar Charts

Bermudagrass Cultivars

Cultivar	Description	Comments
Midiron	Dark green with medium texture.	The most winter-hardy Bermudagrass. Good tolerance to winter traffic. Vigorous, fast rate of establishment. Not a hybrid, but a seedling selection made in Manhattan, Kansas. Develops a purplish cast in the fall. Used primarily for tees, fairways, and athletic fields.
Midway	Blue-green with medium texture and density.	Good resistance to leaf spot and Bermudagrass mites. Excellent tolerance to low-temperature stress. Susceptible to billbugs. Does not thatch as much as some other cultivars.
Ormond	Blue-green with medium-fine texture.	Vigorous and rapid spreading. Does not tend to thatch as much as other Bermudagrasses. Is subject to winterkill and diseases. Highly susceptible to Bermudagrass mites. Used mostly in Florida for golf-course fairways, athletic fields, and home lawns.
Santa Ana	Dark green with fine texture.	Short dormant season and vigorous growth. High tolerance to air pollution. A seedling selection made in Los Angeles, California. Grows dense and may require regular dethatching.
Texturf 10	Dark green with medium texture and shoot density. Low growth habit.	Good tolerance to low temperature. Good spring green-up. Moderately good establishment and growth rate. Susceptible to leaf spot, especially in humid areas. Used in the Southwest for parks, athletic fields, and home lawns. Superior wear tolerance. Low nitrogen and water-use rates.
Tifdwarf	Dark green with fine texture and high density.	Good tolerance to low temperatures and close mowing (to ⅛ inch). Moderately slow establishment and growth rate. Susceptible to leaf spot, sod webworms, and smog. Used primarily on golf and bowling greens.
Tifgreen	Medium green with fine texture.	Tolerates low mowing and heals rapidly. The most popular grass for putting greens in the Southeast and some golf courses of the Southwest. Also used for high-quality home lawns, grass tennis courts, bowling greens, and some fairways.
Tifway	Dark green with fine texture.	Forms a dense, weed-resistant turf. Frost tolerant; takes a lot of wear. Less maintenance compared with other hybrid Bermudagrasses. Good tolerance to herbicides. Popular for home lawns and athletic fields. Commonly used as tee and fairway grass. May be subject to winterkill in northern transitional climatic zone.
Tifway II	Dark green with fine texture and good density.	Excellent resistance to rust and leaf spot. Good tolerance to close mowing and low temperatures. Excellent spring green-up.
Tufcote	Medium dark green with medium texture and density. Low growth habit.	Good tolerance to low temperatures, traffic, and salt. Susceptible to spring dead spot and Bermudagrass mites. Used for athletic fields and home lawns in eastern transitional climatic zone.
Vamont	Light green with medium-coarse texture and medium-high density.	Good spring green-up. Excellent tolerance to low temperatures. Good tolerance to close mowing. Rapid establishment and growth rate. Developed for sports fields in eastern transitional climatic zone.

The improved Bermudagrasses of the Tif series were developed or discovered and released through the University of Georgia's Coastal Plains Experiment Station and the U.S.D.A. In contrast to common Bermudagrass, the Tif cultivars are more disease resistant, have greater density, better weed resistance, fewer seed heads, and finer, softer textures with better color. They are especially suited to playgrounds, football fields, and golf courses.

Kentucky Bluegrass Cultivars

Cultivar	Description	Comments
Adelphi	Dark green with good density and medium texture.	Widely adapted. Good summer performance and spring green-up. Good resistance to leaf spot, stem rust, and summer patch. Moderately good resistance to stripe smut. Moderately good tolerance to shade.
America	Dark green with fine texture and high density. Low growth habit.	Good resistance to leaf spot and leaf and stem rust. Moderately good resistance to stripe smut. Moderately good tolerance to shade and low mowing.
Baron	Dark green with medium texture and density.	Widely adapted. Moderately good summer performance. Moderately good resistance to leaf spot and dollar spot. Moderately susceptible to stripe smut.
Bensun (A-34)	Light green with good density and fine texture.	Good shade performance and wear resistance. An aggressive cultivar. Good resistance to stripe smut. Moderately good resistance to leaf spot.
Birka	Moderately dark green with good density and fine texture.	Moderately good shade performance. Good resistance to leaf spot, stripe smut, and powdery mildew.
Bristol	Dark green with a medium-coarse texture and good density.	Moderately good shade tolerance. Good resistance to leaf spot, stripe smut, stem rust, and powdery mildew.

Kentucky Bluegrass Cultivars (continued)

Cultivar	Description	Comments
Challenger	Glossy dark green with medium-fine texture and medium-high density. Low growing.	Excellent resistance to leaf spot. Good resistance to dollar spot, stripe smut, and leaf, stem, and stripe rust. Moderately good resistance to summer patch. Excellent color in early spring and late fall.
Cheri	Medium dark green with medium texture and medium-high density. Moderately low growth habit.	Moderately good resistance to leaf spot. Moderately susceptible to stripe smut, dollar spot, powdery mildew, and leaf and stem rust. Good seedling vigor.
Columbia	Moderately dark green with good density and fine texture.	Good winter color and spring green-up. Moderately good heat tolerance. Good resistance to leaf spot, stripe smut, stem rust, and summer patch.
Eclipse	Dark green color with medium texture and good density. Vigorous with low growth habit.	Good resistance to leaf spot and stripe smut. Moderately good resistance to powdery mildew, dollar spot, and summer patch. Good tolerance to shade, cold, heat, and drought.
Fylking	Moderately dark green with fine texture.	Forms sod well. Good resistance to leaf spot. Moderately resistant to stripe smut. Susceptible to summer patch. Best kept mowed 1½ inches or lower.
Glade	Dark green with good density and fine texture.	Moderately good shade tolerance. Moderately good resistance to leaf spot. Good resistance to stripe smut and powdery mildew.
Kenblue	Medium green with an upright growth habit and moderate density.	Best at low maintenance levels—high cutting and low fertility. Susceptible to leaf spot.
Majestic	Dark green with medium texture and good density.	Good winter color and spring green-up. Good resistance to leaf spot. Moderately good resistance to stripe smut, stem rust, and dollar spot.
Merit	Medium dark green with medium-coarse texture and medium density. Moderately low growth habit.	Moderately resistant to leaf spot, stem rust, and dollar spot. Susceptible to powdery mildew. Medium spring green-up and good seedling vigor.
Midnight	Deep dark green with fine texture and high density. Slow leaf extension rate. Low growth habit.	Good resistance to leaf spot, stem rust, stripe smut, and dollar spot. Persistent. Good tolerance to heat, cold, and low mowing. Fair shade adaptation.
Newport	Dark green with medium texture and density.	Good winter color. Susceptible to leaf spot and summer patch.
Nugget	Dark green with fine texture and high density. Poor color in winter.	Extremely hardy. Good resistance to leaf spot and powdery mildew. Susceptible to dollar spot.
Parade	Medium green with good density and fine texture.	Good winter color and spring green-up. Good resistance to leaf spot, stripe smut, stem rust, and summer patch.
Park	Moderately dark green with an upright growth habit and moderate density.	Best at low maintenance levels—high cutting and low fertility. Susceptible to leaf spot and summer patch. Prone to yellowing in alkaline soils.
Plush	Medium green with medium texture and density. Aggressive and moderately low growth habit.	Good resistance to stripe smut and dollar spot. Moderately good resistance to leaf spot and stem rust. Good spring green-up and heat tolerance.
Ram I	Dark green with medium texture and high density. Low growth habit.	Good resistance to stripe smut and powdery mildew. Moderately good resistance to leaf spot and stem rust. Moderately susceptible to leaf rust and dollar spot. Good spring color and low mowing tolerance.
Rugby	Medium dark green with medium texture and good density. Moderately low growing.	Moderately good resistance to leaf spot, dollar spot, stripe smut, summer patch, and leaf and stem rust. Retains color well in early spring and late fall.
Sydsport	Medium green with good density and medium texture.	Widely adapted. Forms sod well. Tolerates wear. Moderately good resistance to leaf spot, stripe smut, and powdery mildew.
Touchdown	Moderately dark green with good density and fine texture.	Moderately good tolerance of low mowing and shade. Good winter color and spring green-up. Good resistance to leaf spot, stripe smut, and powdery mildew. Moderately susceptible to dollar spot and stem rust.
Victa	Dark green with medium texture and density.	Widely adapted. Moderately good summer performance. Moderately good resistance to leaf spot and stem rust. Moderately susceptible to stripe smut.

Fine Fescue Cultivars

Cultivar	Description	Comments
Aurora	Hard type. Moderately dark green with fine texture, high density, and a slow growth habit.	Good resistance to red thread, leaf spot, anthracnose, powdery mildew, and fusarium patch. Improved performance in summer, in shade, and at low fertility. Good drought tolerance.
Banner	Chewings type. Dark green with good density and fine texture.	Moderately good disease resistance. Tolerant of low mowing. Very competitive with Kentucky bluegrasses in mixtures. Susceptible to powdery mildew.
Boreal	Creeping type. Moderately dark green with medium texture and density.	Good seedling vigor. Good winter hardiness; poor summer performance. Susceptible to leaf spot.

Fine Fescue Cultivars (continued)

Cultivar	Description	Comments
Cascade	Chewings type. Medium green with a fine texture.	Good establishment rate. Susceptible to leaf spot.
C-26	Hard type. Dark green with fine texture and good density.	Good disease resistance compared with the other fine fescues. Good drought tolerance. Should perform well in mixtures with Kentucky bluegrass.
Dawson	Semicreeping type. Medium green with good density and fine texture.	Moderately good resistance to leaf spot. Tolerant of low mowing. Good for overseeding Bermudagrass. Can be severely damaged by dollar spot and red thread.
Ensylva	Creeping type. Medium green with medium density, moderately fine texture, and vigorous rhizomes.	Moderate resistance to leaf spot and fusarium patch. Moderately susceptible to red thread. Good seedling vigor.
Flyer	Creeping type. Moderately dark green with medium texture and density. Vigorous rhizomes.	Moderate resistance to leaf spot and red thread. Good resistance to fusarium patch. Good seedling vigor and shade adaptation. Good in mixtures.
Fortress	Creeping type. Forms extensive rhizomes. Dark green with medium texture and density.	Good resistance to powdery mildew and good seedling vigor. Blends well with Kentucky bluegrass and recovers well from summer injury.
Highlight	Chewings type. Medium green with fine texture and good density.	Moderately good disease resistance. Tolerant of low mowing. Very competitive with Kentucky bluegrass in mixtures.
Jamestown	Chewings type. Dark green, good density and fine texture.	Moderately good disease resistance. Tolerant of low mowing. Very competitive with Kentucky bluegrass in mixtures. Susceptible to powdery mildew.
Koket	Chewings type. Medium green with fine texture and good density.	Moderate resistance to leaf spot and red thread. Good spring color. Tolerant of low mowing. Moderate seedling vigor.
Pennlawn	Predominantly a creeping type. Medium dark green, good density, and fine texture.	A widely adapted cultivar with moderate disease resistance. Used widely in mixtures with Kentucky bluegrass.
Reliant	Hard type. Medium to dark green with fine texture, high density, and low growth habit.	Good resistance to red thread, anthracnose, fusarium patch, and powdery mildew. Good heat and drought tolerance. Good shade adaptation and low fertility performance.
Ruby	Creeping type. Dark green, medium texture and density.	Good seedling vigor. Blends well with Kentucky bluegrass. Poor summer performance. Susceptible to leaf spot.
Scaldis	Hard type. Dark green with fine texture, good density, and low growth habit.	Good resistance to red thread, anthracnose, and fusarium patch. Moderate resistance to leaf spot. Improved summer performance and shade adaptation. Good drought and low-fertility tolerance.
Shadow	Chewings type. Medium dark green with fine texture, good density, and low growth habit.	Moderately good resistance to red thread and leaf spot. Good resistance to powdery mildew and fusarium patch. Good tolerance to shade. Good seedling vigor.
Waldina	Hard type. Dark green with fine texture, good density, and low growth habit.	Good resistance to red thread, anthracnose, and fusarium patch. Moderately good resistance to leaf spot. Susceptible to powdery mildew. Good tolerance to drought. Improved performance in summer, in shade, and at low fertility.

Tall Fescue Cultivars

Cultivar	Description	Comments
Adventure	Medium dark green with medium-fine texture and improved density. Moderately low growth habit.	Good resistance to brown patch and crown rust. Moderately good resistance to leaf spot. Good shade, heat, drought, and wear tolerance. Better vigor and color retention at low fertility.
Alta	Medium green. Upright growth and coarse texture.	Drought tolerant. Moderately persistent in turf. Susceptible to leaf spot. Do not plant around young trees.
Apache	Dark green with medium-fine texture and improved density. Moderately low growing.	Good resistance to brown patch and leaf spot. Moderately good resistance to crown rust. Improved heat, drought, shade, and wear tolerance. Good color retention at reduced fertility.
Bonanza	Dark green with medium-fine texture, improved density, and reduced vertical growth rate.	Good resistance to brown patch, leaf spot, and crown rust. Improved heat, drought, shade, and wear tolerance. Good color retention at low fertility. Lower growing than most other cultivars.
Clemfine	Medium green with coarse texture and medium-low density.	Moderately good resistance to brown patch. Moderately susceptible to leaf spot. Resembles 'Kentucky 31' with better persistence in turf.
Falcon	Medium dark green with medium-fine texture and improved density. Moderately low growth habit.	Moderately good resistance to brown patch, leaf spot, and crown rust. Good tolerance to heat, drought, and shade. Improved persistence in turf and wear tolerance.

Tall Fescue Cultivars (continued)

Cultivar	Description	Comments
Fawn	Medium green. Upright growth and coarse texture.	Drought tolerant. Moderately persistent in turf. Susceptible to crown rust. Not as persistent in turf as 'Alta' and 'Kentucky 31'.
Finelawn I	Medium dark green with medium texture and density. Moderately low growth habit.	Moderately good resistance to brown patch, leaf spot, and crown rust. Good heat, drought, shade, and wear tolerance.
Houndog	Medium dark green with medium texture and density. Semiprostrate growth habit.	Moderately good resistance to brown patch and leaf spot. Good heat, drought, and shade tolerance.
Jaguar	Medium dark green with medium-fine texture and good density. Moderately low growth habit.	Good resistance to brown patch, leaf spot, and crown rust. Good heat, drought, wear, and shade tolerance. Good color retention in the fall.
Kentucky 31	Medium green. Coarse texture and somewhat lower growing than 'Alta' and 'Fawn'.	Widely adapted to many soil types. Drought tolerant. Moderately disease resistant. Susceptible to leaf spot. Fair persistence in turf in transition zone. Good winter recovery and spring green-up.
Mustang	Dark green with medium texture and density. Moderately low growth habit.	Good resistance to leaf spot. Moderately good resistance to brown patch. Good shade tolerance and spring and fall color retention.
Olympic	Dark green with medium-fine texture and improved density. Moderately low growth habit.	Good resistance to leaf spot and crown rust. Moderately good resistance to brown patch. Good tolerance to heat, drought, shade, and wear. Good spring and fall color retention. Less iron chlorosis in alkaline soils.
Rebel	Medium dark green with medium-fine texture and improved density. Moderately low growth habit.	Good resistance to brown patch. Moderate resistance to leaf spot. Moderately susceptible to crown rust. Good tolerance to heat, drought, shade, and wear.

Turf-Type Perennial Ryegrass Cultivars

Cultivar	Description	Comments
All Star	Dark green with fine texture and good density. Low growth habit.	Good resistance to brown patch. Moderately good resistance to leaf spot and above-ground insects. Moderately susceptible to stem rust. Good mowing qualities, heat tolerance, and spring green-up.
Birdie II	Medium dark green with fine texture and good density. Low growth habit and reduced rate of vertical growth.	Good resistance to brown patch, leaf spot, and stem and crown rust. Moderate resistance to red thread and above-ground insects. Good mowing qualities and heat tolerance.
Blazer	Medium dark green with fine texture and good density. Low growth habit and reduced vertical growth rate.	Good resistance to brown patch, leaf spot, and crown rust. Susceptible to stem rust. Good mowing qualities and heat and cold tolerance.
Citation II	Dark green with fine texture and high density. Low growth habit and reduced vertical growth rate.	Good resistance to leaf spot, brown patch, stem and crown rust, and above-ground insects. Moderately good resistance to red thread and dollar spot. Good mowing qualities and heat and wear tolerance.
Cowboy	Medium dark green with medium texture and density. Low growth habit.	Good resistance to stem and crown rust, leaf spot, and brown patch. Moderately good resistance to above-ground insects. Good heat and wear tolerance. Improved mowing qualities.
Derby	Moderately dark green. Good density and texture.	Moderately good heat and cold tolerance. Good resistance to brown patch. Moderately good resistance to leaf spot. Good mowing qualities.
Loretta	Light green with good density and fine texture.	Moderately good cold tolerance. Very good mowing qualities. Good resistance to crown rust. Susceptible to stem rust. No stemming period in spring, and low performance in the summer.
Manhattan II	Medium dark green with fine texture and high density. Low growth habit and reduced rate of vertical growth.	Good resistance to leaf spot, brown patch, and stem and crown rust. Improved heat tolerance and summer performance. Very good mowing qualities and low mowing tolerance.
Omega II	Dark green with medium-fine texture and high density. Low growth habit and reduced vertical growth.	Good resistance to leaf spot, brown patch, and stem and crown rust. Moderately good resistance to red thread and above-ground insects. Good heat tolerance and mowing qualities.
Palmer	Dark green with fine texture and good density. Low growth habit.	Very good resistance to brown patch. Good resistance to crown rust. Moderately good resistance to leaf spot. Moderate resistance to above-ground insects. Susceptible to stem rust. Good tolerance to heat, wear, and low mowing.
Pennant	Moderately dark green with medium-fine texture and moderate density.	Good resistance to brown patch and above-ground insects. Moderate resistance to leaf spot, dollar spot, and crown rust. Susceptible to stem rust. Moderately good mowing qualities and heat tolerance.
Pennfine	Moderately dark green with good density and texture.	Good heat tolerance. Good resistance to brown patch. Susceptible to leaf spot. Good mowing qualities with stemming period in the spring.

Turf-Type Perennial Ryegrass Cultivars (continued)

Cultivar	Description	Comments
Prelude	Dark green with fine texture and medium-high density. Low growth habit.	Very good resistance to brown patch and crown rust. Moderately good resistance to leaf spot and above-ground insects. Susceptible to stem rust. Good tolerance to heat, wear, and low mowing. Good mowing qualities.
Premier	Dark green with medium-fine texture and good density. Low growth habit.	Good resistance to brown patch. Moderately good resistance to leaf spot, dollar spot, and crown rust. Improved mowing qualities and heat and wear tolerance. Susceptible to stem rust.
Regal	Dark green with moderately good density and texture.	Moderately good heat tolerance. Moderately good resistance to brown patch. Susceptible to leaf spot and crown rust. Moderately good mowing qualities.
Yorktown II	Dark green with good density and fine texture.	Moderately good heat and cold tolerance. Good resistance to brown patch and crown rust. Very good mowing qualities.

Northern Native Grasses

Grass	Description	Culture	Comments
American Beachgrass (*Ammophila breviligulata*)	A tough grass that grows tall, to about 5 feet. A deep root system and aggressive underground runners allow rapid growth and spread in shifting, infertile beach sand. Similar to European beachgrass, but has a longer planting season and greater persistence.	Dig old clumps in fall just before complete dormancy. Cut stems back to about 2 feet. Plant clumps about 8 inches deep. Adding fertilizer at planting time will promote more rapid growth.	Used for first-stage stabilization of shifting dune areas. As soon as the grass covers, begin planting more permanent woody plants. Beachgrass grows naturally on the shores of the Great Lakes, along the Atlantic Coast from Newfoundland to North Carolina, and along the Pacific Coast.
Blue Grama (*Bouteloua gracilis*)	Grayish green and fine textured. Excellent heat and drought tolerance. Used in rangeland seedings or similar never-water situations.	Use 1 to 3 pounds of seed per 1,000 square feet. Slow to establish. Sow in fall or spring, allow about 30 days to germination. Mow to 2 or 3 inches. Minimal fertilizer required.	Basically a warm-season grass but remains hardy to –40° F. An important native of the Great Plains, it is found in Wisconsin, Manitoba, Alberta, and south to Arkansas. Good in arid, alkaline soil.
Buffalograss (*Buchloe dactyloides*)	Finely textured blades are grayish green. One of the most dominant grasses of the short-grass prairie. Grows during the summer and has outstanding heat tolerance. Is only green during the growing season.	Easily started from seed. Use 0.5 to 1.5 pounds of seed per 1,000 square feet in the fall. Should come up in 14 to 21 days. After watering deep to establish, little is needed. Give 0 to 0.3 pounds of actual nitrogen per 1,000 square feet per growing month. Mow to about 1½ to 2 inches.	Favored by settlers for building sod houses, it makes a dense turf. Thrives in areas that receive 12 to 25 inches of rain per year (Minnesota to central Montana; south to Iowa, Texas, Arizona, and northern Mexico). Does well in heavy soil.
Fairway Wheatgrass (*Agropyron cristatum*)	Not a true native—introduced from Russia. Tolerates temperatures as high as 110° F and as low as –20° F. Related to the nuisance weed quackgrass.	Sow 3 to 5 pounds of seed per 1,000 square feet. Germination is in 7 to 21 days. Water deeply until established; no supplemental water should then be necessary. Mow between 2 to 3 inches.	Grows best in moist, alkaline soil. Commonly found throughout much of western Canada, the northern Great Plains, and other northern mountain regions of the United States. Sometimes grows as far south as Texas and as far west as northeast California, Oregon, and Washington.

Native grasses make excellent low-maintenance ground covers. Although they do not make the most attractive home lawns, they can be used to stabilize banks and roadsides. Fertilizer and water needs are minimal. Growth is slow, so mowing only needs to be done three or four times per season. Some native grasses may be difficult to find; availability is usually limited to their adaptation and usefulness in your area. Check with your nursery staff or local seed supplier.

Lawn Grass Comparisons

The lists that follow compare the specific types of grass in general terms. They are based on the personal observations of many specialists and are not absolute. The specific qualities of one grass could vary, and newly developed cultivars could have different positions in the lists.

While a particular grass may seem perfect for your home lawn, you should take into account many other factors, such as how it adapts to your climate and how difficult it is to maintain.

High Temperature Tolerance

Tolerant
zoysiagrass
improved Bermudagrass
common Bermudagrass
St. Augustine grass
centipedegrass
bahiagrass
tall fescue
dichondra
Kentucky bluegrass
perennial ryegrass
creeping bentgrass
Intolerant
rough bluegrass

High temperature tolerance depends on the cultivar, maintenance practices, and a whole range of climatic factors that affect growth habits. Raising the cutting height of a cool-season grass will improve its temperature tolerance. Tolerance to high temperatures is more important in transitional areas, since the grass is not as well adapted.

Accepts Low Mowing

Best
creeping bentgrass
(¼ inch or less)
improved Bermudagrass
common Bermudagrass
zoysiagrass
centipedegrass
rough bluegrass
fine fescues
perennial ryegrass
Kentucky bluegrass
St. Augustine grass
tall fescue
Worst
bahiagrass

Mowing height is primarily determined by the growth habit of the grass. Those that spread horizontally can be clipped lower. In general, Kentucky bluegrass cut above 1½ inches is much easier to keep.

Drought Tolerance

Tolerant
common Bermudagrass
improved Bermudagrass
zoysiagrass
centipedegrass
tall fescue
fine fescues
St. Augustine grass
dichondra
Kentucky bluegrass
perennial ryegrass
creeping bentgrass
Intolerant
rough bluegrass

While a grass may tend to remain green and resist short periods of drought, it may die out completely if subjected to severe drought.

Fertilizer Requirements

Least
fine fescues
bahiagrass
zoysiagrass
tall fescue
centipedegrass
St. Augustine grass
perennial ryegrass
Kentucky bluegrass
rough bluegrass
common Bermudagrass
improved Bermudagrass
dichondra
Most
creeping bentgrass

While a lawn may exist on low amounts of fertilizer, a high-quality lawn can only be grown with increased amounts. The cultivar, soil type, and climate greatly influence fertilizer needs.

Cold Tolerance

Tolerant
creeping bentgrass
rough bluegrass
Kentucky bluegrass
fine fescues
tall fescue
perennial ryegrass
dichondra
zoysiagrass
common Bermudagrass
improved Bermudagrass
annual ryegrass
bahiagrass
centipedegrass
Intolerant
St. Augustine grass

Unlike cool-season grasses, warm-season grasses are usually not tolerant of cold weather. Most warm-season grasses grow vigorously in the warm summer months, then become dormant, turning brown in cold weather.

Shade Tolerance

Tolerant
St. Augustine grass
fine fescues
rough bluegrass
dichondra
tall fescue
perennial ryegrass
creeping bentgrass
bahiagrass
zoysiagrass
centipedegrass
Kentucky bluegrass
improved Bermudagrass
Intolerant
common Bermudagrass

The shade tolerance of a grass depends upon many conditions. If the site is quite damp, rough bluegrass could persist while fine fescues die out completely. Just the opposite could occur on a dry site. Cultivars also have significant differences.

Establishment Time

Fast
improved Bermudagrass[1]
common Bermudagrass
perennial ryegrass
creeping bentgrass[1]
St. Augustine grass[1]
rough bluegrass
tall fescue
fine fescues
bahiagrass
centipedegrass
Kentucky bluegrass
creeping bentgrass[2]
dichondra
Slow
zoysiagrass

The point at which a new planting becomes a lawn depends on the lawn owner. If the lawn is for appearance and to keep the soil in place, a new heavy seeding of perennial ryegrass or tall fescue can do the job in 2 to 3 weeks.

[1]Seeds only
[2]Stolons only

Wearability

High
zoysiagrass
improved Bermudagrass
bahiagrass
common Bermudagrass
perennial ryegrass
tall fescue
Kentucky bluegrass
fine fescues
St. Augustine grass
centipedegrass
creeping bentgrass
rough bluegrass
Low
dichondra

Often turfgrass cannot tolerate heavy traffic, although there is quite a lot of variability between cultivars. For example, 'Bensun' and 'Baron' Kentucky bluegrass bear traffic rather well.

Installing a Lawn

A new lawn can have a dramatic effect on a home or building. Landscape plantings are accentuated, and the strong lines of walls, driveways, and sidewalks are softened by an expanse of grass.

With the goal of a lush, green lawn in mind, it is tempting to hurry through the initial steps of its establishment—and nothing could be more unfortunate. Your first decisions and procedures are important to the future of your lawn.

Answers to such questions as "Which grass should I plant?" "Do I want to sow seed or use sprigs, plugs, or sod?" "How will I water?" all should be fully thought out in advance of any labor. Look through this entire book before beginning work; some forethought will save you many future headaches.

Preparing for a Lawn

There are many different ways of progressing from bare ground to a new lawn. Some people simply spread seed over the ground without preparing the soil. Few of these lawns reach their optimum level of appearance—if they survive at all. New techniques such as hydroseeding are becoming increasingly popular. Regardless of the planting method, success is still measured by long-term results.

The amount of work necessary to prepare the soil before seeding or sodding depends on its present condition. If you are lucky enough to have a rich loam soil and a proper grade, probably little needs to be done beyond thorough tilling, fertilizing, and raking. Usually, though, more work is required. Following a logical order of events prevents costly backtracking or the repetition of similar steps.

◀ *The essence of freshness—new blades of grass, as yet unmowed, glisten with dew in the early morning light.*

How to Prepare for a New Lawn

1. Examine the soil
2. Remove debris
3. Control weeds
4. Establish a rough grade
5. Measure the lawn area
6. Add soil amendments (if needed)
7. Add high-phosphorus fertilizer
8. Install underground sprinkler system (if desired)
9. Establish the final grade
10. Roll and water

Step 1: Examining the Soil

Much of the success of your lawn depends on how you prepare the soil. Remember that, unlike a vegetable garden where the soil can be rebuilt each year, grass roots grow in the same soil year after year. Although most nutrient deficiencies can be corrected after the lawn has been established, changing the soil texture under growing grass is difficult and expensive. The effort you put into preparing the growing medium will be reflected in the health and beauty of your lawn for years to come. This is true for seed

Hydroseeding is a new and different way to start a new lawn. Seed is mixed with a paper mulch and water, and sprayed through a hose onto the seedbed.

lawns as well as for sod lawns. Even though sod has a little soil already attached, site preparation is still critical to its success.

Types of Soil: Gardeners use many terms to describe the soil in their area including heavy, light, poor, lean, sandy, clayey, and loamy. Scientists and horticulturists classify soil by the proportion of sand, silt, and clay it contains. These three classifications are based on the size of the soil particles, clay being the smallest, silt larger, and sand the largest. Soil texture is determined by the blend of these various particles.

For proper growth, lawns need air in the soil, sufficient moisture (but not standing water), and a supply of mineral nutrients. If soil has plenty of clay, holding onto nutrients is no problem, but the small clay particles cling together so closely that they hold water and leave little room for air. When clay soil is packed down under a lawn, water penetrates slowly to lawn roots. If it drains too slowly, the lawn may die. Clay soil is usually hard when dry and sticky when wet.

Sandy soil has lots of room for air, but moisture and nutrients disappear quickly. Water sinks into sandy soil without spreading, and dries up in just a few days after watering. When sandy soil is packed down, it quickly falls apart when it is released.

In between a sandy or clay soil—and the one best for lawn growth—is a loam soil. Containing a combination of clay, silt, and sand, it retains nutrients and water while allowing sufficient room for air.

Chances are your soil is not the perfect loam, in which case it would benefit from the addition of organic matter (see page 23). Even if it is an ideal soil, heavy foot traffic or perhaps construction activity around new homes can severely compact it, closing air spaces and restricting water and nutrient penetration. You have seen the effects of compaction in foot paths worn across a lawn.

Soil Tests: The first step in preparing any soil for a future lawn is to have your soil tested. A soil test eliminates guessing the amount of nutrients, lime, or sulfur to be added and often provides useful information on the texture of the soil.

Many land-grant colleges and universities test soils for residents of their state. Check the chapter entitled "Lawns in Your Area," beginning on page 87, for the address of a local soil-testing facility. In states that do not offer soil-testing programs, check the Yellow Pages under "Laboratories, testing" for private laboratories, or ask your county extension agent for help. Some facilities give specific recommendations, while others supply instructions on how to interpret results and take appropriate steps.

How to Take a Soil Test: First, obtain any necessary forms or questionnaires from your local cooperative extension service office or private soil lab. Typical questions include: "How large is the sample area?" "Has fertilizer or lime ever been added?" "To what degree is the land sloped?"

To collect the soil, you need a clean, nonmetal bucket or container, a soil sampler, garden trowel or spade, pencil and paper, and mailable container that holds about a pint of soil.

To get reliable soil-test results, gather the soil from several spots in the area you are planning to install your lawn. Low spots, trouble spots, and areas with obvious soil type differences should be treated as separate sampling areas.

Take soil samples to the depth specified by the soil-testing lab, using a soil-sampling tube. The hollow shaft of an old golf club or curtain rod suffices. If you don't have a sampler, dig a V-shaped hole 4 inches deep with a spade or garden trowel. Remove a ½-inch slice from the smooth side. Discard any thatch or surface debris. Mix the soil from one sampling area and allow to dry before proceeding.

Place about a pint of this soil into your waterproof carton or plastic bag, label it properly, and mail it to the soil lab. Record where each sample was taken. Also provide the lab with any additional information on the history of the land, if pertinent.

Step 2: Removing Debris

To start with, clear all debris—wood, stones, and other items—from the planting area.

Rotting wood can cause low spots in a lawn as it decomposes, and can serve as a food source for termites. A tree stump, though often difficult to remove, can cause mushroom growth

How to Take a Soil Test

½-inch slice from center

Using a spade or sampling tube, take separate samples of individual areas at a depth of 4 inches.

Test individual areas separately. The above areas are examples of the soil differences a lawn area can have. Most areas usually have only one or two different soil types.

Mix soil well. (Do not mix soil from separate sampling areas.) Place about 1 pint of this soil into a labeled container. Repeat this process for each test area.

on the lawn above its roots. If you want to remove the stump, do it now.

Stones and cement can damage rotary tillers and other equipment. Piling the stones in a wheelbarrow to be removed will save you the trouble of later picking them up many times.

Step 3: Controlling Weeds
Save yourself time and trouble later on by eliminating weeds now. There are three effective methods.

Use method one in late summer, when most of the weeds have set seed. Remove existing weeds with a hoe. Water the soil every few days to germinate any weed seeds in the soil. Every week or two, as more weeds germinate, kill them with a contact herbicide or by shallow cultivation. Continue this process until no more weeds germinate, then plant the lawn.

The second method is most effective in the spring and summer, when most of the weeds are actively growing. Spray the existing weeds with glyphosate, an herbicide that kills all weeds, even the most difficult ones. Some weeds, such as quackgrass, may require a second treatment after 6 weeks. Glyphosate breaks down on contact with the soil, so seeding or sodding may be done a week after treatment.

The third method is fumigation; it kills everything in the soil and can be done at any time. Fumigants, such as methyl bromide and metam, are dangerous and should be applied by professionals. After three weeks, test to see if the soil is safe by planting some fast-germinating seeds, such as radishes. If they sprout and begin normal growth, it is safe to sow seed or lay sod.

For more information on weed control, see page 58.

Step 4: Establishing a Rough Grade
Next, establish a rough grade by filling low spots and leveling hills. Most lots have fixed grade points, such as house foundations, sidewalks, driveways, and trees. When grading, both rough and finished soil must be distributed so that the elevation changes between fixed points are gradual.

Prevent water from draining toward a house foundation by establishing the grade at a 1- to 2-percent slope away from the house. That measures about a 1- to 2-foot drop per 100 feet. A long string and a level are useful in determining slope.

Lawn borders keep creeping grasses out of neighboring planting beds. Bender board is one material that is flexible enough for curved areas. Install borders before planting your lawn.

If rough grading will be extensive, remove and stockpile the topsoil beforehand. This prevents it from being buried under the subsoil. When the rough grade is finished, spread topsoil out again.

Where underlying hardpan or heavy clay soil creates poor drainage, you may need to install drain tiles. Consult a drainage contractor for advice. Drainage work should be done after the rough grade, but before adding topsoil and amendments.

Trees are sensitive to the amount of soil above their roots. Try to avoid adding or removing more than 2 inches under large trees. Trees in the lawn deserve special care. For further advice, see page 80.

At this point, consider installing a lawn border. Wood, stone, or concrete borders prevent grass from creeping into neighboring flower beds and make trimming easier. For a simple wood border, lay 1 by 4s or 2 by 4s on edge. For other borders, lay bricks in a row or make a band of concrete 4 to 5 inches wide. If you plan to install sod, remember the final, settled grade should be ¾ to 1 inch lower than the grade for a seed lawn, so that the sod fits flush against sprinklers and sidewalks.

Step 5: Measuring the Lawn Area
Determine the dimensions of the lawn area with a tape measure. Methods for figuring lawn dimensions are explained on page 108. Write down the lawn measurements for future reference. They are helpful for estimating the amount of grass seed, sod, and amendments you need to use.

Step 6: Adding Soil Amendments
Once the grade is sloped the way you want it, add soil amendments as a soil test indicates. Replace or add topsoil at this time. Spread half of the topsoil over the area and till it in. This creates a transition zone between underlying soil and new soil. Add the remaining soil, then add any appropriate soil amendments.

Organic Matter: The best way to improve either a heavy, clay soil or a light, sandy soil is by adding organic matter—not just a little, but a lot.

The addition of organic matter—compost, peat moss, manure, sawdust, ground bark—makes clay soil more friable and easier to work. In clay soil, organic matter improves drainage, and allows air to move into soil more readily. In sandy soil, it holds moisture and nutrients in the root zone. The more organic matter you add to a sandy soil, the more you increase its moisture-holding capacity.

Adding decomposed organic matter supplies your soil with needed nitrogen. Using fresh organic matter, however, causes what is known as a "nitrogen draft." This means that while the fresh matter decomposes on your lawn, it also creates a nitrogen deficiency, causing yellowing and slow growth. Common culprits include fresh ground bark, straw, and manure containing large amounts of sawdust or straw. If you use fresh matter, add enough nitrogen to counteract the negative effects on your lawn. Or, better yet, switch to a decomposed organic matter.

Enough organic matter should be added to physically change the texture of the soil to a depth of 6 to 8 inches—the area where most grass roots grow. The final soil mixture should be 25 percent organic matter by volume—about 2 inches of organic matter mixed into the top 6 inches of soil is usually sufficient. For amounts of organic matter needed to cover a lawn, see the chart below.

The type of organic matter you choose usually depends on what is locally available. Although decomposed barnyard manure and compost work well, they often contain troublesome weed seeds. Peat moss is generally problem free and available, but expensive. Other types of organic matter you can look for in your area include ground bark, straw, redwood sawdust, grape pomace, buckwheat hulls, peanut hulls, cotton screenings, and shredded tobacco stems.

Lime and Sulfur: Soil acidity is measured by its pH. On a scale of 14, pH 7 is neutral, above 7 is alkaline, and below 7 is acid. A soil pH between 5.5 and 7.5 is good for most grasses and 6.8 to 7 is ideal. For proper grass growth, if your soil pH is below 5.5, add lime to the soil; if it is above 7.5, add soil sulfur. (Centipedegrass is an important exception—it prefers more acid soil. Add lime if the pH is below 4.5, enough to raise the pH to 6.)

In areas of the country with heavy rainfall, soils are typically acid. Grasses grow poorly in highly acid soils, usually because of a phosphorus deficiency and, in extreme cases, because of aluminum toxicity. The only sure way to know whether your soil needs lime is by conducting a soil test. However, applying lime periodically to the soil is a way of life in many areas. In these areas, you probably already know that your soil needs lime.

The easiest and best form of lime for lawns is ground limestone. Dolomitic limestone (dolomite) is the best type in many areas because it adds magnesium as well as calcium. Alternatives are hydrated lime, ground seashells, marl, and chalk. Lime is best applied with a mechanical spreader. For information on spreaders, see page 56.

Where low rainfall is common, soil pH may rise above 7, which can significantly reduce lawn growth. To lower a high soil pH, use soil sulfur (also called flowers of sulfur). Other acidifying materials are aluminum sulfate, ferrous sulfate, lime-sulfur solution, and fertilizers containing ammonium.

For approximate amounts of ground limestone or soil sulfur to correct soil pH, see the chart on below.

Step 7: Adding High-Phosphorus Fertilizer

Adding phosphorus encourages new lawn grass to thicken quickly. Add a high-phosphorus fertilizer, such as formula 0-20-0, and thoroughly mix it with the top 6 to 8 inches of soil. Make several passes with a tiller in opposite directions to ensure that the soil, organic matter, lime or sulfur, and fertilizer are properly blended.

Step 8: Installing an Underground Sprinkler System

Once soil and amendments are mixed together, install an underground sprinkler system, if you have decided to have one. Waiting until the tilling is finished avoids potential damage to pipes. See pages 45 to 48 for information on underground sprinkler systems.

Step 9: Establishing the Final Grade

Do the final grading just before you plant. A smooth bed can be ruined if it is left too long. Take time raking and smoothing the planting area to be sure it is free of rocks and as level as possible. It will be difficult to correct high and low spots later. A chain link fence or wooden drag can help to smooth large areas. See the top photo on page 30.

Step 10: Rolling and Watering

Rolling the freshly prepared soil lightly with a water-filled roller firms up the area to create a more uniform planting depth for seeds, to improve soil contact of seeds or sod, and to reduce dustiness. Fill the roller half or less than half full of water. Water the area well after rolling to settle the soil.

A common problem with new lawns is that soil settles unevenly. This occurs primarily where trenches have been dug for underground sprinkler pipes. If your carefully prepared grade changes after watering, repeat Steps 9 and 10 until the soil settles properly.

Soil Amendments

Organic Matter: Coverage in Cubic Yards*

| Area in Square Feet | Percent Organic Matter Mixed Into 6 Inches of Soil | | | | |
	10%	15%	20%	25%	30%
300	0.6	0.8	1.1	1.4	1.7
500	0.9	1.4	1.9	2.3	2.8
1,000	1.9	2.8	3.7	4.6	5.6
3,000	5.6	8.3	11.1	13.9	16.7
5,000	9.3	13.9	18.5	23.1	27.8
10,000	18.5	27.8	37.0	46.3	55.6
20,000	37.0	55.6	74.1	92.6	111.1
40,000	74.1	111.1	148.1	185.2	222.2

*To a depth of 1 inch, 3 cubic feet will cover 36 square feet. There are 27 cubic feet in a cubic yard.

Ground Limestone: Amounts to Raise Soil pH

| Change in pH Desired | Pounds of Ground Limestone per 1,000 Square Feet** | | | | |
	Sand	Sandy Loam	Loam	Silt Loam	Clay Loam
4.0 to 6.5	60	115	161	193	230
4.5 to 6.5	51	96	133	161	193
5.0 to 6.5	41	78	106	129	152
5.5 to 6.5	28	60	78	92	106
6.0 to 6.5	14	32	41	51	55

**In the southern and coastal states, reduce the application by approximately one half.

Soil Sulfur: Amounts to Lower Soil pH

| Change in pH Desired | Pounds of Soil Sulfur per 1,000 Square Feet | | |
	Sand	Loam	Clay
8.5 to 6.5	46	57	69
8.0 to 6.5	28	34	46
7.5 to 6.5	11	18	23
7.0 to 6.5	2	4	7

Seed Lawns

Regardless of the quick effect of sodding, certain pleasures are afforded to those who choose to start a new lawn from sprigs, plugs, or seed. Few colors are as bright yet as soft as young, green grass. Growth occurs so rapidly that the feeling of growing something is immediate and intense, and the part you play in nature's drama seems important. People who grow their own lawns feel "more the gardener."

In most of North America, seed is the most common way to start a new lawn. Years ago, what was swept from the barn was scattered around the yard, eventually causing a lawn of sorts to grow. This casual and haphazard approach has been superseded by a sophisticated industry that supplies about 120 million pounds of lawn seed for growing turf each year.

Kentucky bluegrass is the most important of the seeds produced; it is the most widely adapted grass of North America. Common Bermudagrass is also planted in large quantities. Fine and tall fescue and ryegrass are the other important lawn seeds. A wider range of mixtures and blends is available as seed, compared with sod.

Buying Seed

One reason that planting seed is the most popular method of starting a new lawn is that it is so economical. Seed usually accounts for no more than 5 percent of the total cost of establishing a new lawn.

Buy seed from a reliable source. Carefully prepared seed is healthy and has a high percentage of germination. It is also weed and disease free. Spending a few more dollars now for the best possible seed can save you hundreds of dollars in the years ahead. You can count on having fewer maintenance problems and a generally healthier lawn.

The kind of seed you select is important. Make sure that both grass type and cultivar you choose are adapted to your area. Read the labels on seed containers carefully. The questions below may seem obvious, but should be considered carefully when choosing seeds or seed mixtures:

• Will your lawn be used primarily for decoration or for recreation?

• Which grasses are best adapted to where you live?

• Will the lawn be partially shaded or receive full exposure to the sun?

• How much time and energy are you willing to put into the care and maintenance of your lawn?

To find out which grasses best suit your needs, refer to the descriptions off different grasses beginning on page 8.

Reading Seed Labels

The variety of lawn seed available in most garden centers and hardware stores can make selecting lawn seed a bewildering experience. Besides the colors and sizes of the containers and the brand names, the only way to comparison shop is to read the labels. Understanding a seed label enables you to make an informed decision. The sample seed label on the next page shows and briefly explains the major parts of a typical label. The following is a more detailed description.

Directions for Use: Most commercial mixes give you two sets of directions: one for seeding a new lawn and the other for reseeding an old lawn. Some packages indicate the spreader setting to use, although there is usually a more informative statement such as "enough seed for 1,000 square feet of new lawn or 2,000 square feet for reseeding." You then know how far the seed goes, regardless of how you intend to spread it.

The directions for use often include brief steps in preparing the site for seeding. (For detailed site preparation, see pages 21 to 24.)

The amount of seed needed to begin a lawn varies according to the seed size and the growth habit of the grass. Most lawns get a good start if seeded at a rate of 3 million seeds per 1,000 square feet, which equals approximately 1½ pounds of Kentucky bluegrass or 5 pounds of fine fescue over the same area. Although cultivars of the same grass type vary in seed size, these differences are inconsequential when determining how much seed to use. For more on determining how much seed to use, look at "Seed Facts" on page 28.

A breeder makes a quick field check of seed production. The seed heads are removed from the grass plant (left) and gently rubbed between the palms (center). The seeds easily separate from the hulls (right).

Fine- and Coarse-Textured: Fine-textured grasses are the backbone of a good seed mixture. Kentucky bluegrass and fine fescues are the most important fine-textured grasses.

Bentgrass is considered fine textured also, and at one time was a component of all quality mixes. Its soft, narrow leaf blades qualify it as fine textured, but because of its growth habit and management needs, bentgrass does not mix well with Kentucky bluegrass, fine fescues, or turf-type perennial ryegrass. It forms unattractive "puffs" that are prone to mower scalping in a lawn that is mowed high. Mowed low, bentgrass eventually crowds out other grasses. Planted by itself and properly cared for, bentgrass makes a handsome lawn.

Bluegrasses other than the Kentucky types (*Poa pratensis*) are considered fine textured. Some shade lawn mixes include rough bluegrass (*Poa trivialis*). Bermudagrass and perennial ryegrass are also listed as fine textured. All other grasses must, by law, be listed as coarse textured. Coarse grasses include tall fescue and annual ryegrass.

Percentages: When a label says that 60 percent of a given mixture is Kentucky bluegrass and 40 percent is red fescue, it means 60 percent and 40 percent by *weight* of the contents. For clarity, take a look at "Seed Facts" on page 28. Note that there are usually over 2 million seeds of Kentucky bluegrass in a pound, and approximately 600,000 seeds per pound of red fescue. When you plant a mixture of 60 percent Kentucky bluegrass and 40 percent red fescue, in actual seed numbers you are planting 84 percent bluegrass and 16 percent red fescue. That is because a red-fescue seed weighs three times more than a Kentucky bluegrass seed. The actual contents of a seed mixture would be clearer if the percentages represented seed counts, rather than weight.

Germination percentages let you know how many of each seed type germinate under ideal conditions as of the test date. By multiplying the germination percentage by the percent of the grass type, you can determine how many seeds of that type have the potential to grow. This calculation is

A Sample Seed Label

This label is an example of what you find on grass-seed boxes or containers. The proportions of grasses listed are only a sample. A good seed mixture is indicated by a low percentage of weed and crop seeds, an absence of noxious weeds, and high percentages of germination.

Attractive lawns depend on fine-textured grasses. Look for common, high-quality grasses here, such as Kentucky bluegrass and fine fescues.

Named cultivars are considered superior to common types, and in most cases are a sign of a good mixture.

Percentages indicate the proportion of the grass by weight, not seed count. See "Seed Facts" on page 28.

Generally, "coarse kinds" tend to clump and do not mix well with other grasses. Course-textured grasses should not exceed half of the mixture. The exception is turf-type perennial ryegrass. Some kinds are listed as coarse by law, but are actually fine textured.

It is virtually impossible to keep all weed seeds out of a seed crop, but look for less than 1 percent. State laws regulate which plants are considered weeds.

When seed quantities account for more than 5 percent of the mixture, the label must show the state or country where the seed crop was grown. This has no bearing on grass adaptation.

Germination is the characteristic most subject to change for the worse as the seed ages. Percentages represent the amount of viable seed that germinate under ideal conditions. This varies with the grass.

Fine-Textured Grasses		Origin	Germination
30%	Kentucky bluegrass	Oregon	80%
20%	'Adelphi' Kentucky bluegrass	Oregon	80%
20%	'Fylking' Kentucky bluegrass	Oregon	80%
29%	Creeping red fescue	Canada	90%

Coarse Kinds	Other Ingredients
None claimed	0.01% Crop seed
	1.05% Inert matter
	0.03% Weed seed
	No noxious weeds

Tested: (No earlier than 9 months of date listed.)

These are seeds from any commercially grown crop. They may be other lawn grasses or real problems such as timothy or orchardgrass. Look for "0.00 %."

The chaff, dirt, and miscellaneous material that manages to escape cleaning is called inert matter. Although it is harmless, it should not total more than 3 or 4 percent.

Noxious weeds are troublesome. In most states, it is illegal to sell seed that contains certain noxious weeds. When present, they must be individually named and the number of seeds per ounce indicated. A good seed mixture should have none.

This is the guarantee that all the information listed on the label is correct. It is best to buy seed that shows a current date. Seed stored in a cool, dry place lasts months longer.

called percent-pure live seed. This percentage is not listed on the label, but it is one way to figure the real value of the seed before purchasing it.

Continuing to use the mixture of 60 percent Kentucky bluegrass and 40 percent fine fescue as an example, if the germination percentage of the bluegrass is 80 percent, then 60 percent multiplied by 80 percent (.60 × .80) equals the percent-pure live seed of Kentucky bluegrass. Usually 90 percent of a fine fescue germinate. So, 90 percent multiplied by 40 percent (.90 × .40) equals the percent-pure live seed of fescue. By these calculations, you see that the mixture is actually 48 percent Kentucky bluegrass and 36 percent red fescue. As the germination percentage goes down, you are buying less viable seed.

If a container of seed is unmixed and unblended, it lists the percentage of purity. Essentially, this has the same meaning as the percentages of grass types in a seed mixture. A box of straight Kentucky bluegrass should be at least 90 percent pure. Multiplying the percentage of purity by the germination percentage tells you how many viable seeds are in the box, and thus the value of the seed.

Percent-pure live seed is a good way to compare value, but it is not the only measure. On the label, judge quality primarily by comparing germination percentages, weed- and crop-seed percentages, and the occurrence, if any, of noxious weeds.

Crop and Weed Seed: Agricultural laws in each state distinguish between crops and weeds. Labeling laws were designed for farmers, not buyers, of lawn seed. That is why some of the most serious lawn weeds may not be listed under "Weed seed." Bromegrass, orchardgrass, tall fescue, and timothy—all serious lawn weeds—are usually classified as crop plants. Just 1 percent of a weedy fescue can contribute 10,000 seeds to every 1,000 square feet of new lawn. A small percentage of these can establish many weeds in a new lawn.

The percentage of weed seeds in a package of lawn seed can represent a few large, harmless weeds or many serious, lightweight weed seeds. The quality of the producer is the only standard to judge by. For example, even when there are only 0.27 percent weeds per seed package, homeowners can plant 30 unwanted chickweed seeds per square foot.

Treat your newly seeded lawn with special care. While it is establishing itself, surround the area with stakes, stretched string, and flags to warn people to stay off the delicate growth.

Noxious Weeds: Noxious weeds are often difficult to eliminate once they are established. Many spread just as aggressively with runners or bulbs as by seed. Each state has a list of weeds it considers noxious.

The specific noxious weeds set forth in the Federal Seed Act are: whitetop (*Lepidium draba*, *L. repens*, *Hymenosphysa pubescens*); Canada thistle (*Cirsium arvense*); dodder (*Cuscuta* sp.); quackgrass (*Agropyron repens*); Johnsongrass (*Sorghum halepense*); bindweed (*Convovulus arvensis*); Russian knapweed (*Centaurea picris*); perennial sowthistle (*Sonchus arvensis*); and leafy spurge (*Euphorbia esula*). Most are field crop weeds, but a few are serious lawn weeds.

Annual bluegrass (*Poa annua*) and Bermudagrass (*Cynodon dactylon*) are considered noxious weeds in a few states. If present in a seed mixture, noxious weeds must be named and the number of seeds per ounce shown. In a high-quality seed mixture, there should be none.

Straights, Mixtures, and Blends

Straights: This describes lawn seed that is composed of just one type of grass. Many warm-season lawns are neither mixed with other grass types nor blended with cultivars of the same grass type. Lawns of common Bermudagrass and St. Augustine grass are examples. Tall fescue and bentgrass are cool-season grasses that are sometimes used alone. Straights can be very uniform and attractive, but are

more susceptible to diseases, so think twice before planting an entire lawn with a single variety.

Mixtures: A mixture contains seed from two or more types of grasses. The strength of one grass type compensates for the weakness of another. For this reason, a mixture is best for the average lawn. For most climates, the best mixtures are insect and disease resistant and have an overall adaptability. In the past, growers weren't sure which seeds would work well, so they threw in a little bit of everything, including a "nursegrass." The idea of a nursegrass, disregarded today, is that a hardy, fast-growing grass prepares the way for slower, more delicate premium grass. We now know that a fast-growing grass competes with and slows the establishment of a premium grass.

The grasses that mix together best have similar colors, textures, and growth rates, and are roughly equal in aggressiveness. Grasses that are similar in these respects are Kentucky bluegrass, fine fescues, and turf-type perennial ryegrass. Seed formulators vary the relative amounts of these ingredients and sometimes add small amounts of other grasses, depending on the intended use of the mixture. For instance, they add more fine fescue for lawns with partial shade and for drought-prone soil. They mix in more turf-type perennial ryegrass to get the lawn off to a fast start. And they add quantities of Kentucky bluegrass to produce a show lawn.

Seed Facts

Name	Uses and Adaptability	Seeds per Pound	Pounds of Seed per 1,000 sq. ft.	Minimum % Purity	Minimum % Germination	Days to Germinate*
Bahiagrass	Low maintenance. Gulf Coast.	175,000	5-8	75	70	21-28
Bentgrass, Creeping	Putting/bowling greens. Cool, moist climates.	6,500,000	½-1	98	90	4-12
Bermudagrass, Common	Good play lawn.	1,750,000	1-2	97	85	7-30
Blue Grama	Low maintenance. Drought tolerant. Northern Plains.	800,000	1-3	40	70	15-30
Bluegrass, Kentucky	All purpose. Widely adapted.	2,200,000	1-2	90	80	6-30
Buffalograss	Tough. Drought tolerant. Low maintenance. Central Plains.	290,000	½-1½	85	—	14-30
Carpetgrass	Low maintenance. Tropical, wet soils.	1,300,000	1-2	—	90	21
Centipedegrass	Low maintenance. Gulf Coast.	410,000	¼-½	50	70	14-20
Dichondra	Lawnlike ground cover. Southwest.	—	1	—	—	14-24
Fescue, Fine	Tolerant of shade, dry soil. Widely adapted.	615,000	5-8	97	90	5-10
Fescue, Tall	Tough play lawn. Use by itself. Good transition-zone grass.	230,000	6-10	97	90	7-12
Ryegrass, Annual	Quick cover for winter overseeding.	230,000	6-10	97	90	3-7
Ryegrass, Perennial	Turf-types called "crisis grass." Good in mixtures. Mild winter areas.	230,000	6-10	97	90	3-7

*Varies according to growing conditions.

Blends: A blend is a combination of cultivars from one species of grass. The benefit of blending cultivars is that it usually produces a lawn with improved resistance to certain diseases while preserving the texture and color of the particular type of grass. For example, a combination of 'Fylking', 'Adelphi', and 'Baron' Kentucky bluegrasses is a blend. Occasionally, a seed container announces that it is "an all-bluegrass mixture." Since this "mixture" has only one type of grass, it is technically a blend. If you are looking for a mixture instead of a blend, remember that a true mixture has more than one type of grass. Many good packaged lawn seeds are available in a combination of a mixture *and* a blend.

Seed Ratings

Almost every state has a program of seed certification. Technically, certified seed only guarantees the purity of each cultivar. In other words, if the label says "Certified 'Adelphi' Kentucky bluegrass," the container contents are guaranteed to be 'Adelphi' Kentucky bluegrass. In most states, certified seed also guarantees there are fewer weed seeds, other crop contaminates, and inert fillers.

"Percent fluorescence" is a special rating for perennial ryegrass. In 1929, researchers discovered that annual ryegrass secretes a fluorescent substance when it germinates on white filter paper. The improved turf-type perennial ryegrasses do not secrete this substance.

In order to certify perennial ryegrass, manufacturers germinate a sample on filter paper. If any fluorescence appears when the sample is exposed to ultraviolet light, the presence of annual ryegrass (or a hybrid of annual and perennial ryegrass) is established. By law, there can be no more than 3 percent fluorescence in a bag of seeds. Not all manufacturers require this test of quality to be indicated on the seed label. If listed, any fluorescing seedlings are found under "other crop" on a seed label.

From Germination to Establishment

Once seeds are in the ground, their ability to germinate and eventually form a full lawn depends on a variety of conditions. Postseeding care is the single most important factor in the success or failure of a seeded lawn.

Watering needs to be done several times a day for newly seeded lawns to keep the soil moist (but not so much that the soil washes away). Traffic, such as children, pets, and equipment, should be kept off the planted area to avoid crushing the emerging blades. This delicate nurturing period extends from the time the seed is sown to the point at which the grass becomes established. The timing depends on the grass type, its germination rate, its initial growth rate, and the day-to-day temperature. Germination can take anywhere from 4 to 30 days, with an average of 14 to 21 days, followed by a 6- to 10-week establishment period prior to use. When you sow seed, keep in mind that seed invariably germinates more slowly in the cool temperatures of late fall or early spring.

To the right are three photographs of four grasses taken at 15-day intervals. These grasses—'Manhattan' perennial ryegrass, 'Merion' Kentucky bluegrass, 'Fortress' creeping red fescue, and common Bermudagrass—were sown on the same day. In this test, the perennial ryegrass came up first, then the creeping red fescue, followed by the common Bermudagrass, and the Kentucky bluegrass. Because of the variations in grass types and local temperature, the seed you plant may not germinate "by the book."

Germination time sequence: Four grasses were sown in an identical soil mixture and lightly covered with a mulch. From left to right: 'Manhattan' perennial ryegrass, 'Merion' Kentucky bluegrass, 'Fortress' creeping red fescue, and common Bermudagrass.

The ryegrass was the first to germinate, followed closely by the fescue. Both the bluegrass and the Bermudagrass took between 13 and 14 days to emerge.

Ryegrass and the fescue grew faster than the bluegrass and the Bermudagrass. After germination, any type of grass grows rapidly when the soil is rich in nutrients and the time of year is favorable.

How to Seed a Lawn

1 Rake and Level the Seedbed

Use a steel rake for final grading and removal of stones. Scouring large areas with a piece of chain link fence or wooden drag can be especially helpful in leveling the ground. Take your time on this step—a level lawn prevents scalping from lawn mowers and water puddles from forming later on. It is difficult to correct the grade after the lawn is established.

2 Sow the Seed

You can sow grass seed with the same equipment used to spread fertilizer if the spreaders are calibrated to distribute seed at the recommended rate. The results will be good as long as you do not drastically overseed or underseed. In small areas, you can easily sow the seed by hand. Regardless of the seeding method, divide the seed into two equal lots. Seed the second lot at right angles to the first, covering the entire lawn area in each direction. When using wheeled spreaders, you may need to touch up edges by hand.

3 Rake in the Seed and Roll

To ensure good contact between seed and soil, lightly rake the entire area. Do not rake too roughly; you can redistribute seed, ruin the final grade, and bury the seed too deeply.

Seeding at a depth of ⅛ to ¼ inch (depending on seed size) is usually sufficient. To establish this depth and to place seeds firmly into the soil, go over the area with a water-filled roller. Surrounding the seeds with soil causes the seeds to assimilate more water, which quickens germination time.

4 Add Mulch

Mulching the area where grass seed has been sown hastens germination by keeping soil moist, while also providing protection for young seedlings. On slopes, mulching can prevent soil erosion during watering and rainfall.

Many materials, such as straw or sawdust, can be used as a mulch. A special roller is shown here applying the mulch in a thin layer. Wind is often a problem with lightweight mulches. In areas that have abundant rainfall or strong winds, a heavy mulch is advisable. The mulch covering should be thin enough to expose some of the soil of the seedbed—never completely cover the area.

5 Water Thoroughly

Improper watering probably causes more newly seeded lawns to fail than any other factor. For seeds to germinate evenly, the top layer of soil—always the first to dry out—must stay constantly moist. Thoroughly soak to a 6-inch depth after sowing, then lightly sprinkle by hand as often as three to four times daily until the young grass is established. How long establishment takes depends on the grass type and cultivar, its germination rate, its growth rate, and the daily weather. Water more frequently if it is hot or windy.

Use a fine spray or a nozzle with a mist setting to minimize soil movement or seed washing away. Avoid standing water.

Stringing the area with brightly colored flags will warn neighbors and children, but not necessarily dogs, to stay off.

Sprig and Plug Lawns

In areas of the United States where warm-season grasses predominate, sprigging and plugging are common methods of starting a lawn. Both methods are economical ways of using sod. Sprigs are pieces of torn-up sod; planting them is similar to seeding. Plugs are small squares or circles of sod; planting them is similar to sodding. Both methods spread by grass stems that run parallel to the soil surface from which new plants root and sprout. (See the grass plant illustration on page 6.) Unlike seeds, planting sprigs or plugs activates the stems to immediately create new grass plants. In time, the grass plants fill in and form an even lawn. This planting method is not practiced with most cool-season grasses, such as Kentucky bluegrass.

With some grasses, hybrid Bermudagrass, for example, it is only possible to plant vegetatively with sprigs, plugs, or sod, because they do not produce viable seed.

Regardless of the planting method, first prepare the soil according to the instructions beginning on page 21.

Sprigs

A sprig can be a short or a long stem. It needs at least one node or joint to spread and develop into a grass plant. Sprigging is simply the planting of individual sprigs at spaced intervals. A suitable sprig should have roots or at least two to four nodes from which roots can develop. Bentgrass, Bermudagrass, and zoysiagrass are grasses that are commonly planted by this method.

You can buy sprigs by the bushel; or you can buy sod and pull or shred it apart into separate sprigs. Sprigs bought by the bushel by mail order are shipped in bags or boxes. Shipping usually takes place within 24 hours after mechanical shredding.

The best time to plant sprigs is from late spring to mid-summer. The onset of warm weather provides optimum growing conditions for warm-season grasses.

The soil should be ready to plant when the sprigs arrive. Keep the sprigs cool and moist until planting time, which should be as soon as possible after delivery. It only takes five minutes of sunlight to damage sprigs enclosed in plastic bags. Even when stored properly, sprigs decay rapidly.

How to Plant Sprigs: There are several ways to plant sprigs. Whichever method you use, it is always best to work with *slightly* moist soil. In any case, *do not let the stems dry out.* Water sections as you plant them, and keep the soil constantly moist until the stems are established.

One planting method is to cut 2- to 3-inch-deep furrows in the soil bed and place the sprigs in the furrows. Dig the furrows with a hoe and space them from 4 to 12 inches apart, depending on the rate of coverage you would like. Close spacing results in more rapid coverage, but naturally involves more material and labor. Place the stems against one side of the furrow so that any tufts of foliage are above ground and the light-colored stem is below ground. Firm the soil around each stem and level the area as well as possible. Rolling with a half-filled roller helps to firm the soil around stems and aid in the leveling.

Another method of planting sprigs is to place the stems on the soil at desired intervals and lightly press them in with a notched stick.

The third and fastest method is called broadcast sprigging, stolonizing, or shredding. Sprigs are shredded

---

Sprigging is an economical way to use sod. Although the finished results take longer than laying sod, the lawn eventually fills in to form a lush, green cover. Once a lawn started from sprigs is established, you cannot tell the difference between it and one started by seed, sod, or plugs.

Planting Methods for Warm-Season Grasses

Grass	Method
Bahiagrass	Seed
Bermudagrass	
Common	Sprigs, Plugs, Sod, Seed
All Others	Sprigs, Plugs, Sod
Carpetgrass	Sprigs, Plugs, Sod, Seed
Centipedegrass	Sprigs, Plugs, Sod, Seed
St. Augustine grass	Sprigs, Plugs, Sod
Zoysiagrass	Sprigs, Plugs, Sod

A square yard of sod provides: 2,000 to 3,000 Bermudagrass or zoysiagrass sprigs; 500 to 1,000 St. Augustine grass or centipedegrass sprigs; 324 two-inch plugs; 84 four-inch plugs; or 1 bushel of sprigs. Row planting requires 2 to 6 bushels per 1,000 square feet. Broadcast sprigging requires from 5 to 10 bushels.

into short stems and spread by hand over the designated area like a mulch. Afterwards, cover them with soil and roll lightly with a water roller. Water once or twice a day for the first week.

Sprigs can be long or short stems of warm-season grasses. Longer stems, such as this one, can be planted in shallow furrows in the soil.

Plugs

Plugging is exactly what it sounds like—plugging small squares or circles of sod into the soil at regular intervals. Square plugs are cut from sod with a shovel or knife, while round plugs are cut with a special steel plugger similar to a bulb planter. You may buy sod and cut the plugs yourself, but it is easier to order precut plugs by mail. When they arrive, place plugs in properly sized holes, spaced 6 to 12 inches apart. (See the photographs on the following page.) Then roll and water them. Although plugs do not dry out as fast as sprigs, keeping the surrounding soil moist is still important. Water daily for the first week. Plant plugs, like sprigs, just before spring weather begins.

St. Augustine grass and centipedegrass are usually cut into plugs 3 to 4 inches in diameter and are planted 1 foot apart. Bermudagrass and zoysiagrass plugs are usually 2 inches in diameter and are planted 6 to 12 inches apart. The spacing between each plug determines the time it takes to achieve complete coverage.

After plugging, it is usually necessary to add soil after initial establishment to level the lawn. Watering and rain may cause the soil to wash out between plugs, yielding an uneven and bumpy lawn.

Plugs are sections of sod that have been cut into small circles or squares. Planted at regular intervals, they spread to become a lawn.

Plugging a lawn is simple. Just use a steel plugger to remove cores of soil at regular intervals. Then fill the holes with similar-sized plugs.

Paving-Block Lawns: Concrete paving blocks combined with turfgrass can produce a "lawn" for use as a driveway or pathway. The appearance is similar to a checkerboard, with squares of grass supported by the ridges of blocks. Paving blocks are manufactured specifically for this use. An average-sized block covers about 3 square feet. Standard concrete building blocks also work well.

Planting a lawn with paving blocks is a simple operation. If the proposed area must support heavy weight, such as a driveway, prepare a solid base for the blocks first. Place the paving blocks in position, side by side, and fill the planting holes with high quality soil. Then plant plugs (or even seeds) the same as you would for any new lawn. After the grass is established, the blocks, rather than the turf, support the weight of vehicles or heavy foot traffic. Keep the grass looking good with proper cultural practices.

There are many advantages to this type of lawn. It is more attractive than a completely artificial surface, and is cooler and produces less glare. During the rainy season, there is less water runoff due to the absorption qualities of the grass.

Different grass types produce different effects. A vertically growing grass, such as tall fescue, obscures the blocks completely. A horizontal grass, such as Bermudagrass, stays low, providing a textured pattern.

The cost of a making a paving-block lawn varies with each situation. But as a general rule it should be the same or even less than poured concrete.

Paving-block lawns provide a cool alternative to concrete or asphalt driveways. The weight of the car is supported by the blocks, not the sod.

Sod Lawns

Sod is turf that is grown commercially, cut into strips, and lifted intact, along with a thin layer of soil held together by runners, roots, or netting. Installing a sod lawn is much like laying a carpet, with the objective of reestablishing the grass roots in well-prepared soil.

Compared with establishing a lawn by seeding, sprigging, or plugging, laying sod yields quick results. A sod lawn can be functional in as little as two weeks, although there should be some restraint on its use until its roots have knitted properly with the soil. Lift the corners of the sod to check. In comparison, Bermudagrass sprigs cover in 8 to 10 weeks, St. Augustine grass plugs take 3 months, and lawn seeds take an average of 14 to 21 days for germination, followed by a 6- to 10-week establishment period.

While timing is critical when seeding a lawn, you can install a sod lawn almost any time of year as long as weather permits and irrigation water is available. Ideal times to install sod are in late summer, early fall, and early spring for cool-season grasses; late spring and early summer for warm-season grasses.

One advantage of sod is that it can be installed in places where a seed lawn may be difficult to establish, such as a heavily trafficked area or a slope that erodes easily.

The drawback of a sod lawn is the initial cost and labor involved, which is substantial compared with a seed lawn. The price tag needs to be weighed against achieving such fast results.

Keys to Starting a Sod Lawn

Selecting the Sod: The first step is to select a high-quality, healthy grass that is well adapted to your area and site. Most nurseries have information on ordering the sod you want. Or look in the Yellow Pages under sod or sodding service companies.

Sod consisting of cool-season grasses is usually available in the same cultivars or blends that are obtainable in seed mixtures. Sod mixtures usually include both shade-tolerant and sun-loving grasses.

Sod usually comes in rolled or folded strips from 6 to 9 feet long and 2 feet wide. The strips should be moist, not too wet and definitely not too dry. High-quality sod will be uniformly green. Do not buy sod that has poor color or yellowing areas.

The thickness of different types of sod varies, but generally from the top to the bottom of the soil should measure ¾ to 1 inch. If the sod is too thick, it will root slowly or poorly; if it is too thin, it will dry out too fast. It should not fall apart easily when handled.

Some states have a sod certification program to ensure that sod is labeled correctly and is relatively free of insects, weeds, and disease. If certified sod is not available, make sure the sod you buy originates from a reputable sod farm.

Preparing the Soil: Before the sod is delivered, prepare the soil thoroughly according to the instructions on pages 21 to 24. Do not be fooled into thinking that because the sod already has soil attached that soil preparation is not important. It is just as important as it is with the establishing a seed, sprig, or plug lawn.

When you are preparing the soil, remember that the final grade should be ¾ to 1 inch lower than you want the lawn to be. This allows for the thickness of the sod to fit flush against sprinklers, sidewalks, and driveways.

Installation

Sod is usually delivered on pallets to the site where it is to be installed. Plan to lay the sod as soon as possible after it arrives. If a lawn service is doing the installation, make sure there are no unnecessary delays.

Do not leave the sod rolled and stacked on pallets more than one day in hot weather. In cool weather, sod can remain rolled for two to three days. Store in a cool, shaded area. Be sure to keep the soil on the outer pieces moist. If you must leave it longer than several days and have the space, you can store sod indefinitely by unrolling it on a hard, shaded surface, such as a garage or carport, and watering it frequently.

Moisten the soil before laying sod. It is best to water a day or two in advance to avoid laying the sod on muddy soil. Work in sections if you are sodding a large area: Lay the sod in one area, roll and water, then move on to another area. This method prevents the sod from drying out, especially if the weather is warm.

Whether you or lawn professionals are installing the sod, you need to be informed about the entire procedure. See the pages that follow for step-by-step instructions and photographs on sod installation.

Where sod comes from: A cutting machine lifts strips of turf at a sod farm.

Slopes: When laying sod on a slope, start from the lowest point and move uphill. Always lay the sod so that it runs perpendicular to the slope. Stagger the joints to avoid excess erosion during irrigation or rain.

Pegging or staking sod strips is advisable on steep slopes. Use soft pine pegs; left in place, they decompose quickly. Three pegs 6 to 8 inches long are usually sufficient to hold each strip of sod. Place one peg in each top corner and one in the center. Drive in pegs at an angle that is vertical, rather than perpendicular, to the slope.

After Installation

Watering: Proper watering is the single most important step in the establishment of a sod lawn. After the sod is in place, it may be necessary to water every day for up to two weeks until the roots have sufficiently knitted with the underlying soil.

After watering, lift a corner of a sod strip to be sure the soil underneath is moist. An inch of water over the area is usually sufficient to wet soil and sod.

Sod strip edges and borders along paths and driveways will be the first to dry out and the last to knit with the soil.

Mowing: Mow newly sodded areas as soon as the grass is 2½ to 3 inches high. Clip it frequently enough to prevent removal of more than one third of the growth at one mowing. See pages 49 to 52 for more mowing information.

How to Install a Sod Lawn

1 Choose High-Quality Sod

You can avoid many problems by buying sod of high quality and proper grass type. Most states have sod inspection programs to ensure that sod is free of weeds, diseases, and insects, and that it is the cultivar or species it is advertised to be. Make sure sod originates from a reputable sod farm. Your county extension agent or local nursery staff should be helpful. Many nurseries also sell and install sod. See the previous page for other characteristics of healthy sod.

2 Prepare the Soil

Because you are laying actively growing grass with soil already attached, you may think that it is unnecessary to prepare the soil. Nothing could be more untrue.

Prepare the soil as you would for a seed lawn (see page 21), but make the final grade ¾ to 1 inch lower, so that the sod fits flush against sidewalks, driveways, and sprinklers. If a soil test indicates the need, add lime or sulfur.

Take the time to make the soil as level as possible. Use a leveling rake, if necessary. Once the sod is laid it is difficult to level. If large quantities of amendments have been added to parts or all of the future lawn area, wet the soil thoroughly to let the soil settle, allow it to dry, then regrade.

3 Spread Fertilizer and Moisten Soil

If the proper amounts of fertilizer have been worked into the soil during site preparation, it is not usually necessary to fertilize again for six weeks or whenever the lawn starts showing the need. If fertilizer has not yet been added, rake in one with a high phosphorus content, such as formula 5-15-5, to a depth of 2 or 3 inches.

Lay sod on moist soil. Muddy soil causes footprints and uneven spots. Dry soil leads to drying and eventual weakening of the sod. If the soil is dry, wet it a day or so before the sod is delivered to give it adequate time to dry to a moist stage.

4 Keep Sod Moist

Be sure you are ready to install the sod by the time it is delivered. In hot weather, sod should not remain rolled or stacked for more than one day. In cool weather, it can remain healthy for two or three days.

Do not allow the soil on the outer rolls to dry out. Occasionally give the rolls a light sprinkling, but take care not to oversaturate them or they will be difficult to handle.

5 Start with a Straight Edge

The easiest way to begin laying sod is to start with a straight edge, such as a sidewalk or driveway. If you have an irregularly shaped lawn, draw a straight line through it or string a line across it, and start laying sod on either side of it. Handle the sod strips carefully to avoid tearing or stretching them.

The rolls of sod are heavy—each strip can weigh as much as 40 pounds. The truck pictured above is loaded nearly to its weight-carrying capacity. Have two or three helpers ready to help unload the rolls as soon as the truck arrives.

On a hot day (like the day on which these photographs were taken), it is a good idea to lightly sprinkle the strips as soon as they are laid.

6 Roll Out the Sod

Place the loose end of the rolled sod tightly against the previously laid strip and carefully unroll it. Stagger the ends of sod pieces much like a brick layer staggers the ends of the bricks.

When rolling out sod strips, stand or kneel on a board or piece of plywood to distribute your weight evenly. Otherwise, you are likely to end up with pockets and uneven spots in the lawn.

7 Place Edges Tightly Together

To avoid unnecessary drying, keep sod edges in the closest contact possible without overlapping. Firm the edges together with your fingers, but do not stretch the sod.

If gaps cannot be avoided, fill them with good soil or organic matter and pay close attention to them when watering; they will be the first areas to dry out. Do not attempt to fill small gaps (less than 3 or 4 inches square) with sod; small pieces of grass usually dry out and die. Assume that the sod will shrink slightly and open gaps, so compress the sod as you install it.

8 Cut Pieces to Fit

Along curved edges or unusually shaped areas, cut with a sharp knife or garden spade to custom fit the turf. A knife with a serrated edge, such as an old bread knife, works best. As mentioned in step 5, begin laying sod in a straight line, and work toward irregular areas.

9 Roll to Ensure Contact

After all the sod has been laid, roll it with a water-filled roller to ensure good contact between sod roots and underlying soil. Roll perpendicular to the length of the strips. If the weather is warm, you may have to roll the sod in sections as it is laid.

Rolling will also have a leveling effect, but it is still better to start with a level sod bed, rather than compacting the soil with repeated rolling.

10 Water Thoroughly

Improper watering after installation is probably the most common cause of failure in sod lawns. Once the sod has been rolled, water it thoroughly. The soil underneath should be wet to a depth of 6 to 8 inches. From then on, watch your new lawn closely. The edges of the sod strips and pieces along sidewalks and driveways are the first to dry out and the last to knit with the soil. They may require spot watering every day, perhaps even more often in hot weather. Make sure the underlying soil is always moist. Once the lawn begins to knit with the soil, you can begin to approach a normal watering schedule (see page 42).

Foot traffic can slow or damage the establishment of a sod lawn. To help avoid this problem, surround the area with stakes, string, and bright flags.

Lawn Care

**This chapter is designed to simplify lawn care—
from mowing and fertilizing to insect, weed, and disease control.
Knowing how these aspects interrelate will help you learn how to
take better care of your lawn.**

Most home gardeners enjoy working with their lawns. Getting outdoors on a Saturday morning is often the perfect opportunity to get some sunshine while you mow and water your lawn. A few minutes of pulling weeds during the week serves as a transition from the bustle of the day's work to the calmer atmosphere of a home and a garden. Lawn care is particularly pleasant when the lawn is lush and attractive. Taking good care of your lawn often involves no more work than taking poor care of it. The difference between good and poor care is not in the amount of effort expended but in *how* the effort is expended.

Level of Maintenance
Walk through your neighborhood and observe some of the lawns that look appealing. Notice how the lawn complements the house and the garden. Look closely. Is it weed free? Are there any yellow or bare spots? You probably won't find many perfect lawns, but lawns don't need to be perfect. Most people are happy with a lawn that is simply appealing and functional.

The degree of lawn maintenance depends a good deal on the amount of time you have to spend on lawn care. When you water, fertilize, mow, or take care of weeds probably depends on when you have the time. These tasks do not have to reduce the pleasure derived from caring for a lawn. Who can say who gets more enjoyment: the lawn connoisseur or the Saturday morning mower?

◀ *Water is just one requirement for a thick, resilient lawn. For a healthy lawn, follow proper lawn care practices.*

Developing a Balanced Program
Although the different aspects of taking care of a lawn can be broken down conveniently into chapters and sub-chapters, actual lawn care is not so precise. A lawn that is properly watered and fertilized has fewer problems with weeds and disease. On the other hand, it also has to be mowed more often. Regular mowing is a good method of weed control.

The key to success, no matter what your maintenance approach, is to develop a balanced program of lawn care. If you mow little, then water and fertilize little, also. If you enjoy getting outdoors and watering, balance this practice with extra fertilizing.

By understanding the needs of your lawn, you will be able to have the lawn you desire. More importantly, you will see that lawn care can be simple and enjoyable.

The pleasure of a having a lawn lies not only in how it looks in the landscape; mowing a lawn on a sunny afternoon provides you with a little exercise and the enjoyable feel and fragrance of a freshly cut lawn.

Watering

More questions are probably asked about watering than any other aspect of lawn care—and rightly so. As for any plant, water is one of the basic requirements for the growth of grass. Without it a lawn cannot survive.

Telling you how much water to apply and how often would be simple if there were set rules for every situation. But too many variables are possible. The water requirements of your lawn depend on a number of things: the type of soil you have, seasonal temperatures, wind velocity, humidity, the frequency of rain, the type of grass, and maintenance practices.

Even with all these variables to keep in mind, certain guidelines, discussed below, remain as basics for a watering program. By combining these guidelines with your own watering experience and a knowledge of the climate in your area, you can develop a good watering program for your lawn.

How Often to Water

The answer to this question is simply: when it needs it. Water your lawn when the soil begins to dry out, before the grass wilts. When a lawn wilts, grass blades either roll or fold, exposing the bottoms of the blades. At this stage, the lawn color appears to change from a bright green to a dull blue-green or smoky color. You are actually seeing the bottoms of the wilted blades, which are grayer than the tops. This first occurs in the most drought-prone spots, especially beneath trees.

Another signal of the need for water is the loss of resilience—the ability of a lawn to bounce back into shape. Take a walk across your lawn. Do the impressions of your footprints remain visible for more than a few seconds? If the answer is yes, especially in the morning, your lawn needs water.

Other ways to check for adequate water are with soil moisture testers or coring tubes. There are two types of moisture testers: mechanical and electrical. The mechanical type, called a tensiometer, has a porous tip and a water-filled tube. Dry soil pulls out the water in the tube. A gauge measures the suction this action creates. Leave tensiometers in place once they are installed. The electrical type of moisture tester operates on the principle that wet soil conducts electricity better than dry soil. A coring tube takes a plug of your lawn and the underlying soil. It allows you to see and feel the moisture level in the soil.

How long your lawn can go between waterings depends on several factors. Roots grow only where there is water. If you constantly wet only the top few inches of soil, the roots do not venture deeper. Eventually, the limited size of the root system forces you into watering more often. That means trouble, because frequent watering keeps the surface wet, which is ideal for weeds and diseases. If roots go deep into the soil, they can draw on a larger underground water supply and the lawn can go much longer between waterings.

Soil conditions affect how often you need to water. For example, 12 inches of loam soil hold about 1½ inches of water, a sandy soil about half that much, and a clay soil twice as much. Lawns in sandy soil need water less often, but water must be applied at a slower rate to avoid wasteful runoff.

Different grasses have different water requirements. Check the water needs of your grass type in "A Gallery of Grasses," beginning on page 8.

Local weather patterns are also important. Seasonal rain can play an integral part in a watering program. When it is hot and windy, more frequent watering is required.

How Much to Water

To keep grass roots growing deeply, moisten the soil to a depth of 6 to 8 inches. This means watering until there is about an inch of water over the lawn surface. In dry weather, an average lawn depletes this amount of water in about three days. To determine whether the water has gone down deeply enough, wait 12 hours, then check with a soil coring tube. Or poke a screwdriver into the ground; if it penetrates 6 inches of soil without much resistance, the lawn is wet enough.

Apply water as uniformly as possible and no faster than the soil can absorb it. Avoid applying so much at one time

Just about everyone has enjoyed this kind of summer fun. Here, sprays of sparkling water refresh more than the lawn.

that it results in wasteful runoff. If runoff occurs, divide the watering into timed intervals. Sprinkle until the soil cannot take anymore, then stop for 20 to 30 minutes to allow for absorption. Continue watering until the desired amount has been applied.

When to Water

Many people think that early morning is the best time to water. Others prefer afternoon or evening waterings. The main consideration of when to water is simply: whenever it is the most convenient time for you. However, certain times of day have their advantages and disadvantages.

Afternoon watering has several disadvantages. During the afternoon, evaporation caused by the wind and sun is at a maximum, which means that less of the water applied actually reaches the lawn. Wind can disrupt sprinkler patterns, causing poor coverage. Local water consumption is usually highest in the afternoon, which can result in low water pressure. Keep in mind, too, that drought symptoms are more evident in the afternoon and evening. These symptoms can be induced by the higher temperatures and winds typical of that time of day, but are not always an indication of water stress. Often the grass regains its bright green color as temperatures and winds subside.

In spite of these disadvantages, syringing (light watering) in the afternoon can benefit your lawn on hot days. When temperatures reach their highest during the day, alleviate the heat stress of your lawn by wetting it just enough to moisten and cool the grass blades.

Most lawns become wet at night naturally by the dew, but you may still water in the evening. In some areas, leaving a water-soaked lawn overnight may promote disease. However, cultural practices, such as proper fertilizing, regular dethatching and aerating, and mowing at recommended heights, do more to prevent disease than switching from evening waterings to a different time of day.

Early morning is the ideal time to water. Morning waterings usually take advantage of less wind, milder temperatures, and adequate water pressure. Unlike the afternoon, water has time to soak down to the roots without evaporating.

The best guideline of all, though, for when to water is: Water when the lawn needs it.

About Hoses

Most gardeners realize the importance of a hose. Improper use or a hose of poor quality can be annoying and harmful. Does your hose have leaky connections? Is it too short? Is it impossible to roll it up? Are the edges of its metal couplings sharp and jagged?

If you answered yes to any of these questions, you probably need to make minor repairs or purchase a new hose. Repair is usually easy and inexpensive. If you decide to buy a new hose, it is worth paying more for one of high quality that will provide excellent service for a long time.

A well-made hose is flexible in any weather. This is usually the case with hoses made of high-grade rubber and laminated filament. It is seldom true of the inexpensive plastic models. The hose you buy should be long enough to reach to all areas of your yard, and should have a wide enough diameter to supply sufficient quantities of water. The larger the diameter of the hose, the more water it can deliver. Garden hoses are available in ¾-inch, ⅝-inch, and ½-inch diameters. A hose that is ⅝ inch in diameter is the usual choice for a medium-sized lawn.

If your hose needs repair, you will find a wide variety of hose repair equipment, as either clamp-on or screw-on connections. Our favorite is the brass screw-on type featured in the photos below.

If you have ever damaged plants while dragging the hose from one area to another, consider placing heavy wooden stakes as barriers in key areas of the garden.

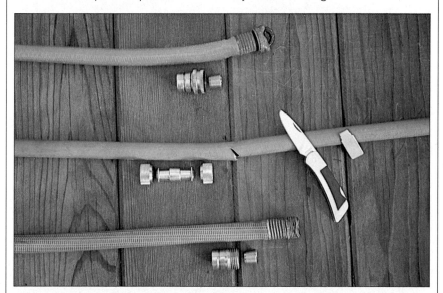

Too many gardeners put up with broken or leaky hoses without realizing how easy and inexpensive they are to repair. The photo above shows some common hose problems. The photo below shows the same hoses after being repaired.

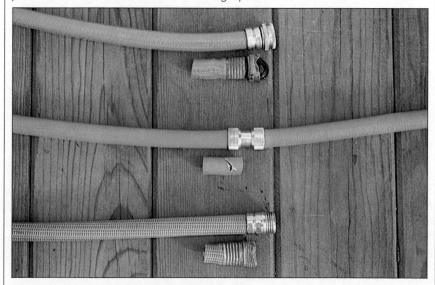

Watering During Drought

When drought conditions exist, a lawn slows its growth, becomes wilted and brown, and may die. If you live in an area where water conservation is requested or enforced, you simply have to hope that your lawn survives the stress. If it dies, replant with a more drought-tolerant grass when suitable weather returns. During times of drought, lawns that are under a system of survival watering may still develop a spotty, thinned appearance. Here are some basic watering rules in case your area experiences a drought:

1. Do not apply nitrogen fertilizer to lawns when drought conditions exist.

2. Mow your grass higher and less often. However, do not let it grow more than twice the recommended mowing height.

3. Reduce weed competition.

4. Irrigate without runoff to root-zone depth (6 to 8 inches) when your lawn shows the need.

There is a difference between a drought-stressed brown lawn and a dormant brown lawn. Cool-season grasses, such as Kentucky bluegrass or fescue, become dormant in the hottest part of the summer, returning to full vigor in the cooler fall weather. If water is abundant and you started an effective watering program the previous spring, it is possible to keep your cool-season lawn green during this dormant period by continuing to water throughout the summer. However, if the lawn becomes dormant, let it stay that way. Too many fluctuations between dormancy and active growth can weaken a lawn.

Check with the local weather bureau for climate information. It should be helpful in setting up your specific watering program. Rain gauges are also a useful tool. By knowing how much rain falls, you can tell how much supplemental water you need. Do not be misled by light drizzles that supply little moisture to the soil. However, watering after a light shower can be an effective way of reducing water loss through evaporation.

If drought is a recurring problem, you may want to plant a more drought-resistant lawn. To check the drought tolerance of different grasses, see the chart on page 19.

Watering New Lawns

A special set of rules applies for watering newly seeded or sodded lawns. Sprinkling is, at the least, an everyday requirement. For seeds to germinate or sod roots to knit, watering is often required more than once a day. For watering information on newly seeded lawns, see page 31; for newly sodded lawns, see page 39.

Water-Efficient Lawns

Besides watering more deeply and less frequently, you can increase watering efficiency by improving other cultural practices. Two major problems that result in poor water penetration are thatch and compacted soil. If the problems are bad enough, either can actually repel water, causing wasteful runoff. Regular dethatching and aerating, as described on pages 81 to 82, increase water penetration, provide air in the root zone, and aid in nutrient assimilation.

You can conserve water by following recommended mowing heights and by adding fertilizers that are high in potassium and low in nitrogen before hot weather arrives.

Fertilizing properly is an important factor in efficient watering. Under-fertilizing invites competition from water-hungry weeds and reduces the capacity of the lawn for wear and tear. Overfertilizing can be just as damaging. It promotes vigorous, water-hungry growth of the lawn, which causes thatch to develop and reduces the ability of a cool-season grass to recover from summer dormancy.

Portable Sprinklers

Besides understanding the requirements of your lawn and its signals for water, you must be familiar with your sprinkling equipment. Whether you choose a reliable portable sprinkler or an automatic underground system, the application rates and the pattern of water distribution vary. If properly designed and installed, automatic systems are usually more precise and predictable than portable ones. If you decide to water with a portable sprinkler, choose yours with a skeptical eye and a thought for uniform coverage and minimum water waste.

Many kinds of portable sprinklers are available with, consequently, many patterns of water distribution. Different brands of the same type of sprinkler—even individual sprinklers—have completely different patterns. Without knowing this, a conscientious waterer can end up with sections of lawn that are either overwatered or underwatered. This produces uneven green and brown areas and unnecessary weeds and disease. Along with knowing about soil, climate, and wind conditions, it is important to be aware of how your sprinkler distributes water.

The Container Test: Measuring the water distribution of your sprinkler is easy. Set up a gridlike pattern of small containers of the same size on a section of the lawn. Even though different types of sprinklers require different grid patterns, it is a good idea to start with a straight line of containers, extending them at set intervals, from

To water efficiently you need to know the water pattern and distribution rate of your sprinkler system. Check how much water falls in specific areas by evenly spacing containers on the lawn.

close to the sprinkler head to just outside the reach of the water. Turn the sprinkler on at the normal operating pressure; leave it on for a set period of time, then record the amount of water deposited in each container. This gives you a good idea of the sprinkler pattern, as well as the amount of water distributed.

Realizing that a lawn generally needs 1 to 2 inches of water per week, the container test is an easy method that helps you to determine how long to turn on the sprinkler and to what degree to overlap the sprinkling pattern for efficient watering.

Types of Sprinklers: Stationary sprinklers deliver water in an irregular pattern. The accumulation of water in the containers may vary from 8 inches an hour in one spot, to 2 inches an hour just 4 feet away, to almost nothing near the sprinkler head. There is no predictable pattern that leads to proper overlapping and efficient watering. However, it is unfair to label this sprinkler ''useless.'' As long you know how it distributes water, it can be valuable for spot watering, supplementing other types of sprinklers.

Oscillating-arm sprinklers deliver water in a rectangular pattern. Many observers believe that this type of sprinkler deposits most of the water near the sprinkler head, with decreasing amounts toward the periphery as the arm moves away from the vertical, central position. While this is true of older models, newer versions stall momentarily when the arm is farthest from its upright position, thus evening out distribution at the periphery.

The whirling-head sprinkler deposits the largest amount of water close to the sprinkler head; the amount decreases the farther away it goes from the source of the spray. Water distribution is uneven when this sprinkler is used without a system of overlapping. With a 50-percent overlap, efficiency increases and the sprinkler becomes quite useful.

Impulse sprinklers are best for large areas and are commonly used for golf-course lawns. An internal jet rotates the sprinkler, which delivers pulses of water covering anywhere from a full circle to a part circle. Coverage to your lawn is quite even.

By combining the knowledge gained from experimentation and an observant eye, it is quite easy to set up a watering schedule for your lawn with a portable sprinkler.

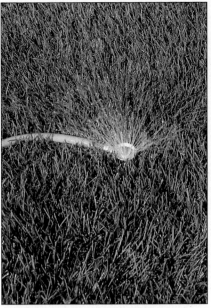
Stationary sprinklers are good for spot watering. Move them often for even coverage.

Oscillating-arm sprinklers apply water over large areas, and are highly adjustable.

Whirling-head sprinklers deposit more water near the head and less at the periphery.

Impulse sprinklers have a rotating head that shoots water out with a pulsating jet action.

Underground Sprinkler Systems

Interest in underground sprinkler systems increases every year. An underground system has many advantages over a portable sprinkler; the most obvious is the convenience of not having to constantly move it. Most underground systems are also more efficient than portable types. Sprinkler heads apply predictable amounts of water over an exact area, eliminating the most objectional grievance of portable sprinklers: uneven water distribution. An underground system combined with an automatic timer can even water while you are away from home.

Before deciding to put in an underground system, consider the initial cost of materials and the labor involved in installing it. Because of the increased popularity of such systems, manufacturers now produce illustrated, easy-to-follow directions for homeowners who do the work themselves. Materials have also become easier to install and less expensive.

Keep in mind, however, that a poorly designed or poorly installed underground system can be as bad as or worse than a portable sprinkler. These pages outline typical installation considerations, potential problems, and how they can be solved.

Installing It Yourself: After you have decided to put in an underground sprinkler system, you need to decide how much, if any, of the work you are going to do yourself. Companies specializing in irrigation can often install a system within a few days. Doing it yourself may take several weekends. If the sprinklers need to be installed before planting a new lawn, the clutter of materials and equipment may not be important. In an established lawn, however, it may be bothersome, even damaging. Cost is also a consideration. If you are handy with tools and have the time, it is much less expensive to do it yourself.

Choosing a System: Once you decide who is doing the work, be sure to choose the manufacturer as well as the supplier carefully. Consult neighbors who have underground systems, as well as irrigation specialists, nursery workers, or your county extension agent for advice about the trade name that best suits your needs. Then either write the manufacturer or see your local distributor to obtain detailed information. If you are installing the system yourself, before purchasing it read the installation instructions to make sure they are easy to follow.

Flow Rate: One of the most important aspects of installing a sprinkler system successfully is determining the available flow rate: the rate at which water travels through a pipe, measured in gallons per minute (GPM). The easiest way to find the available GPM is by using a special gauge. Many sprinkler suppliers loan this gauge on request.

Another way to deduce the available GPM is to measure how many seconds it takes an outdoor faucet, turned wide open, to fill a 1-gallon container. Dividing the total number of seconds into 60 gives you the flow rate in gallons per minute. For example, if a 1-gallon bucket fills in 5 seconds, divide 5 into 60 to determine that the flow rate is 12 GPM.

Piping: For most sprinkler systems, galvanized steel and copper pipes have gradually given way to lightweight PVC (polyvinyl chloride) plastic pipe and flexible polyethylene pipe.

Ease of handling, assembly, durability, flow characteristics, cost, and availability are all reasons for recommending PVC pipe and solvent-welded fittings as the piping for sprinkler installations. Use the heavy-duty schedule 40 for all pressure-holding lines. To save money and materials, use class 200 or class 315 pipe for lateral lines that will never be required to hold constant pressure.

A less expensive but less substantial substitute for PVC pipe is flexible polyethylene pipe. It comes in 100-foot and 200-foot rolls and can be cut with a knife. Fittings are inserted into the pipe and held in place with stainless-steel clamps tightened with a screwdriver or wrench. The advantage of polyethylene pipe is that it does not restrict you to following straight lines. However, this pliability is a disadvantage as well. You can cut through it with a spade while digging in your garden without being aware of it. Rodents, especially gophers, like to chew holes in it. And it cannot handle enough pressure for it to be used between the water meter and the control valves.

In general, unless you have a large lawn, ¾-inch pipe is sufficient for the entire system. If water needs to travel more than 100 feet, the friction of water through the ¾-inch pipe may reduce the available GPM. Use 1-inch pipe for distances over 100 feet to avoid this occurence.

Sprinkler Heads: Although a wide variety of sprinkler heads is available for every conceivable application, most residential lawns are best served by adjustable, pop-up sprinkler heads with full, half-circle, and quarter-circle watering patterns. When not in use, the head rests flush on the ground, out of the way of the mower and foot traffic. Each sprinkler head discharges a specific number of gallons per minute (GPM) over a given radius, and each requires a certain water pressure in order to achieve its designed throw.

Most sprinkler heads have a flow control to adjust how far the water is thrown. Heads set for a specific arc are the most popular, such as three-quarter, 30-degree, and 60-degree

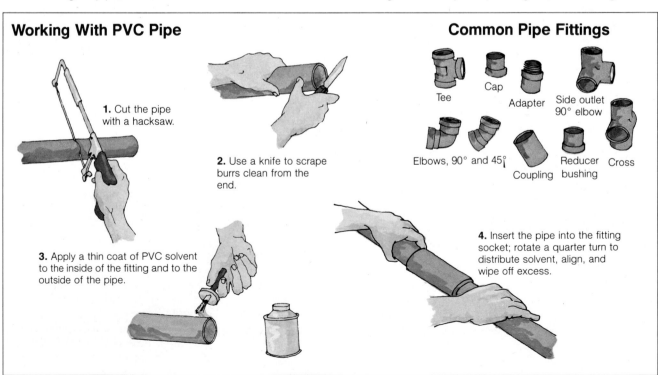

Working With PVC Pipe

1. Cut the pipe with a hacksaw.

2. Use a knife to scrape burrs clean from the end.

3. Apply a thin coat of PVC solvent to the inside of the fitting and to the outside of the pipe.

4. Insert the pipe into the fitting socket; rotate a quarter turn to distribute solvent, align, and wipe off excess.

Common Pipe Fittings

Tee

Cap

Adapter

Side outlet 90° elbow

Elbows, 90° and 45°

Coupling

Reducer bushing

Cross

arcs. Heads with adjustable arcs are hard to find and expensive. If you do buy a head with an adjustable arc, check specifications to make sure that this feature does not drastically affect the flow rate. This could change your watering strategy.

Sprinkler heads with a square pattern and a low precipitation rate are also available. A square pattern is useful in narrow areas such as side yards and parking strips. Use a low-precipitation head where runoff is a problem due to a sloping grade or clay soil.

Whenever possible, group sprinkler heads by the requirements of an area. Besides pop-up spray heads, impulse sprinklers are useful for watering large areas. However, they are difficult to use efficiently for small lawns. If wind is a problem, place a pop-up sprinkler with rotary action in the center of a lawn area; it will disperse water evenly in large drops rather than a spray.

Risers: Risers bring the water from the underground pipe to the sprinkler heads. The height of the risers must be carefully adjusted. Several types of risers are available to make this adjustment easier. Cutaway risers have sections of thread in short increments along its entire length. It is easy to cut away small ½-inch pieces, one or two at a time, until the proper height is reached. Flexible risers also require proper height adjustment, but if the attached sprinkler head is accidentally kicked or hit by a mower, the risers flex rather than break.

Valves and Circuits: The manifold is the control unit of the sprinkler system. It is composed of a group of control valves that deliver water to different parts of the lawn. Position it in a convenient spot, where you can turn it on and off without getting wet. Try to conceal it with a cover or box, since the plumbing is seldom attractive. One manifold *each* is needed for a front lawn and a back lawn.

The control valves that make up the manifold are usually globe valves, the same type of valves used for faucets in a house. Globe valves shut off the flow of water by pressing a soft disc against a smooth valve seat.

Control valves often have antisiphon valves attached to them. Antisiphon valves, also known as vacuum breakers, prevent the backflow of water into the house supply. They are sometimes required by local ordinances and are always a good idea to include.

Pop-up sprinkler heads are used in most residential systems. When not in use, they rest flush on the ground, out of the way of the mower and foot traffic. Use full-circle arcs for center areas of a lawn, half-circle arcs for the sides, and quarter-circle arcs for the corners.

Each control valve controls several sprinkler heads. This group of heads is called a circuit. Two factors control the number of circuits you need. One is the available flow rate. If too many sprinklers are turned on at one time, the water pressure drops, preventing the heads from spraying as far as they are supposed to. For proper coverage, it is best to turn on one circuit at a time. The other factor to consider is the watering needs of different areas. For example, if a shrub bed is on the same circuit as a lawn, the shrub bed will be watered as often as the lawn, even though it does not need as much water.

Drawing a Plan: Drawing your plan on paper helps you to visualize your underground sprinkler system. A carefully prepared plan helps when ordering materials; makes it easier to get advice from your garden center, irrigation specialist, or hardware dealer; and serves as a detailed record of where the pipelines are laid.

Begin your sprinkler system with graph paper (10 grids to an inch is fine), a soft-lead pencil, a dime-store compass, and a measuring tape. Make your plan complete. A good plan is actually a bird's-eye view of your property drawn to scale, preferably 1 inch equaling 20 feet. It should show shrubs, trees, paved areas, fences, mailboxes, raised planters, buried drainage or power lines, and other features that could affect the sprinkler design and installation. If significant,

note prevailing wind direction, sun and shade areas, as well as high and low spots in your landscape.

Draw the plan for both front and back yards, even if you plan to install the system only in one area. You may want a similar system in another area at a later time. If you want to include sprinklers for trees and shrubs, indicate any water-sensitive or especially thirsty plants on the plan.

Next, draw in the location of the sprinkler heads. Set your compass to match the radius of the sprinkler head pattern (available from the manufacturer's catalog). Locate a quarter-circle head in each corner of the lawn, set the compass point on each head location, and draw a quarter circle to show the area covered by that head. Next, locate half-circle heads along the edges of the lawn. Space the heads so that their spray patterns overlap at least 60 percent. If you live in a windy area, overlap them 100 percent, so that the spray from each head touches adjoining heads. Finally, fill in the center areas of the lawn with full-circle heads.

It is all right to overlap spray patterns more than is needed to make everything fit, but do not space heads too far apart. If one section of the lawn receives less water than the rest, it will die from underwatering unless you water it by hand.

Once you have located the heads, draw light circles around those that are to be on the same circuit. Follow these rules when arranging the circuits:

1. Areas covered by one circuit must be watered together, so they should have the same watering needs.

2. Each circuit should use no more than 75 percent of the available flow rate. To determine the flow rate of each circuit, add together the flow rate of each sprinkler head, as given in the catalog description.

3. Do not mix different types of sprinkler heads (impulse, spray, shrub bubblers) on one circuit.

Take your time planning the circuits. It may take two or three tries to get it right.

Next, draw in the pipe going from the house water supply to the manifold. From there, draw in every valve going to every head on its circuit. Plan to use the same trench for installing two or more water lines wherever possible. Avoid going under walks or driveways or near trees. If you are using PVC or other rigid pipe, draw straight lines with right-angle turns; you can lay polyethylene pipe in curves.

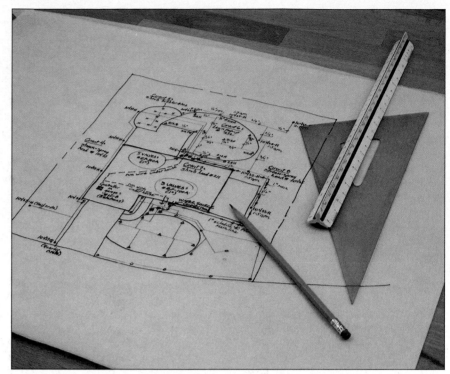

A drawing helps you to visualize your sprinkler system. If you decide to include sprinklers for shrubs, trees, and flower beds, be sure to put them on different circuits than the lawn.

Make a Shopping List: On the plan, write the catalog number of each sprinkler head and valve. At each intersection or turn in the pipe line, write the fitting needed. Measure the number of feet of pipe needed. Now make a shopping list, transferring items one at a time from the plan to the list. Include PVC cement. If you are using an automatic controller, add it to the list, along with enough wire and wire connectors to wire each valve to the controller.

To avoid costly problems, have your plan checked by a specialist before you begin. The retail dealer who supplies your equipment may offer help, in which case you can have it checked free of charge. Otherwise, it is money well spent to engage the services of an independent installer.

Installation: Here are the basic steps:

1. *Install the Manifold.* First turn off the water to the house. Cut a 1¼-inch section from your service pipe and install a tee fitting. Several special tees are available for cutting into lines. Ask at a local hardware store.

Install a length of pipe and a shut-off valve in a valve box. The shut-off valve is usually a gate valve, and allows you to turn off the water to the sprinkler system without turning off the house water. Once the valve is turned off, you can turn the house water back on. Run lines to the manifold location and install the control valves. It is usually easiest to assemble the manifold at a shop bench, then carry it to the site and install it. Close the valves, open the shut-off valve, and test the manifold for leaks.

2. *Install the Controller.* If you are using automatic valves and an electric timer, install it according to the manufacturer's instructions, and lay the connecting wire to the valves. Most timers run on a voltage that is low enough (24 volts) to let you bury the wire directly, without enclosing it in a conduit. Position the timer where it is protected from sun and rain and is close to an electrical outlet; a garage is ideal. The position of the timer may influence the location of your control valves.

3. *Mark the Layout on the Lawn.* Drive a stake into the ground at each sprinkler head location. Sprinkle agricultural lime on the ground to mark where trenches are to be dug.

4. *Dig Trenches.* Next to your pipe layout, use a spade or rented trencher to dig trenches. Make the trenches at least 8 inches deep.

5. *Install Pipe, Risers, and Sprinkler Heads.* Lay out pipe and fittings on the ground. Working backward to the manifold, assemble and solvent-weld pipe and fittings in the trench.

Measure the trench depth at each sprinkler head location, making the head flush with the soil surface. If you are installing sod, make the head 1 inch higher than the soil surface. Install risers, making further height adjustments as needed.

In areas where the soil freezes in winter, install drain valves at the lowest point in each circuit and between the control valves and the first gate valve near the water meter (usually in the basement). Use a level to avoid having any water pockets in the system. Slightly tilt the drain valves downward in each circuit, cover them with a short piece of pipe, surround them with gravel, then cover them with plastic film. Never put a drain valve in a fitting before attaching the fitting to the pipe; PVC solvent may clog the valve.

After the pipe and risers have been installed, wait 12 hours for the solvent to dry. Then turn on the water to flush out any dirt, stones, or scraps of PVC from pipe lines. When the pipes appear to be clear, install the sprinkler heads.

6. *Test for Coverage.* Turn on each circuit one by one; inspect the sprinkler pattern carefully to make sure that every part of the ground is receiving adequate coverage. At this point, it is easy to add sprinkler heads if they are needed.

7. *Backfill the Trenches.* Replace the soil in the trenches a little lower than the final soil line. Flood the trenches with water to settle the soil, then add more soil so that the backfill is mounded slightly. It will settle later.

Mowing

In spite of cartoons to the contrary, most people enjoy mowing their lawns. Mowing is a good way to stretch muscles and see the neighbors. Perhaps the best reward is the smell and feel of a freshly cut lawn.

Many people who want a handsome lawn do not realize the importance of mowing. A lawn that is mowed to the right height at the right time resists weeds, insects, and disease, and appears lush and healthy. Infrequent mowing often results in the removal off too much grass at one time, and eventually produces a lawn that looks thin, spotty, or burned. Unfortunately, grass can also be weakened by mowing too frequently, especially if it is kept short.

How Often to Mow
How often your lawn needs mowing depends on three things: how often and how much you water and fertilize, what time of year it is, and the type of grass in your lawn.

The fertilizer you apply affects the growth rate of your lawn, and, consequently, the frequency of mowing. Lawns that are fertilized often require more frequent mowing. Golf course greens, for example, are usually mowed daily.

Cool-season and warm-season grasses respond differently to seasonal climate changes. When cool-season grasses slow down or become dormant during summer heat, mowing may only be necessary once every two or three weeks. However, during spring and fall, cool-season grasses grow more vigorously and usually need mowing at least once a week. Warm-season grasses do not grow at all in the winter and slowly in the spring and fall. Mowing is infrequent during these times. But during the high temperatures of summer, growth is vigorous and mowing should be more frequent.

Although not widely available for home use, chemicals that slow grass growth are being researched by turfgrass scientists. In past experiments, lawn growth has been slowed five to eight weeks. Delayed growth means that lawns need to be mowed about half as often. The growth regulators that are presently available are best adapted for difficult mowing situations, such as along fences and walls or on steep, unmowable slopes.

During periods of vigorous growth, most people find it convenient to mow their lawns on a weekly schedule, such as every Saturday morning. Unfortunately this is not appropriate for all lawn grasses. Even though you can establish a general schedule for both cool-season and warm-season grasses, different types of grass still grow at different rates. For example, although common Bermudagrass may do well when mowed once a week during midsummer, well-fertilized improved Bermudagrass may need to be mowed every two or three days. If you can, match your mowing schedule to the growth rate of the grass.

The Right Height
Proper mowing height depends primarily on the type of grass. The chart on this page recommends mowing heights for the major lawn grasses. The rule of thumb is: Mow when the grass grows from one-fourth to one-third taller than its recommended mowing height. For example, if the recommended mowing height for your lawn is 2 inches, mow when it is about 3 inches high.

The penalty for not paying attention to the recommended mowing height is a stiff one. By letting grass grow too high and then cutting away half or more at once, you expose stems that have been shaded and may burn in strong sunlight. If the lawn is yellowish after you mow, you have waited too long. More importantly, roots are severely shocked by heavy mowing and may need several weeks to recover. Research has shown a direct relationship between the height of the cut and the depth of roots. When grass is properly mowed to its recommended height, roots grow deeper. In turn, a deep root system makes lawn care much easier.

Grasses tend to spread either horizontally or vertically. For instance, bentgrass and Bermudagrass spread horizontally by creeping stems. Because these stems parallel the ground as well as the cut of the mower, they are not normally mowed off. Unless these grasses are mowed low, preferably with a heavy reel mower, they will have problems with thatch.

Think of it this way: "X" amount of leaf surface is necessary to keep the grass plants healthy and growing. If that leaf surface is spread out over a wide area, the lawn can be mowed close to the ground without reducing the necessary leaf surface.

Mowing Heights

Grass	Height in Inches
Bahiagrass	2–3
Bentgrass	¼–1
Bermudagrass	
Common	¾–1½
Improved	½–1
Bluegrass	
Common	2–3
Improved	1½–2½
Rough	1–2
Buffalograss	1½–2
Carpetgrass	1–2
Centipedegrass	1–2
Dichondra	½–1½
Fescue	
Chewings, Hard	1–2½
Red	1½–2½
Tall	2–3
Annual Ryegrass	1½–2
Perennial Ryegrass	1–2
St. Augustine Grass	2–3
Zoysiagrass	1–2

Vertically growing grasses, such as bahiagrass, common Kentucky bluegrass, tall fescue, and St. Augustine grass, cannot be mowed too low (below 1½ to 2 inches) because they do not have enough leaf surface to support the plants.

Mowing too low probably ruins more Kentucky bluegrass lawns than any other practice. This is especially true in transitional areas where adaptation is marginal. Cut high, Kentucky bluegrass is more disease resistant and can successfully compete with weeds and insects. The tall growth shades the soil, keeping temperatures lower for cool-loving roots.

Exceptions are some of the new Kentucky bluegrass cultivars, which are essentially dwarfs. They are more compact and have more leaf surface in less area. In shade, mow another ½ inch higher.

Mowing New Lawns
Newly seeded lawns are more delicate than established ones, which is why you have to be more careful when mowing them. The soil is soft and the grass plants usually are not deeply rooted by the first mowing. On the other hand, mowing young lawns, especially those planted vegetatively, helps the plants to spread, thus promoting a thicker lawn. Use common sense and apply the same principles for properly mowing any lawn.

Mow a new lawn for the first time after it has grown a third higher than the regular mowing height. For example, a lawn that should be maintained at a 2-inch height should be mowed when it reaches 2½ to 3 inches. Do not remove more than a third of the total height of the grass.

If you can, use a mower that is not too heavy, especially if the soil is still soft. A lightweight rotary or a push reel mower is your best bet. Make sure the mower blades are sharp; the young grass plants can be easily pulled from the soil by dull blades.

If the soil remains too soft or if the new grass is too loosely knit to mow without damage, wait. Let the lawn continue to grow, then lower the cut gradually until it is down to the proper height. Reduce the cutting height by ½ inch or ¾ inch every second mowing until you reach the recommended mowing height.

Grass Clippings

Whether to leave clippings on a lawn or to pick them up is a question of many gardeners. There are advantages and disadvantages to leaving grass clippings on your lawn, depending on the type of grass you have and how well you maintain it.

Leaving clippings of cool-season grasses on the lawn does not cause or contribute to thatch. It is the woody, slow-to-decompose stems below warm-season grass blades that contribute most to thatch buildup.

Use grass clippings as a mulch in a vegetable garden. Spread them in a thin and even layer to avoid decaying odor. Do not use clippings treated with weed killers.

Clippings return nutrients to the lawn. Although it is difficult to measure, some estimates suggest that as much as one third of the nitrogen requirement of a lawn can be supplied by decaying grass clippings.

At certain times, however, it makes sense to remove clippings from your lawn. First of all, clippings can be unsightly. They are removed from many intensely maintained lawns for just this reason. Secondly, if you do not mow your lawn frequently enough, you will cut off too much grass at one time. If clippings mat down and block light from the lawn, remove them so only a light cover of clippings remain.

Some people remove clippings to use as a compost or mulch in a vegetable garden. This is fine provided they are free of 2,4-D and other broadleaf herbicides. Continually mulching tomatoes with herbicide-treated clippings, for example, has resulted in distorted plants. Also, watch for weeds in the clippings—they can create havoc in your garden.

To remove clippings from your lawn, use a steel-tine lawn rake after mowing. The tines are made of spring steel, and snap back into position even when bent back. Do not substitute a steel-wire leaf rake for collecting clippings; its wire tines are more likely to tear the grass. An easier solution is to purchase a grass catcher bag for your lawn mower.

Lawn Mowers

Almost every homeowner with a lawn has a lawn mower. The number of available varieties and styles grows each year. It pays to shop around until you find the mower that fits your specifications.

The two most common mowers are the reel and the rotary. Each basic type has its variations: gas or electric power, walking or riding, pushing or self-propelled. Some have bagging attachments or grass catchers.

Before buying a lawn mower, look it over carefully. Consider its maneuverability. Make sure the grass catcher is easy to take on and off. Ask about the safety features. These points will help you choose the right mower.

Mowers can be specialized. Some are designed to cut high weeds, others are engineered to produce the carpet-like nap of a putting green. There are some unusual types, too, such as the one that rides on a cushion of air and the one that cuts with spinning monofilament line.

Rotary Mowers: The power rotary mower is the most popular model. It is generally lower priced, more versatile, and easier to handle and maintain than a reel mower. It stands rougher use. Its blades cut like a spinning scythe, which is better for taller growing, less intensively maintained lawns. The blades are also easier to sharpen.

However, power rotary mowers require greater caution in use. They need larger motors with more horsepower; they do not cut as cleanly as a properly sharpened reel mower; and few can mow lower than 1 inch. The mower also shakes if its blades get out of balance.

The type that rides on a cushion of air, rather than on wheels, is the easiest to use if your lawn is smooth and level. It is almost frictionless and can be swept sideways as well as forward and backward. However, it does not hover properly on rough ground, and its tendency to skim downhill makes it difficult to use on sloping lawns.

You probably need a riding mower if your lawn is large. Riding mowers come in rotary and reel models, but rotaries are the most common types available. Although they are fun for adults to drive, they are not toys; do not let children play with them.

Reel Mowers: Reel mowers are available in manual (push) models or powered with gasoline or electric engines. They cut with a scissor action, which produces the cleanest cut. They conform better to land contours than do rotaries, but are impractical on rough, uneven ground or for tall-growing grass. Because they can be adjusted to cut quite low, they are the preferred mower for bentgrass or Bermudagrass lawns. In general, reel mowers are preferred for fine lawns but perform poorly on tall grasses and lawns with high, wiry seed heads.

Power reel mowers discharge clippings from either the rear or the front (rear throw, front throw). The rear-throw type is widely available and less expensive.

Front-throw reel mowers are used primarily by professional landscape gardeners. They are usually well made and can stand constant use. The weight and power of these mowers makes them perfect for the low-mowing requirement of Bermudagrass or zoysiagrass lawns. Height is easy to adjust, usually with just a lever. Some can be adjusted low enough to cut at the soil line.

Lawn Mowers

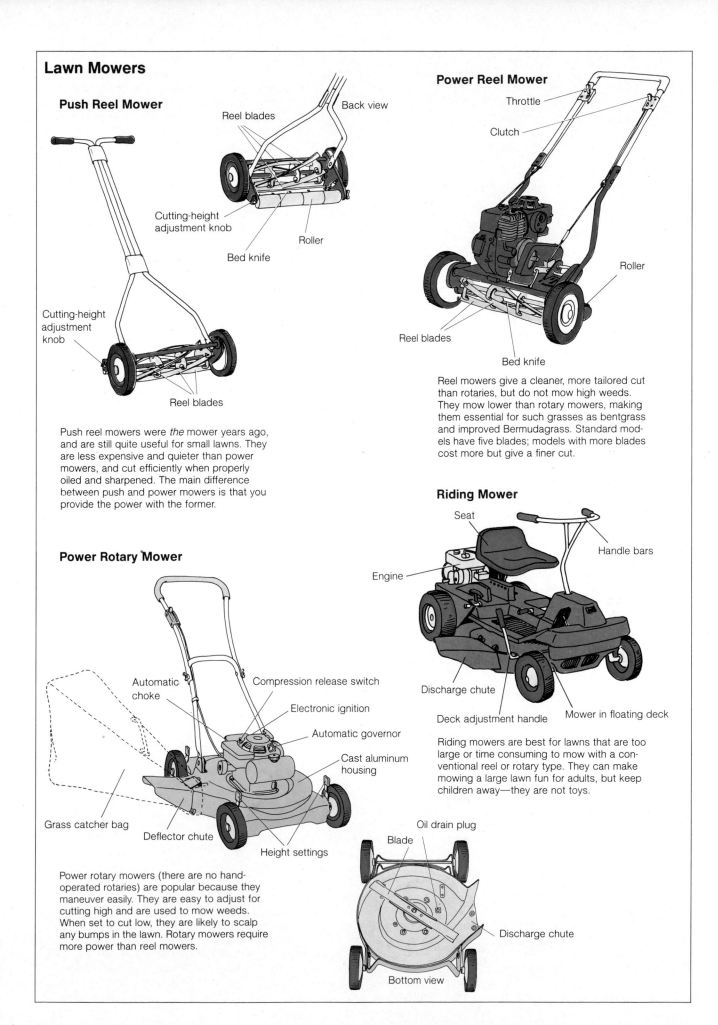

Push Reel Mower

Back view

Reel blades

Cutting-height adjustment knob

Bed knife

Roller

Cutting-height adjustment knob

Reel blades

Push reel mowers were *the* mower years ago, and are still quite useful for small lawns. They are less expensive and quieter than power mowers, and cut efficiently when properly oiled and sharpened. The main difference between push and power mowers is that you provide the power with the former.

Power Rotary Mower

Automatic choke

Compression release switch

Electronic ignition

Automatic governor

Cast aluminum housing

Grass catcher bag

Deflector chute

Height settings

Power rotary mowers (there are no hand-operated rotaries) are popular because they maneuver easily. They are easy to adjust for cutting high and are used to mow weeds. When set to cut low, they are likely to scalp any bumps in the lawn. Rotary mowers require more power than reel mowers.

Power Reel Mower

Throttle

Clutch

Roller

Reel blades

Bed knife

Reel mowers give a cleaner, more tailored cut than rotaries, but do not mow high weeds. They mow lower than rotary mowers, making them essential for such grasses as bentgrass and improved Bermudagrass. Standard models have five blades; models with more blades cost more but give a finer cut.

Riding Mower

Seat

Handle bars

Engine

Discharge chute

Deck adjustment handle

Mower in floating deck

Riding mowers are best for lawns that are too large or time consuming to mow with a conventional reel or rotary type. They can make mowing a large lawn fun for adults, but keep children away—they are not toys.

Oil drain plug

Blade

Discharge chute

Bottom view

Riding mowers are expensive compared to other mower types, but they can be worth the cost if your lawn is large.

Other Mowers: Electric nylon mowers cut grass with nearly the same efficiency as steel-bladed mowers and are much safer. Two counter-rotating disks powered by separate electric motors spin monofilament line to mow and trim your lawn.

Several other less common types of mowers are available for special jobs. Flail mowers, also known as hammer-knife mowers, use loose, T-shaped blades revolving on a horizontal shaft to cut grass. They are useful in maintaining rough areas such as vacant lots and the sides of highways. Sickle bar mowers are perfect for an empty lot overgrown with weeds. They are the same sort of mower that farmers use to cut field oats and other hays and grains. Heavy reel mowers are useful for the one or two times you need to cut the lawn extra low for thatch removal. High-wheel rotary mowers cut higher than most rotary mowers—about 4 inches—and are easy to maneuver over rough terrain.

Mower Maintenance

Taking care of your lawn mower will lengthen its life as well as eliminate many time-consuming problems. The manufacturer's maintenance manual for your mower is the best guide.

Mow at the proper cutting height for your lawn. Adjust a reel mower by raising or lowering the roller by the knobs or screws at each end. Measure the distance between the bed knife and a hard surface to check the cutting height. Adjust a rotary mower by raising or lowering the wheels. Some rotary mower blades are at the same level as the skirt, so check the cutting height by measuring the height of the skirt above a hard surface. You can always determine the cutting height by cutting a small section of lawn and measuring the height with a ruler.

Keep the mower blades sharp. The blades of rotary mowers are easy to sharpen at home. Only a small portion at the end of the blade actually cuts the grass. Sharpen the edge with a file or grindstone, making sure to even out any rough spots. Check the balance before remounting. Because of their position, blades of reel mowers are tricky to sharpen at home. Take any mower to a shop if you have doubts about sharpening its blades.

Remember that every mower has other maintenance needs to keep it in working order. Be sure the motor oil is at the proper level. Clean the mower blades after use with a soft spray of water. Forceful cleaning with water or air can push dirt into delicate bearings. Do not spray water onto a hot engine. Keep gaskets and fittings tight; gas or oil leaks kill the grass.

If you store your mower in the winter, clean it and drain the gas tank. In the spring, change the oil, clean the spark plug, and refill the gas tank.

Safety Tips

Power lawn mowing equipment is so common that it is taken for granted. But power mowers are responsible for thousands of accidents yearly. Follow the guidelines below, along with those provided by the mower manufacturer, and you can avoid becoming another injury statistic.

Do not disconnect the manufacturer's safety features and always keep in mind the possible dangers.

Many fingers have been lost by unclogging discharge chutes of rotary mowers. Make a habit of turning off the power and disconnecting the spark plug before reaching into the clogged grass.

Use common sense when mowing steep or uneven terrain. Check the stability of the mower first, and be aware that a slipping mower can injure both you and your lawn. Mow slight slopes either across or up and down. If there is a chance of slippage, tie a rope to the mower and mow it down the slope from the top. Perhaps the safest way to handle a slope is to plant a ground cover that does not need to be mowed.

Walk over the lawn area before mowing, looking for rocks, toys, sprinkler heads, and other possible obstructions.

Do not allow children to use a power mower until they are strong enough and mature enough to handle the job.

Lawn Mowing Hints

• Don't cut wet grass. It causes uneven mowing, the clippings are messy, and they can mat and block light from the grass. There is also the danger of slipping on wet slopes.

• Pick up stones and sticks before mowing.

• Alternate mowing patterns. Mowing the same direction every time tends to compact the soil and causes wear patterns.

• If you are using a reel mower, give the lawn an attractive "checkered" finish by mowing it twice, traveling in opposite directions.

• Check the blade height by measuring the grass after cutting.

• Sharp turns with a mower can cause uneven cutting. Make wide turns or take advantage of sidewalks and driveways, but be aware of rocks or debris on pavement areas.

• If the ground is uneven in some areas because the soil has settled, be careful not to scalp the high spots.

Fertilizing

People accept the fact that they must mow and water to maintain the health of their lawn. But some may question the need for fertilizer. They shouldn't.

Lawn grasses live in an unnatural environment. The grass plants are crowded together and compete with each other, along with neighboring trees and shrubs, for water and nutrients. They are mowed regularly, which is highly irregular in nature, and their clippings, a source of nutrients, are often removed.

Because of this competition and the unnatural demands placed on lawns, they must be fertilized. Just as a balanced diet works best for people and animals, the same is true of lawns—they need fertilizer for sustenance. When properly fertilized, a lawn maintains good color, density, and vigor, and does not easily succumb to insects, weeds, or diseases. When underfertilized, the lawn is not only less attractive, but also is considerably more susceptible to environmental stress and damage.

The Nutrients a Lawn Needs

Sixteen different mineral elements are essential to the growth of all lawns. Some are common, such as oxygen from air and hydrogen from water. Others, such as zinc or boron, are needed in only the minute amounts usually found naturally in most soils.

Nitrogen: This is by far the most important element that a lawn needs. It promotes rapid shoot growth and gives lawns a healthy color. Nitrogen is the mineral most often in short supply. Growing lawns need a plentiful and continual supply of water, but watering also flushes nitrogen from the soil. Without sufficient nitrogen, growth stops and the lawn becomes pale and yellowish. On the other hand, if there is too much nitrogen, thatch and disease develop.

Phosphorus: This nutrient is less important, but is still essential for the healthy growth of lawn grasses. It stimulates the early formation and strong growth of the roots, which is why new lawns need it at such a high percentage. It is not readily flushed from the soil by watering and is needed by established lawns in small quantities, so most balanced lawn fertilizers contain only a low percentage. Phosphorus is supplied by phosphoric acid.

Potassium: Next to nitrogen, potassium is second in importance. And like nitrogen, it is flushed out by water, but at a slower rate. It strengthens lawn grasses, enabling them to withstand traffic and resist disease. Potassium is needed in about the same quantity as nitrogen, but since the soil supplies a considerable amount, not as much is added to fertilizers. The major source of potassium in fertilizers is potash.

Calcium, Sulfur, and Magnesium: It takes relatively large amounts of these nutrients to meet the needs of most lawns. Calcium is either present in adequate quantities in the soil or is added through periodic applications of lime. Dolomite (or dolomitic limestone) supplies magnesium as well as calcium. Most soil sulfur reaches a lawn through the air, water, or organic matter. For more information on lime and sulfur, see page 24.

Micronutrients: These are elements needed in small amounts. If your lawn does not become greener with an application of nitrogen, the problem may be a shortage of iron. This is particularly true in areas where soil pH is high. Yellowing can also be caused from a sulfur deficiency, overwatering, manganese deficiency in sandy soils, or a pH less than 5.0. A soil test may help find the cause of persistent, soil-related problems such as these.

Types of Fertilizers

A little shopping in a garden store reveals an abundance of lawn fertilizers. You see labels proclaiming "fast acting," "slow release," and so on. But if they all contain the same basic minerals, what is the difference? Here is a description of these products.

Organic Fertilizers: A chemist might argue that some manufactured fertilizers are technically "organic." Here organic refers to a fertilizer derived from plant or animal waste.

The variety of organic fertilizers is endless. There are manures of all kinds, municipal sewage sludge, blood meals, and seed meals. They all share advantages and disadvantages. In some areas, they may be inexpensive and easy to obtain, yet the reverse is often true. Most have distinctly beneficial soil-building properties, which are covered on pages 23 and 24.

Since the action of organics is slow, overfertilizing is usually not a problem. This is the major difference between organic fertilizers and soluble synthetic fertilizers: their nutrients are released slowly.

Organic fertilizers are bulkier, heavier, and more difficult to handle than other types of fertilizer. They have a low percentage of nitrogen, so it is necessary to apply a much greater quantity at one time. They may also have an unpleasant smell.

Cycles of Lawn Growth

Fertilizer application ▬   **Grass growth rate** ▬

J F M A M J J A S O N D

Cool-season grasses grow actively in the cool weather of spring and fall, and slowly in summer heat. Fertilize in the spring and fall.

J F M A M J J A S O N D

Warm-season grasses grow actively in the warm summer months, then become dormant in cold weather. Fertilize throughout the growing season.

Prevent "lawn stripes" by fertilizing in a easy-to-remember pattern: Fertilize the edges of the lawn first, then travel the length of the lawn in straight lines back and forth.

The release of nutrients from organic fertilizers depends on the weather and is, therefore, unpredictable. Soil microbes must digest the organic material to release its nutrients. Because the activity of microbes depends on soil temperature, nutrients may not be available in early spring and late fall—times when cool-season grasses are growing actively—but be abundant in summer, when cool-season grass should not be fertilized heavily.

Soluble Synthetic Fertilizers: These are the most common fertilizers used on lawns today.

The big advantage of this type of fertilizer is predictability. Because their characteristics are known precisely, you can learn the exact effect they have on a lawn. This is an important feature for many lawns. Soluble synthetic fertilizers become available to the lawn before the soil has thoroughly warmed in the summer, they are less expensive than organic fertilizers, and they are easier to handle. Less fertilizer needs to be applied since the percentage of nitrogen is usually high.

However, more work is usually required of those gardeners who use them. More applications are necessary because the effects are short term. If your lawn requires 4 to 6 pounds of actual nitrogen a year, that many separate applications are necessary.

Further, because of the high percentage of nitrogen, there is the possibility of fertilizer burn. To avoid this, apply the fertilizer at recommended rates, spread it on a dry lawn, and water it thoroughly after application.

The exceptions are some "weed-and-feed" products that are formulated with soluble fertilizers and are designed for use on wet grass during moderate temperatures—under 85° F.

Slow-Release Fertilizers: To some extent these fertilizers combine the characteristics of the organics and the soluble synthetics. Usually they have a high percentage of nitrogen, so spreading large quantities is not necessary. The possibility of fertilizer burn is greatly reduced, since the nitrogen does not become available to the plant all at once.

Several types are available. Some are categorized on the fertilizer bag as W.I.N., meaning water-insoluble nitrogen. Many commonly available lawn fertilizers are actually a combination of soluble nitrogen and W.I.N.

Slow-release fertilizers are favored by many lawn growers because they make heavier applications of nitrogen possible, hence making fewer applications necessary. However, they do not provide a quick green-up. Your control of greening response is slightly more than with organics.

Water-Insoluble Nitrogen

A high percentage of water-insoluble nitrogen (W.I.N.) means that a fertilizer is less likely to burn the lawn after application and is less subject to being flushed from the soil by water. Fertilizers with more than 30 percent of W.I.N. are basically slow release; between 15 percent and 30 percent are medium acting; and any less than 15 percent are fast acting.

In order to determine the actual percentage of W.I.N., it is necessary to do a little arithmetic. For example, if you have a 25-3-7 formula fertilizer with 7.6 percent of W.I.N., multiply the 7.6 by 100 to equal 760. Divide the 760 by the total percentage of nitrogen shown on the bag. In this case, dividing 760 by 25 equals 30.4. Thus 30.4 percent of the nitrogen is water insoluble.

Complete Fertilizers

Complete fertilizers are those that contain all three of the primary nutrients: nitrogen, phosphorus (in the form of phosphoric acid), and potassium (in the form of potash). Every state requires that the percentages of these three elements be prominently displayed on every bag of fertilizer. The first number is nitrogen, the second is phosphorus, and the third is potassium. An example is 24-4-8. These numbers state the percentages by weight of nutrients in the bag compared to the total contents of the bag. The percentages are called the analysis or the formula grade.

A 3-1-2 ratio of nutrients has proven to be generally good for fertilizing home lawns. However, factors such as local climate, soil conditions, and the form of nitrogen in the fertilizer influence what is best in various localities. A fertilizer with a 3-1-2 ratio could, for example, have a formula of 21-7-14. Although it is not critical for a fertilizer to have exactly this ratio, something close to it is recommended. A higher nitrogen ratio of 6-1-2 (formula 24-4-8) is common.

For proper application follow the directions on the label. Some complete fertilizers are manufactured for general use, while others are designed to be used on specific grasses.

Fertilizer and Pesticide Combinations

In recent years, combinations of fertilizers and pesticides (fungicides, herbicides, and insecticides) have become available. Many combinations contain herbicides for broadleaf weed or crabgrass control. Some products include insecticides and fungicides for insect and disease control.

These products have definite advantages. Considerable time, labor, and equipment are saved by accomplishing two or more jobs in one. Less total material needs to be handled and less storage space is required. In addition, the cost of the combined material may be less than the cost of the ingredients when purchased separately. But most important of all, the pesticide can often be applied more evenly than if it is sprayed on the lawn.

The disadvantage of combining fertilizers and pesticides is the difficulty in applying the products at the proper time, since the best time to fertilize is not always the best time to control disease, weeds, or insects. For best results, apply a combination product during the growth cycles of disease, weeds, and insects. A fertilizer combined with preventive chemicals is most useful if the advantages and limitations are understood.

How Much Fertilizer to Apply

Since fertilizers vary in formula and type, application rates are different. In order to know how much fertilizer to use, you first need to determine the amount of actual nitrogen you need to apply. For these rates, see the actual nitrogen requirements chart on the next page. Then, to calculate the amount of fertilizer to use, divide the number of pounds of actual nitrogen you need to apply by the percentage of nitrogen. For example, if you need to apply 1 pound of actual nitrogen to your lawn using 24-4-8 fertilizer, dividing 1 by .24 gives you 4.17, which indicates the pounds of fertilizer you need to apply.

Most labels recommend application rates that supply approximately 1 pound of actual nitrogen per 1,000 square feet. Exceptions are slow-release fertilizers—those with high percentages of W.I.N.—which are often applied at higher rates.

When to Fertilize

The amounts recommended here are guidelines. The amount you fertilize should be based on your own experience. If the lawn grows too rapidly, and you have to mow it more than once a week, fertilize less. If it turns yellow, and you have been watering it regularly, it may either be the signal of an iron deficiency (see page 79) or the need to fertilize more.

Cool-Season Grasses: Spring fertilizing begins in late fall. After top growth is stopped by cold weather but the grass is still green, the roots grow for several weeks before becoming dormant. Feed one fourth of the yearly total of actual nitrogen as soon as the grass stops growing. This will stimulate strong, fast growth for next spring.

As soon as the grass is growing vigorously in the spring, feed another one fourth of the yearly total.

About 6 weeks later, or when the grass begins to lose its bright green color, feed one eighth of the yearly total. At this feeding, use a fertilizer that is high in potassium as well as nitrogen. As hot weather weakens cool-season grasses, the potassium protects them against diseases. If the lawn begins to turn yellow during the summer, fertilize it again, but lightly.

A Sample Fertilizer Label

Manufacturers must supply the same basic information on lawn food labels. State laws and agencies that control plant food stipulate the specific information that must appear on a label. Although labels differ, the most important characteristics, described below, are found on every bag of fertilizer sold as lawn food.

In this example, "Lawn Food" is the equivalent of a brand name.

Referred to as the formula grade or the analysis, these three numbers indicate the percentages of nitrogen, phosphate, and potassium, in that order, of the contents. The percentages indicate that the ratio of this fertilizer is 6 to 1 to 2.

Guaranteed analysis is the manufacturer's warranty that at least the stated analysis by weight is present in the container. The guaranteed analysis is always stated in this order and form.

The percentages of available nitrogen, phosphoric acid, and soluble potash are listed here because their presence is claimed in the formula grade. If a fertilizer contains nitrogen only, such as 17-0-0, the zero percentages for the absent primary nutrients are not listed here.

The percentages of the sources of nitrogen are not always required, but most manufacturers supply this information. Nitrogen sources have different characteristics, so it is useful to know which ones are used in the fertilizer you buy. The percentage of water-insoluble nitrogen (W.I.N.) shown in the sample indicates that the fertilizer is medium acting.

The primary nutrients in this fertilizer—nitrogen, phosphorus, and potassium—are derived from these basic products.

Many fertilizers have an acid effect on the soil. In order to completely neutralize the acidifying effects of 1 ton of this fertilizer, you would have to add 800 pounds of calcium carbonate (limestone).

Lawn Food 24-4-8

Guaranteed Analysis:

Total Nitrogen (N) 24%
- 4.1% Ammoniacal Nitrogen
- 15.9% Urea Nitrogen
- 4.0% Water-Insoluble Nitrogen

Available Phosphoric
Acid (P_2O_5) 4%

Soluble Potash (K_2O) 8%

Primary Nutrients from Urea, Ureaform, Ammonium Sulfate, Ammonium Phosphate, and Muriate of Potash.

Potential Acidity 800 lbs. Calcium Carbonate Equivalent per ton.
Net Weight 20 lbs.

As soon as the weather cools in the fall, feed the remaining ⅜ of the yearly total. This heavy fertilizing helps the grass recover from hot weather.

Warm-Season Grasses: The growth of warm-season grasses peaks in mid-summer, tapers off in the fall, and continues at a slower pace until frost occurs. The first sign of spring green-up comes when the soil is still cold. Fertilize as soon as new growth appears, then feed the same amount every 6 weeks until the fall. In most areas this will be 4 or 5 times a year.

An additional fertilizing in October keeps the lawn green longer into the winter, but can increase its susceptibility to winter kill, and can stimulate the growth of winter weeds. If your lawn is bothered by either of these problems, do not fertilize after September.

How to Apply Fertilizer
The three basic methods of applying fertilizers are by spraying, broadcast spreading, and drop spreading. Use a sprayer to apply a liquid fertilizer, and either a broadcast spreader or drop spreader to apply a dry, granular fertilizer.

Sprayers: The most common type of sprayer used to apply a liquid fertilizer is a hose-end sprayer. This sprayer has a plastic body suspended beneath a nozzle that attaches to the end of a hose. Because of the water pressure the hose provides, up to 15 gallons of diluted spray can be applied, which eliminates refilling the sprayer frequently. Simply measure the liquid fertilizer into the sprayer and dilute it with water. Spray the entire contents of the sprayer onto your lawn, providing equal coverage to all sections of the lawn. Read the directions on both the liquid fertilizer and the sprayer carefully. Be accurate about the ratio of fertilizer to water, and make sure all parts of the sprayer are attached properly and operational.

Broadcast Spreaders: The easiest way to apply a dry fertilizer is to use a broadcast spreader. There are two types: hand held and push wheel. Each model throws the dry fertilizer over a wide area via a whirling wheel. Because it requires fewer passes to completely cover the lawn, a broadcast spreader is easier to use than drop spreaders, especially on large lawns. Make sure you measure the throw width so that you can calculate how far to space your passes. You can

Actual Nitrogen Requirements

To determine how much fertilizer to apply each year, use these figures in the "Fertilizer Worksheet" to the right. Apply the lesser amount if your lawn is shaded or is growing too rapidly, and the higher amount if your lawn is in full sun or is growing too slowly.

Grass Type	Pounds of Actual Nitrogen Per Growing Month
Cool-Season Grasses:	
Bentgrass, Creeping	0.5–1.0
Bluegrass, Kentucky	0.25–0.8
Bluegrass, Rough	0.3–0.5
Fescue, Chewings	0.1–0.5
Fescue, Hard	0.1–0.3
Fescue, Red	0.1–0.5
Fescue, Tall	0.1–0.5
Ryegrass, Annual	0.3–0.5
Ryegrass, Perennial	0.3–0.5
Warm-Season Grasses:	
Bahiagrass	0.5
Bermudagrass, Common	0.5–1.0
Bermudagrass, Improved	1.0
Centipedegrass	0.1–0.3
Dichondra	0.5–1.0
St. Augustine Grass	0.4–0.8
Zoysiagrass	0.3–0.5

Fertilizer Worksheet
To determine how much fertilizer to use and how often to use it, complete the following calculations:

Pounds of actual nitrogen to apply per growing month
(from the actual nitrogen chart)　[   ]

×

Growing season in your area
(number of months)　[   ]

_____

Pounds of actual nitrogen to apply per year　[   ]

÷

Percentage of nitrogen in fertilizer　[   ]

_____

Pounds of fertilizer to apply per year　[   ]

*Pounds of fertilizer for first feeding　[   ]

Pounds of fertilizer for second feeding　[   ]

Pounds of fertilizer for third feeding　[   ]

Pounds of fertilizer for fourth feeding　[   ]

Pounds of fertilizer for fifth feeding　[   ]

Pounds of fertilizer for sixth feeding　[   ]

*To determine the number of feedings per year for your type of grass, read the section on "When to Fertilize" beginning on page 55.

Liquid fertilizers are applied with hand-held sprayers attached to the hose. Some people may have trouble applying spray evenly.

Uneven applications are common when spreading dry fertilizer by hand. For the best results, use a spreader.

Drop spreaders are useful on small lawns. Make sure you overlap applications just enough so that no strips are left unfed.

determine the throw width easily by running the spreader over dark-colored pavement for a short distance. Usually, overlapping passes by one third of their width is sufficient for uniform coverage.

The best technique for applying fertilizer is to cover the ends of the lawn first, then go back and forth the long way. To avoid double applications, shut off the spreader as you approach the end strips. Keep the spreader closed while you are turning around, backing up, or stopped. For even and thorough coverage, walk at normal speed and keep the spreader level.

Fill spreaders over a sidewalk or driveway. If you happen to spill or drop dry fertilizer on the lawn, scrape or vacuum it up, then flood the area with water to avoid fertilizer burn.

Drop Spreaders: Drop spreaders are more precise, but slower, than broadcast spreaders. They are most useful on small- and medium-sized lawns. When using a drop spreader, overlap the wheels enough so that no strips are left underfertilized, but also be careful not to double-feed any sections. If this happens, your lawn will become green unevenly, or worse, it will develop fertilizer burn.

Drop spreaders have adjustable settings. A chart that comes with the spreader or the fertilizer tells you which setting to use for each fertilizer. Although the settings are fairly accurate

when the spreaders are new, they should be calibrated (the actual application rate tested) at least once a year.

To check calibration of a drop spreader, draw a square 10 feet by 10 feet on a clean, smooth patio or driveway. Fill the spreader, then spread fertilizer over the square. Sweep up the fertilizer in the square and weigh it.

Multiply the weight of the fertilizer by 100 to find how much will be spread over 1000 square feet. If the amount is not what you want it to be, try another setting and repeat.

Drop spreaders are also used to spread seed. Again, calibration is necessary to make sure you apply appropriate quantities of seed.

Hand-held broadcast spreaders operate by turning a side-arm crank; the fertilizer flies out from a whirling wheel.

Push-type broadcast spreaders are ideal for large lawns. Before using, measure the "throw" to avoid uneven applications.

Weeds

Weeds are simply plants that are growing in the wrong place. The finest lawn grass is a weed in a vegetable garden; likewise, dandelions are cultivated in some vegetable gardens, but certainly not in lawns.

Weed seeds permeate most soils by the millions. They find their way into the soil in many ways: wind, lawn equipment, organic matter. Once in the soil, they wait, dormant, until brought to the surface or until the lawn dies, giving them more light and moisture to start growing. Some seeds remain alive in the soil for many years, which is why some weed treatments are useful before putting in a lawn.

You can eliminate most lawn weeds easily. Mowing at the right height, fertilizing adequately, and watering sensibly goes a long way in achieving a weed-free lawn.

A healthy lawn is not troubled much by weeds. If your lawn has weed problems, check the following six pages for the most common lawn weeds and their controls.

Types of Weeds

Weeds are categorized according to several traits. First, they are either annuals or perennials. Annual weeds are those that live only one year, while perennial weeds are those that live for two or more years.

Weeds are further classified by their leaf types: either broadleaf or narrowleaf. Broadleaf weeds have obvious, showy flowers. Their leaves have a network of small veins originating from a principal point or vein that often divides the leaf in half. Dandelion is a typical broadleaf weed. Grassy weeds are narrowleaf. They usually have hollow stems and long, narrow leaf blades

Control annoying weeds before they choke the desirable grasses in your lawn. For existing lawns, use a postemergence herbicide. Make sure the weed bothering your lawn is on the label.

with parallel veins. Crabgrass is a common narrowleaf weed. Sedges are another, much less common weed type. They look similar to grasses, but have triangular stems.

Before Planting

The more weeds you eliminate before planting a new lawn, the fewer you have to battle later on. One of the best methods of eliminating weeds begins with keeping the soil bare and moist for three or four months. During this time, till or spray the area with a contact herbicide every three weeks as the weed seeds germinate. If it is awkward to leave your soil bare that long, try another method.

Fumigation is another preplanting weed treatment. It, too, involves time—at least three weeks. (Check the directions on the label.) Metam makes a gas that kills many weed seeds and other soil organisms. While it is effective, it is neither inexpensive nor simple to apply. Also, it may harm nearby tree or shrub roots. Methyl bromide kills

weeds thoroughly and quickly—in two to three days—but it is the most dangerous of the soil fumigants to use and is best applied by a professional. A special permit is usually required for homeowner use.

The only other preplanting weed-control method is to use a preemergence herbicide. This type of herbicide is effective against germinating seeds—it kills the plants before they emerge to the soil surface. Several preemergence herbicides are listed below and at the top of the next column by their chemical names. For a list of trade names, see the chart on page 109.

Atrazine: Controls several annual grasses and broadleaf weeds only in lawns of centipedegrass, St. Augustine grass, or zoysiagrass. May also be applied as postemergence control if weed seedlings are less than 1½ inches high. Does not damage woody ornamental plants.

Benefin: Controls annual grasses in most lawns. Do not use on bentgrass. Benefin prevents all seeds from germinating for up to eight weeks.

Bensulide: Another control for annual grasses and certain broadleaf weeds. Do not try to reseed for four months after application. Safe for use on bentgrass lawns.

DCPA: Especially effective on germinating grasses and the seeds of certain broadleaf species, including chickweed and purslane. Do not use on new lawns and do not reseed for 10 to 12 weeks after use. Avoid using on bentgrass or dichondra lawns.

Soil fumigation is an effective weed treatment to use before planting a lawn. Although some fumigants must be applied by a professional, others are available for use by home gardeners.

Oxadiazon: Effectively controls goosegrass and other annual grasses. Do not use on fine fescue or bentgrass. Do not try to reseed for four months after application.

Pendimenthalin: Controls many annual grasses and some broadleaf weeds. Do not use on bentgrass.

Siduron: Effectively controls weedy grasses, such as crabgrass, foxtail, and barnyardgrass. It has the unique quality of not interfering with the germination of cool-season grasses, such as Kentucky bluegrass.

Existing Weeds

Pulling lawn weeds by hand can be a tiresome, overwhelming, and usually futile job. The most effective way to remove existing weeds is to apply a postemergence herbicide. Postemergence types are categorized as either contact or systemic herbicides. Contact herbicides kill those above-ground plant parts that become covered by the spray. Systemic herbicides affect plant systems. After plants absorb the chemical, it circulates inside them and kills all parts, including the roots and

stems. Some of the most effective postemergence herbicides are listed below by their chemical names. For a list of trade names, see the chart on page 109.

Cacodylic Acid: Kills only on contact. Although effective, repeat treatments are necessary before it kills tough perennials, if at all. Kills all green-growing leaf tissue; does not move within plants to roots. Often used to clear lawns of existing growth prior to renovation or to selectively remove weeds in dormant Bermudagrass lawns.

CAMA, MAMA, MSMA: These chemicals (organic arsenicals) control grassy weeds, such as crabgrass and foxtail. They kill mostly by foliage activity. Effective against some hard-to-kill nutsedges. Requires two applications.

Dalapon: Effective against all grasses. Usually used to spot-treat undesirable clumps of Bermudagrass or tall fescue. In the West, use it to eliminate Bermudagrass from dichondra lawns. Use carefully; excessive rates can damage dichondra. Residual toxicity can last from two to four months.

Dicamba: Particularly effective against clover, beggarweed, chickweed, knotweed, and red sorrel. Like 2,4-D, dicamba affects plant hormones. It is absorbed through roots and leaves. Be careful using it around trees and shrubs or in areas where roots lie under the area to be treated.

Glyphosate: Nonselective and systemic: It kills both grasses and broadleaf weeds. It is an effective herbicide for the control of Bermudagrass, and is useful against most other perennial grassy weeds.

MCPP: Related and similar to 2,4-D, but safer to use on new lawns or sensitive grasses, such as bentgrass or St. Augustine grass.

2,4-D: Widely available in many forms and products. It is essentially a growth-influencing hormone that singles out the broadleaf weeds in the lawn and kills them without damaging most lawn grasses.

2,4-DP: Similar to 2,4-D, it effectively controls difficult-to-kill broadleaf weeds, such as oxalis and mugwort.

Annual Bluegrass
Scientific Name: *Poa annua*
Weed Type: Narrowleaf. Annual/Perennial.
Season of Fast Growth: Prefers the cool weather of spring and fall. Tends to die out in the summer. A winter annual in the South.
Preemergence Control: Use benefin, bensulide, or DCPA. Apply in early August. Several applications may be necessary.
Postemergence Control: No selective control. Spot-treat with glyphosate and reseed.

Bermudagrass, Devilgrass
Scientific Name: *Cynodon dactylon*
Weed Type: Narrowleaf. Perennial.
Season of Fast Growth: Summer. Grows fast when temperatures are high.
Preemergence Control: None.
Postemergence Control: No selective control. Spot-treat with glyphosate and reseed.
Comments: Where Bermudagrass is well adapted to the climate, it can either be your lawn or a troublesome weed if you have a different type of lawn, such as zoysia.

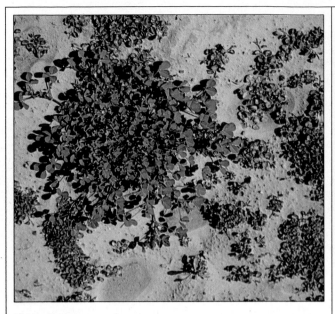

Burclover
Scientific Name: *Medicago hispida*
Weed Type: Broadleaf. Annual.
Season of Fast Growth: Spring and fall.
Preemergence Control: None.
Postemergence Control: Use a product containing dicamba or MCPP in spring or fall.

Crabgrass
Scientific Name: *Digitaria* species
Weed Type: Narrowleaf. Annual.
Season of Fast Growth: A summer weed. Begins in early spring and grows fast until the seed heads form in late summer to early fall.
Preemergence Control: Products containing benefin, bensulide, DCPA, oxadiazon, pendimenthalin, or siduron. Weed killer must be applied in the spring before seedlings appear. For regional recommendations, see ''Lawns in Your Area'' beginning on page 87.
Postemergence Control: Use organic arsenicals such as CAMA, MSMA, or MAMA. Apply when weeds are small and easier to control. If needed, repeat treatment after 7 to 10 days.

Dallisgrass
Scientific Name: *Paspalum dilatatum*
Weed Type: Narrowleaf. Perennial.
Season of Fast Growth: Dallisgrass is a summer weed, but grows the year around in mild climates.
Preemergence Control: None.
Postemergence Control: Use organic arsenicals such as CAMA, MAMA, or MSMA as a spray every 10 days or as the label directs. Do not use on bahiagrass, centipedegrass, or St. Augustine grass.
Comments: Thrives in low, wet areas. Try to drain the soil first for control. Bahiagrass is a close relative and sometimes infests Bermudagrass lawns. Control with a similar treatment.

Dandelion
Scientific Name: *Taraxacum officinale*
Weed Type: Broadleaf. Perennial.
Season of Fast Growth: Spring and fall.
Preemergence Control: New herbicides are being developed, but are not yet available to the home gardener.
Postemergence Control: Sprays containing 2,4-D or MCPP are effective. Apply during spring or fall when growth is active but before yellow flowers appear. Spray on a windless day when temperatures are above 60° F but less than 80° F.
Comments: Improved cultivars usually resist dandelion invasion quite well.

Dock

Scientific Name: *Rumex* species
Weed Type: Broadleaf. Perennial.
Season of Fast Growth: Spring and fall.
Preemergence Control: None.
Postemergence Control: Use 2,4-D or dicamba in midspring or midfall.

English Daisy

Scientific Name: *Bellis perennis*
Weed Type: Broadleaf. Perennial.
Season of Fast Growth: The cool weather of spring and fall, in all seasons if protected from drought and high heat.
Preemergence Control: None.
Postemergence Control: Difficult to control. Dicamba, MCPP, or 2,4-D give fair control. Apply in late spring.

Henbit

Scientific Name: *Lamium amplexicaule*
Weed Type: Broadleaf. Annual.
Season of Fast Growth: Spring and fall.
Preemergence Control: New herbicides are being developed, but are not yet available to the home gardener.
Postemergence Control: Use dicamba, MCPP, or 2,4-D in the fall or spring. Two applications may be required.
Comments: This weed is from the mint family—notice its four-sided stem. It appears in late winter or early spring.

Knotweed

Scientific Name: *Polygonum aviculare*
Weed Type: Broadleaf. Annual.
Season of Fast Growth: Early spring through early fall.
Preemergence Control: New herbicides are being developed, but are not yet available to the home gardener.
Postemergence Control: Dicamba or MCPP are the favored treatments anytime during active growth, which begins in early spring.
Comments: This weed is commonly seen in hard, compacted soils. Thorough aeration may help to eliminate it.

Mallow, Cheeseweed

Scientific Name: *Malva* species

Weed Type: Broadleaf. Annual.

Season of Fast Growth: Has a long growing season. Gets started in early spring and survives through the fall.

Preemergence Control: None.

Postemergence Control: Use dicamba, MCPP, or 2,4-D from midspring to late spring.

Mouse-Ear Chickweed

Scientific Name: *Cerastium vulgatum*

Weed Type: Broadleaf. Perennial.

Season of Fast Growth: The cool weather of spring or fall.

Preemergence Control: New herbicides are being developed, but are not yet available to the home gardener.

Postemergence Control: Use dicamba or MCPP. Apply in the fall or early spring when temperatures are between 60° F and 70° F.

Oxalis

Scientific Name: *Oxalis* species

Weed Type: Broadleaf. Perennial.

Season of Fast Growth: Spring and late summer to fall.

Preemergence Control: None.

Postemergence Control: Products containing dicamba, MCPP, 2,4-D, or 2,4-DP may be used. Apply in the spring or fall on a day when the wind is still and air temperatures will remain above 60° F but below 80° F. In many areas, treatment in late summer to fall is most effective. Usually requires several treatments.

Plantain

Scientific Name: *Plantago* species

Weed Type: Broadleaf. Perennial.

Season of Fast Growth: A cool-season weed. Forms rosettes with prominently veined leaves.

Preemergence Control: New herbicides are being developed, but are not yet available to the home gardener.

Postemergence Control: MCPP or 2,4-D are effective when applied in spring or fall before flower spikes form.

Purslane

Scientific Name: *Portulaca oleracea*

Weed Type: Broadleaf. Annual.

Season of Fast Growth: Summer.

Preemergence Control: DCPA applied from early to midspring.

Postemergence Control: Use dicamba or 2,4-D from midsummer to late summer.

Quackgrass

Scientific Name: *Agropyron repens*

Weed Type: Narrowleaf. Perennial.

Season of Fast Growth: Spring and fall.

Preemergence Control: None.

Postemergence Control: No selective control. Spot-treat with dalapon or glyphosate.

Comments: The underground stems are vigorous; even digging them out by hand is rarely successful.

Spotted Spurge

Scientific Name: *Euphorbia maculata*

Weed Type: Broadleaf. Annual.

Season of Fast Growth: A summer weed, the most aggressive growth is from late spring through early fall.

Preemergence Control: Use DCPA or siduron in early spring before germination, then again in midsummer.

Postemergence Control: Products containing dicamba or 2,4-D may be used. May require repeat applications.

Comments: Minor damage may result to turfgrasses from summer treatments.

Tall Fescue

Scientific Name: *Festuca elatior*

Weed Type: Narrowleaf. Perennial.

Season of Fast Growth: Spring and fall.

Preemergence Control: None.

Postemergence Control: Spot-treat only. Use either repeated sprays with a contact herbicide or dalapon. Glyphosate also controls well if applied when the weed is actively growing.

Comments: Frequently confused with crabgrass. Can be dug out by hand. Makes a good lawn where adapted, but is a weed when it occurs in a finer-textured lawn.

Thistle

Scientific Name: *Cirsium* species

Weed Type: Broadleaf. Perennial.

Season of Fast Growth: The strongest growth occurs in the cool weather of fall and spring.

Preemergence Control: None.

Postemergence Control: 2,4-D is effective. Spray in the fall. Two applications may be necessary. Otherwise, spot-treat with glyphosate.

Comments: There are several different types of thistle, all commonly found in northern regions. Leaf forms frequently vary. Roots may spread underground horizontally.

Veronica, Speedwell

Scientific Name: *Veronica filiformis*

Weed Type: Broadleaf. Annual.

Season of Fast Growth: Spring and fall.

Preemergence Control: None.

Postemergence Control: Spray 2,4-D in the fall or DCPA at flowering time in spring. Two applications may be necessary.

Comments: Dense patches of veronica become established below mowing height. It is a tough weed to kill. There are several slightly varying species. Flowers are light blue and seed pods are heart shaped.

White Clover

Scientific Name: *Trifolium repens*

Weed Type: Broadleaf. Perennial.

Season of Fast Growth: The cool seasons of fall and spring. Profuse flowering in early summer.

Preemergence Control: None.

Postemergence Control: Apply dicamba or MCPP in spring or fall. Choose a warm and windless day for treatment.

Wild Onion, Wild Garlic

Scientific Names: *Allium canadense, A. vineale*

Weed Type: Broadleaf. Perennial.

Season of Fast Growth: Spring to midsummer.

Preemergence Control: None.

Postemergence Control: Use 2,4-D; 2,4-D wax-impregnated bars are the most effective. Several treatments may be required. Use in late fall when the weeds are still small. Once mature they are difficult to control.

Comments: Wild onion differs from wild garlic in two ways: Wild onion does not produce the underground bulbs common to wild garlic, and garlic has a hollow leaf.

Insects and Other Pests

Hundreds of kinds of insects and other creatures live in a typical lawn. Some are so tiny they are hardly visible; others are quite large. Most do little damage to the lawn, and you are usually not even aware of their presence. Other insects are troublesome to people but do not damage the grass. Fleas and ticks are in this category. Only a few lawn pests, such as sod webworms, grubs, and chinch bugs, can destroy a lawn within a short time.

Diagnosing the Problem

In trying to discover the source of lawn damage, the easiest and most reliable method is to look—and look closely. Chances are you can see the pests in action. Some appear only at night, or only in a shady or sunny corner. Look for evidence of pest infestation. For example, look for the green, pellet-shaped droppings left by sod webworms. Note the habits and characteristics of the most common pests described on the following pages.

Many insects are only troublesome to certain kinds of grass. For instance, chinch bugs are by far the most damaging to St. Augustine grass. Wireworms rarely attack grasses other than bahiagrass or centipedegrass. Such examples abound. So, to the extent possible, choose a grass that is not bothered by specific pests or at least doesn't have a number-one enemy.

Keep your lawn in good health. While a well-maintained lawn does not keep insects away entirely, it is less subject to damage. It is also able to recover quickly when problems occur. However, if you frequently water and fertilize your lawn, be prepared for some extra pest-related chores. This is a prime environment for insect eggs to grow and hatch.

Insecticides

Insecticides are not the only solutions to lawn pest problems. If and when you decide they are necessary, it is important to know about their differences. Many forms of insecticides are available. When used properly, they are a safe and effective way of ridding your lawn of insects.

The most complete information on pest control products is on the product labels. Always read the label in the nursery or garden center before purchasing a product.

Here are some brief descriptions of insecticides and biological controls commonly used to control lawn pests. The insecticides are listed by their chemical names. For a list of trade names, see the chart on page 109.

Acephate: A good control of armyworms, greenbugs, leafhoppers, and sod webworms in lawns.

Bacillus thuringensis: A biological control. Kills only caterpillars (butterfly and moth larvae). It is useful in many situations, although it is not widely used on lawns.

Carbaryl: This chemical has been around for a long time and is available in a wide variety of forms from many manufacturers. It has several uses for home lawn insect control.

Chlorpyrifos: This provides effective control of chinch bugs, grubs, sod webworms, and many other insect pests. It remains effective for four to six weeks.

Diazinon: Like carbaryl, it is widely available in many forms. It is one of the most effective chemicals for the control of grubs. It protects against several other lawn pests for up to six weeks.

Isofenphos: Provides long-term control of chinch bugs, grubs, mole crickets, and sod webworms. For best results, apply several weeks before insect damage is expected. Remains effective longer than most other insecticides.

Metaldehyde: Look for this ingredient in slug and snail baits. Use it in their hiding places, such as in ground covers. Both snails and slugs hide in cool, moist areas during the day and come out at night. They love new lawns and dichondra.

Methiocarb: Effectively kills slugs and snails. Lightly water the area before spreading the bait.

Methoxyclor: A common ingredient in many spray mixes. It is generally useful as a lawn insecticide and has residual effects for about two months.

Milky Spore Disease: A biological control. This disease is natural only to Japanese beetle grubs. It has no effect on any other insects. It becomes established in soils over a number of years where Japanese beetles are present. While it is slow to establish and control is not 100 percent, it does keep the beetles in check.

NPD: A good control of chinch bugs and sod webworms. It works fast and is effective for about two months. Water the lawn before spraying, then withhold water for two or three days to permit the chemical to do its job. Do not walk on the lawn until the chemical has been washed into the soil.

Propoxur: Similar to carbaryl. Frequently used in baits. Controls chinch bugs, earwigs, and leafhoppers.

Trichlorfon: Effective for grubs and sod webworms.

Only a few insects, such as these grubs, can damage your lawn to this extent. Check your lawn periodically for the presence of insects and other pests, and treat them accordingly.

Identifying the Pest

Here, lawn-damaging insects are grouped according to where they are the most active—above or below the ground—and according to the type of damage they do. Control methods are different for each group.

Group 1: Live above the soil surface and suck plant juices—chinch bugs, leafhoppers, spider mites, and similar pests.

To control:
- Mow the lawn.
- Remove clippings.
- Water heavily.
- Wait until grass blades are dry, then apply insecticide according to label directions.
- Do not water for two days.

Group 2: Live at the soil surface and feed on leaves—armyworms, cutworms, fiery skipper larvae, and sod webworms.

To control:
- Mow the lawn.
- Remove clippings.
- Water heavily.
- Wait until grass blades are dry, then apply insecticide according to label directions. Best applied in late afternoon when insects are active.
- Do not water for two days.
- Fertilize to aid in lawn recovery, if the season is appropriate.

Group 3: Live below the soil surface and feed on roots—ground pearls, grubs, and wireworms.

To control:
- Mow the lawn.
- Remove clippings.
- Apply recommended insecticide according to label directions. Water heavily immediately after spraying, but not so much that the insecticide washes away.
- Fertilize to aid in lawn recovery, if the season is appropriate.

Armyworms, Cutworms, and Fiery Skippers

Symptoms: These three moth larvae chew off the grass blades above the soil surface. The damage they cause is similar to that of sod webworms. Armyworms cause round, bare areas in a lawn. If there are many of them, the grass is eaten to the soil level. Cutworms also feed on the grass blades, cutting them off near the surface. Fiery skippers are usually a minor problem, but can be serious pests of bentgrass and Bermudagrass lawns, especially hybrid Bermudagrass. They can also be a problem for bluegrass lawns in some areas.

Descriptions: Armyworms are yellowish white and have an upside-down "Y" on their heads. Cutworms are plump, smooth, and almost always curled up when you find them. They are usually brown to black; some are spotted or striped. Fiery skippers are easy to distinguish from other pests: They are about an inch long and brownish yellow, with dark brown heads and thin necks.

Control: Products that contain acephate, carbaryl, chlorpyrifos, or diazinon are all useful.

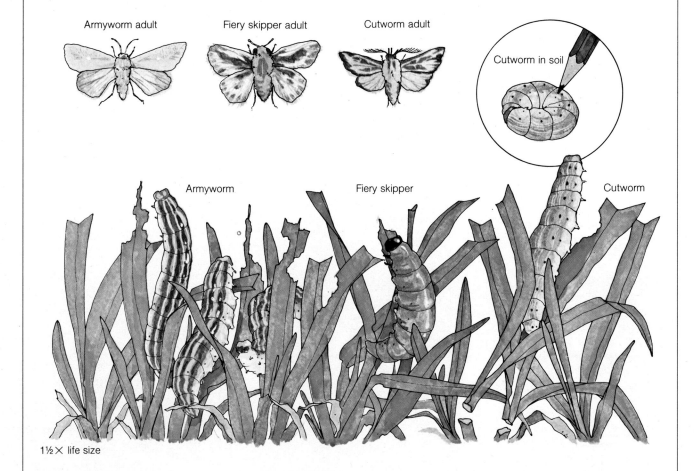

Armyworm adult

Fiery skipper adult

Cutworm adult

Cutworm in soil

Armyworm

Fiery skipper

Cutworm

1½ × life size

Billbugs

Symptoms: A small and distinct circular pattern becomes yellowish or brown. Since adult billbugs feed on roots, grass stems within the dead areas lift easily out of the soil.

Description: Different species of billbugs prefer different types of grass. In the southernmost regions, Bermudagrass and zoysiagrass are commonly attacked, while in the northern regions, Kentucky bluegrass is preferred. Most damage is caused in late summer.

Control: Use an insecticide, such as diazinon or propoxur, in midsummer if you find more than one billbug grub per square foot.

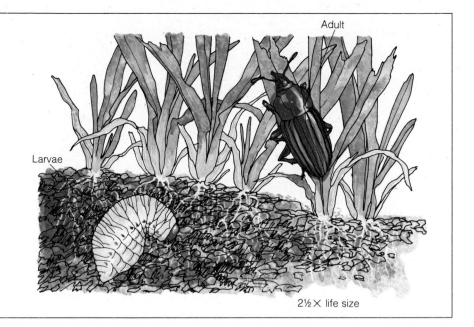

Adult

Larvae

2½ × life size

Chinch Bugs

Symptoms: You will see large, distinct, circular patches, especially on St. Augustine grass lawns. Kentucky bluegrass and creeping bentgrass are occasionally affected. The yellowish spots are distinctly worse toward the center and are confined to sunny areas of the lawn.

Description: Chinch bugs crawl down into the leaves and stems of the grass and suck the plant juices. They thrive in hot, dry weather. To check for chinch bugs, push a bottomless metal can into the affected lawn area and fill it with warm water. Chinch bugs congregate where the grass is just beginning to turn yellow, not in dead or green areas. Where they are abundant, they float to the surface of the water.

Control: Grow resistant 'Floratam' St. Augustine grass, or use chlorpyrifos, diazinon, isofenphos, NPD, or propoxur.

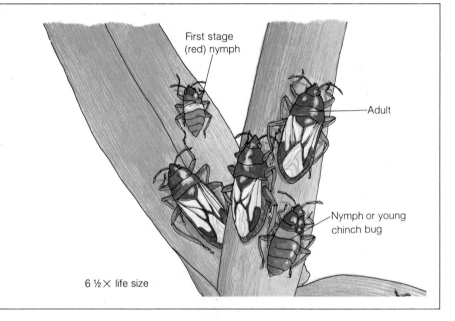

First stage (red) nymph

Adult

Nymph or young chinch bug

6 ½ × life size

Clover Mites

Symptoms: You may first become aware of these pests when they move inside your house looking for a warm place to spend the winter. They live primarily on clover and similar plants in the lawn.

Description: Tiny green to red-brown spiders that live and feed on the undersurface of grass blades. Sometimes their webbing is visible.

Control: Usually kept in check by other insects, predators, or insecticide treatments for other pests. If treatment is necessary, use diazinon or dicofol, a miticide, as the label directs.

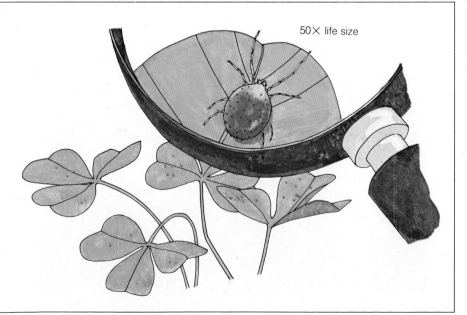

50× life size

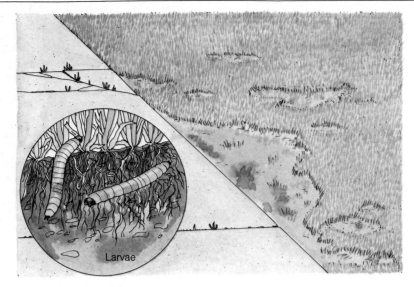

Life size

Crane Flies

Symptoms: A lawn bothered by crane flies loses patches of grass, often beginning at the edge of the lawn. When an area is heavily infested, you will see a brownish paste covering the soil over the missing grass. Brownish gray grubs, about an inch long, may be found just below the soil surface.

Description: Adult crane flies look similar to mosquitos; they do not bite. The adults do not damage the lawn, but they do lay eggs in lawns in late summer. The grubs that hatch damage a lawn by feeding on grass blades. Winter cold does not kill them. The worst damage occurs in the spring.

Control: Use a product containing diazinon when damage first appears. Treatment is most effective in the spring.

Life size

Earthworms

Symptoms: Small mounds or clumps of granular soil are scattered throughout the lawn. At night or after a heavy rain, you may see slender, 2- to 10-inch worms moving accordion-like through the soil.

Description: Earthworms thrive on dead grass roots and stems. Their presence helps your lawn by mixing the organic matter on top with the soil below, reducing thatch build up, and improving air and water movement through the soil. Earthworms and their castings (digested soil) are found primarily in moist, fertile soil.

Control: Earthworms are beneficial to the soil, so control measures are not usually required or recommended. If soil mounds are a nuisance, the best solution is to break them up with a rake.

10× life size

Greenbugs

Symptoms: Rust-colored patches of grass appear under trees. These patches of grass turn brown and die. The damage then spreads to the sunny parts of the lawn. Blades may also have yellow to rust-colored spots with dark centers.

Description: Greenbugs are tiny aphids that suck sap from and inject a poison into grass blades. They can kill an entire lawn if left uncontrolled. Underwatered or overfertilized Kentucky bluegrass lawns are particularly susceptible to greenbugs. Damage occurs primarily after mild winters and cool springs.

Control: At the first sign of damage, spray the lawn with a product containing acephate. Repeat if the symptoms continue. Follow proper watering and fertilizing guidelines.

Grubs

Symptoms: Look for brown patches, irregular in shape, in late spring or early fall. Dead patches roll back easily, like a section of carpet. Birds, moles, raccoons, and skunks may damage a lawn looking for grubs.

Description: Grubs are the larvae of many kinds of beetles. They are whitish or grayish in color with brown heads and dark hind parts. They have three pairs of legs, which distinguishes them from the legless billbug grubs. The adult beetles appear around the garden in late spring or summer.

Control: If your lawn is already infested with grubs (two C-shaped grubs per square foot), keep in mind that they are insulated by a layer of grass leaves, thatch, and soil. The insecticide must get below the soil surface by repeated heavy waterings. Remove thatch, then use a product containing chlorpyrifos, diazinon, isofenphos, or trichlorfon.

Adult grub · Young grub · Maturing grub · Eggs · Pupa · 1½ × life size

Leafhoppers

Symptoms: These tiny insects are nearly always present to some degree on lawn surfaces. When severe, they can wipe out a newly seeded lawn and cause a mature lawn to look bleached and unhealthy.

Description: Leafhoppers are tiny, even when full grown. They are usually green, but may be yellow or gray. If your lawn is infested, each step through the grass will kick up a swarm of them.

Control: Insecticide treatments are usually not necessary; they are more of a nuisance to you than to the lawn. Acephate or diazinon will effectively control them, if necessary.

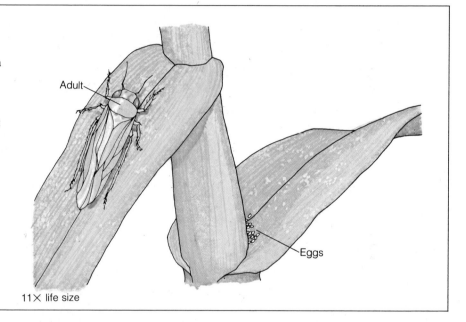

Adult · Eggs · 11× life size

Mole Crickets

Symptoms: Mole crickets cause irregular streaks of brown and wilted grass. They are found in such warm-season grasses as bahiagrass, Bermudagrass, centipedegrass, St. Augustine grass, and sometimes zoysiagrass. The dead grass pulls up easily. You can find the tunnels with your fingers or even see them if the ground is bare.

Description: Mole crickets are about 1½ to 2 inches long and brown or grayish brown. They look similar to a common cricket, except that their heads and their front legs are notably large. They feed on grass roots and by tunneling cause nearby roots to dry out.

Control: The most common control is a mole cricket bait, containing propoxur. Apply the bait the evening before a warm night, watering the lawn first. Or use diazinon in the spring, about a week after seeing the first signs of mole cricket activity.

1⅓× life size

Moles and Gophers

Symptoms: When moles are present, you will notice raised ridges, 3 to 5 inches wide, on the lawn. These ridges sometimes turn brown. Gophers create crescent-shaped mounds of soil on the lawn. Upon close probing, you will find a hole underneath each mound. Gophers are primarily found in western regions.

Description: Both moles and gophers are rodents that live underground. Moles feed on grubs, earthworms, and other insects, while gophers eat plant roots or entire plants. Each causes damage to the lawn by severing grass roots, raising sod, and, in the case of gophers, eating sections of the lawn.

Control: Trapping is the best way to eliminate gophers from your yard. This can be time consuming for moles, however, because of the structure of their surface tunnels and the temporary way they are used. Rid your lawn of moles by eliminating grubs, a favorite food.

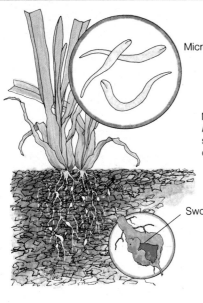

Microscopic

Nematodes can be controlled *before* planting a new lawn by soil fumigation. For information on fumigating soil, see page 58.

Swollen root infected by nematode

Nematodes

Symptoms: The grass is slow-growing, thin, yellowish, and susceptible to drought in the summer. It does not respond to treatments such as aeration, fertilization, or watering. Roots are stubby and shallow, and possibly show swellings or galls. Complete diagnosis requires a professional laboratory analysis.

Description: Nematodes are common in the soil. These small worms are so small that you need a microscope to see them, but scientists say they are the most common form of life on earth. There are thousands of different kinds, but only a few damage plants.

Control: Keep the grass as healthy as possible. If the presence of damaging nematodes is confirmed by a professional, consult with an experienced pest-control operator or your county extension agent.

Slugs and Snails

Symptoms: Their silvery trails in the morning are a giveaway. Be on the lookout for slugs or snails if you have a border of ivy or a dense ground cover. These pests are capable of eating the grass or dichondra adjacent to their hiding places.

Description: These are pretty well-known creatures. They hide in cool and shady spots during the day and feed at night.

Control: Use baits containing metaldehyde or methiocarb.

Sod Webworms

Symptoms: In late spring or summer, dead patches from 1 to 2 inches in diameter are seen among normal-growing grass. Break apart damaged areas to check for webworms. Other evidence is their green-tan excrement. Birds and moles feeding on the lawn may indicate a large population.

Description: The adult form of the webworm is a buff-colored moth that flies in a zigzag pattern, just a few feet above the lawn. The moths themselves do not damage the lawn, but drop eggs into the grass that, on hatching, develop into hungry caterpillars.
  Sod webworms feed at night. They chew grass blades off just above the thatch line and pull the blades into a silken tunnel to eat them.

Control: Use acephate, carbaryl, chlorpyrifos, diazinon, isofenphos, NPD, propoxur, or trichlorfon. Remove thatch to make lawn less desirable to webworms.

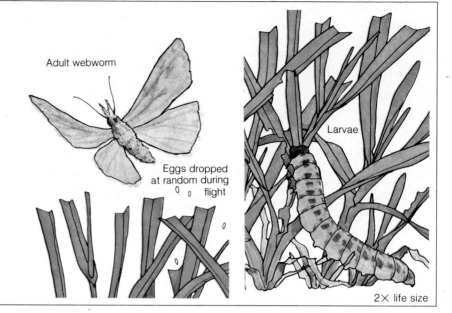

Adult webworm

Eggs dropped at random during flight

Larvae

2× life size

Nuisance Pests

2½× life size

1½× life size

50× life size

Ants
Ants are a problem in lawns because of the nest mounds they make, not because they feed directly on or otherwise harm the grass. Chlorpyrifos or diazinon sprays or granules control ants for as long as two months.

Brown Dog Ticks
This pest is common to lawns that are near wooded areas. Ticks are the most active in spring and early summer. Suffocate ticks on skin with petroleum jelly. Spray lawns with carbaryl, chlorpyrifos, or diazinon.

Chiggers
Chiggers are not insects; they are actually spiders or mites. They lay their eggs in the soil. After hatching, the larvae crawl up onto the grass or weeds and wait for an animal to brush by. Repellents containing diethyltoluamide are effective, as are sprays of diazinon or chlorpyrifos.

1½× life size

4× life size

5× life size

Earwigs
These hard, dark reddish brown insects hide in dark places during the day. Their pincers aren't nearly as dangerous as they look; they are only useful against other earwigs. Baits containing propoxur, scattered in the evening, are effective, or spray with carbaryl, chlorpyrifos, or diazinon.

Fleas
Fleas are certainly well-known pests to dog or cat owners. They may fall off a pet and wait in the lawn for another host animal. The insecticides carbaryl, chlorpyrifos, diazinon, or malathion are good controls.

Gnats
A type of tiny fly, gnats are similar to mosquitoes in many ways; most need water to lay eggs. They can be annoying when they swarm around the lawn. The best treatment is a fogging spray.

Occasional Pests

Some of the insects and other pests included in this group can, in specific situations, cause extensive damage. None of them are nearly so common as chinch bugs, grubs, or sod webworms. Several are problems only in relatively confined regions. Others, such as centipedes, millipedes, pillbugs, sowbugs, and wireworms, are widespread but rarely cause serious damage.

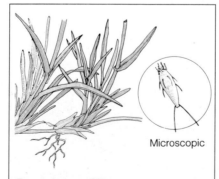

Microscopic

Bermudagrass Mites
These are microscopic pests known best by the damage they cause. Infested Bermudagrass lawns have shortened spaces between leaves. These infested areas become clumps that interrupt the texture of the lawn, gradually causing it to yellow and die. You can sometimes see Bermudagrass mites by shaking infested grass over white paper. Control by thatch removal or use diazinon.

Life size

Crickets
Crickets won't eat much of your lawn, but they may cause a problem if they try to move into your house for the winter. For control, use a chlorpyrifos spray, diazinon granules, or a similar chemical control around the house.

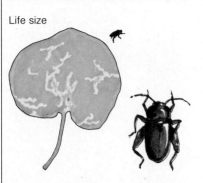

Life size

5× life size

Dichondra Flea Beetles
These tiny beetles look harmless enough, but they can quickly destroy a dichondra lawn. They are easily visible against a white piece of paper. Depending on your area, be ready for them anytime from April to June. Control with chlorpyrifos or diazinon.

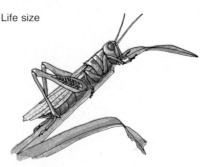

Life size

Grasshoppers
Grasshoppers damage your lawn only if many converge at once. They are usually the most abundant in late summer in rural or suburban areas. Chemical control is rarely necessary, but chlorpyrifos is effective.

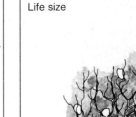

Life size

Ground Pearl
These tiny "pearls" are attached to the roots of Bermudagrass and centipede-grass. About ⅛ inch in diameter, they damage the grass by feeding on the roots. Prevent by following recommended fertilization, watering, and mowing practices. No chemical control is presently used.

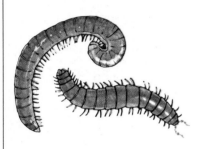

1½× life size

Millipedes and Centipedes
Even though they rarely damage lawns, these segmented wormlike creatures are often found in or near lawns. Like sowbugs, they like cool, moist hiding spots. If there are too many in your yard, cleaning up piles of trash or wood should control them. If serious, control with diazinon.

Life size

Pearl Scale
A serious problem of hybrid Bermudagrass lawns in the Southwest. Starting in mid-May, spot-treat with diazinon every 7 to 14 days throughout the month of June.

Life size

Periodical Cicadas
These large insects live deep in the soil for several years. When they leave the ground, they make a great number of holes. The adults damage nearby shrubs and trees rather than the lawn.

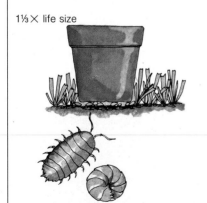

1⅓× life size

Sowbugs and Pillbugs
These bugs are similar in appearance and behavior, but pillbugs are the ones that roll themselves into a ball. Both usually feed only on decaying organic matter. Control by removing their cool, moist hiding places, such as leaves and organic debris, or treat with chlorpyrifos or diazinon.

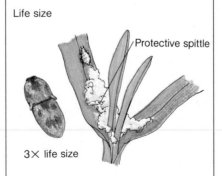

Life size

Protective spittle

3× life size

Spittlebugs
Spittlebugs are rarely responsible for much lawn damage, but are a common inhabitant of lawns. They do damage other plants, however. While feeding, they hide under a material that looks just like spittle, hence the name. If necessary, they can be controlled by either carbaryl or diazinon.

3× life size

Wireworms
These larvae of click beetles feed on lawn roots. They are brown and about 1 inch long. They damage lawns only when present in excessive numbers. Look for them as you would for grubs—in the root zone of sections of dead grass. Control with diazinon.

Diseases and Cultural Problems

Diagnosing lawn problems is often difficult, especially if considerable time has elapsed between the cause of the damage and the diagnosis. A problem that is attributed to an insect or disease may actually be caused by environmental conditions or cultural practices. Improper watering and mowing height, competition from tree roots, iron deficiency, soil compaction, and herbicide damage are some of the many factors that either cause the symptoms or are related to the development of a disease.

Proper Lawn Care

The adage that proper maintenance reduces lawn problems is especially true concerning lawn diseases. Most of the diseases that attack home lawns do so because of improper lawn management. Thatch is one of the most important factors governing the frequency of disease in lawns. Thatch restricts the movement of air, water, and fertilizer into the soil, generally weakening a lawn and making it more prone to disease.

When and how much you fertilize also has an important impact on disease development. Both overfertilizing and underfertilizing makes your lawn more susceptible to disease. Timing is critical. For example, if you give a cool-season lawn heavy doses of growth-stimulating fertilizer in late spring and summer (periods of slow growth), it becomes increasingly vulnerable to leaf spot and summer patch. Always follow a fertilizer program that conforms to the growth cycle of your particular lawn grass. Let the grass grow, don't make it grow.

Watering practices can affect the susceptibility of your lawn to disease. Lawns that are watered deeply but infrequently usually have fewer disease problems. Grass that is constantly wet and that grows in poorly drained soil promotes disease.

Lawn diseases are easier to prevent than to cure. Follow these guidelines to prevent diseases from becoming established in your lawn:

• Plant a grass type and cultivar that is adapted to your climate.

• Mow at the proper height as recommended in the chart on page 49.

• Fertilize at recommended rates and on a schedule that fits the growth cycle of your grass type.

• Water deeply and only when the lawn needs it.

• Dethatch regularly.

When a serious disease does attack your lawn despite adherence to these preventive measures, chemical control is necessary.

Fungicides

To prevent and control disease, over a dozen available fungicides are commonly sprayed on lawns by homeowners. These fungicides are categorized as either *systemic* or *nonsystemic*.

Because systemic fungicides work from inside plants, they are usually the most effective. However, systemic fungicides are specific—they only control certain diseases.

Nonsystemic fungicides work on the outside of plants. They are best used before diseases start. For example, if you know from past experience that a particular disease attacks your lawn at a certain time of year, prevent the disease by spraying the appropriate fungicide two weeks beforehand.

Follow proper cultural practices to keep your lawn healthy and disease free.

Look at the chart below for the type and uses of various fungicides. Fungicides are listed in this chart by their chemical names. For a list of trade names, see the chart on page 109. Use the succeeding pages to help identify and control any diseases that occur in your lawn.

Common Lawn Fungicides

Chemical Name	Type	Uses
Anilazine	Nonsystemic	Brown patch, dollar spot, gray leaf spot, leaf spot, red thread, rust, and typhula blight
Benomyl	Systemic	Brown patch, dollar spot, fusarium patch, necrotic ring spot, powdery mildew, and summer patch
Captan	Nonsystemic	Damping off, gray leaf spot, and leaf spot
Chloroneb	Nonsystemic	Pythium blight
Chlorothalonil	Nonsystemic	Brown patch, dollar spot, gray leaf spot, leaf spot, red thread, and rust
Cycloheximide	Nonsystemic	Gray leaf spot, leaf spot, powdery mildew, and rust
Etridiazole	Nonsystemic	Pythium blight
Fenarimol	Systemic	Brown patch, dollar spot, fusarium patch, necrotic ring spot, summer patch, and typhula blight
Iprodione	Systemic	Brown patch, dollar spot, fusarium patch, leaf spot, red thread, summer patch, and typhula blight
Mancozeb	Nonsystemic	Fusarium patch, gray leaf spot, leaf spot, and red thread
Maneb	Nonsystemic	Gray leaf spot and rust
Metalaxyl	Systemic	Pythium blight
PCNB	Slight systemic activity	Gray leaf spot and stripe smut
Propamocarb	Systemic	Pythium blight
Thiophanates	Systemic	Brown patch, dollar spot, stripe smut, and summer patch
Thiram	Nonsystemic	Damping off. Combine with other fungicides
Triadimefon	Systemic	Brown patch, dollar spot, fusarium patch, powdery mildew, red thread, rust, stripe smut, summer patch, and typhula blight

Brown Patch
July to August

Description: Brown patch is recognized by large, irregular, circular areas up to several feet in diameter. The patches usually have a brown to gray discoloration, with a water-soaked appearance around the edges of the patch. Brown patch usually only attacks leaves and stems.

Favorable Climatic Conditions: High temperatures (75° F to 95° F), excessive thatch, high humidity, lush growth from overfertilizing, and excessive moisture are perfect conditions for this disease.

Susceptible Grasses: A serious disease in the South on centipedegrass and St. Augustine grass. It also attacks bentgrass, Bermudagrass, dichondra, fescues, ryegrass, and zoysiagrass.

Resistant Grasses: Improved Kentucky bluegrass.

Cultural Control: Avoid heavy doses of nitrogen fertilizer, reduce shade and thatch, and water deeply when necessary.

Chemical Control: Apply anilazine, benomyl, chlorothalonil, fenarimol, iprodione, thiophanates, or triadimefon.

Damping Off
Seedling Lawns

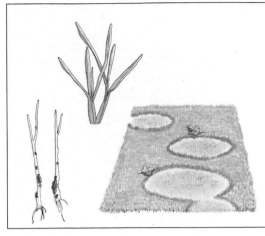

Description: Damping-off disease may be present when new seedlings fail to fill in properly. Look closely to see whether young seedlings have emerged from the soil but collapsed. Damping off is caused by a number of different fungal organisms.

Favorable Climatic Conditions: The most common cause is overwatering after seeding, especially if the soil is heavy and the days are overcast. Damping off does not cause a problem to lawns started from sprigs or plugs.

Susceptible Grasses. Any seeded grass.

Resistant Grasses: None.

Cultural Control: Make sure the pH is close to neutral. Do not overwater. Provide good drainage.

Chemical Control: Use seeds treated with captan or thiram, or spray captan or thiram at the first sign of trouble.

Dollar Spot
May to November

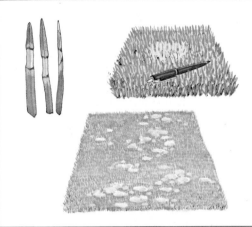

Description: Dollar spot is a common fungus disease that attacks several different types of grass, but it is the most severe on bentgrass and Bermudagrass. It kills in small spots, 3 to 12 inches in diameter, but the spots may fuse into large areas. Diseased spots usually range from tan to straw colored.

Favorable Climatic Conditions: Moderate temperatures, excess moisture, and heavy thatch all contribute to this disease. Underfertilized lawns are prone to attack.

Susceptible Grasses: Bentgrass, Bermudagrass, fescues, Kentucky bluegrass, and ryegrass.

Resistant Grasses: Some of the new, improved cultivars of Kentucky bluegrass and perennial ryegrass.

Cultural Control: Increase nitrogen, keep thatch at a minimum, and water deeply when necessary.

Chemical Control: Apply anilazine, benomyl, chlorothalonil, fenarimol, iprodione, thiophanates, or triadimefon.

Fairy Ring
April to November

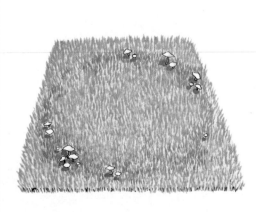

Description: This disease appears as rings of dark green grass surrounding areas of dead or light-colored grass. The rings are produced by any one of over 50 different kinds of fungus. The dying grass inside a ring is caused by lack of water penetration.

Favorable Climatic Conditions: Fairy ring develops in soils that contain undecomposed, woody organic matter, such as dead tree roots or old construction materials. It is primarily a problem in acid soils and old lawns.

Susceptible Grasses: All grasses.

Resistant Grasses. None.

Cultural Control: Try to keep the lawn growing by applying adequate nitrogen fertilizer to hide the problem. Aerate rings and use a wetting agent to improve water penetration. Keep areas wet for about two weeks and mow frequently. You can also dig up the entire area of a ring, to a depth of 12 inches, and replace it with fresh soil and new plantings.

Chemical Control: It is best to try to live with this disease. It is difficult to eradicate it with a soil fumigant.

Fusarium Patch
September to May

Description: This disease, also called pink snow mold, develops under snow or at the margins of a melting snow bank. It occasionally develops without snow being present, however. Fusarium patch causes white or pink circular patches, 1 to 8 inches in diameter. Tiny masses are sometimes found on dead blades of grass. Check for fungal threads in early morning.

Favorable Climatic Conditions: Cool (40° F to 60° F), moist conditions are the most favorable.

Susceptible Grasses: Look for fusarium patch on common Kentucky bluegrass, colonial and creeping bentgrass, fescue, ryegrass, and zoysiagrass.

Resistant Grasses: Improved Kentucky bluegrass.

Cultural Control: Reduce shade, if any. Improve soil aeration and drainage. Avoid excess nitrogen fertilizing in the fall. Remove thatch buildup.

Chemical Control: Apply benomyl, fenarimol, iprodione, mancozeb, or triadimefon.

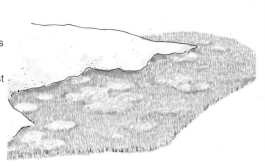

Gray Leaf Spot
June to August

Description: Gray leaf spot attacks St. Augustine grass, especially recently sprigged or plugged lawns. The spots on the grass blades are ash to brown in color and surrounded by a dark margin. The most serious effect of the disease is when blades scorch or die back.

Favorable Climatic Conditions: Warm, rainy periods during the summer.

Susceptible Grasses: St. Augustine grass.

Resistant Grasses: 'Roselawn' and 'Tamlawn' St. Augustine grass has shown some resistance.

Cultural Control: Do not overfertilize with nitrogen. Water as infrequently as the lawn tolerates. When you do water, be sure the moisture penetrates to at least 5 inches. Prune shade trees, if possible, to increase light and air circulation.

Chemical Control: Apply anilazine, captan, chlorothalonil, cycloheximide, mancozeb, maneb, or PCNB.

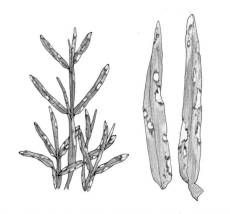

Leaf Spot
April to November

Description: Leaf spot, also known as melting out, refers to a number of diseases that favor Bermudagrass, fescue, and Kentucky bluegrass. The most obvious symptom of the disease is elongated, circular spots on grass blades. These spots have brown or straw-colored centers with black to purplish borders.

Favorable Climatic Conditions: Cool (50° F to 70° F), moist conditions are the most favorable to leaf spot. It first appears in the shade. It is the most severe in closely mowed lawns.

Susceptible Grasses: 'Delta', 'Kenblue', and 'Park' Kentucky bluegrass are the most susceptible.

Resistant Grasses: 'Adelphi', 'Challenger', 'Eclipse', and 'Midnight' Kentucky bluegrass are the most resistant. Many new bluegrass cultivars also have good resistance.

Cultural Control: Reduce the amount of shade. Improve aeration and water drainage. Mow at the recommended height.

Chemical Control: Apply anilazine, captan, chlorothalonil, cycloheximide, iprodione, or mancozeb.

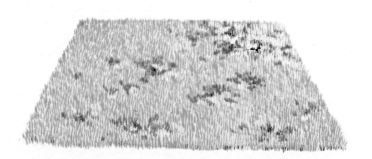

Powdery Mildew
July to November

Description: The first symptoms of powdery mildew are light patches of dusty, white to light gray growth on grass blades. The lowest leaves may become completely covered. While it is usually not too serious a problem, coverage can be severe. It commonly occurs in shady areas.
Favorable Climatic Conditions: Slow or nonexistent air circulation and shade are the most common causes.
Susceptible Grasses: Bermudagrass, Kentucky bluegrass, and zoysiagrass.
Resistant Grasses: 'Birka', 'Glade', and 'Nugget' Kentucky bluegrass; 'Aurora', 'Flyer', 'Fortress', 'Reliant', and 'Shadow' fine fescue.
Cultural Control: Reduce shade, if possible. Do not overwater. Avoid overfertilizing.
Chemical Control: Apply benomyl, cycloheximide, or triadimefon.

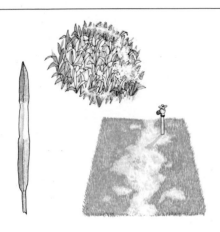

Pythium Blight
July and August

Description: This disease, also known as cottony blight or grease spot, usually only occurs on newly established lawns, but can be a problem for any lawn if conditions are favorable. The diseased area may be a few inches to several feet in diameter. It frequently appears on closely cut lawns as circular spots about 2 inches across. Look for it in early morning while the dew is still on the grass, or during humid weather. The diseased areas are surrounded by blackened blades covered with a white or gray fungus. Dry weather stops the disease.
Favorable Climatic Conditions: High temperatures and excess moisture.
Susceptible Grasses: Bentgrass, Bermudagrass, bluegrass, tall fescue, and ryegrass.
Resistant Grasses: None.
Cultural Control: Avoid excessive watering during warm weather and do not overfertilize. Seed late in the fall.
Chemical Control: Use a fungicide such as chloroneb, etridiazole, metalaxyl, or propamocarb at the first sign of the disease.

Red Thread
September to November

Description: This disease, also known as pink patch, is common in the Pacific Northwest, although it occasionally occurs in the northeast. The first symptoms are small patches of dead grass. Under wet conditions, the fungus is visible as bright pink threads.
Favorable Climatic Conditions: Besides moist air, low levels of nitrogen favor the development of this disease. It is the most prevalent when grass growth slows.
Susceptible Grasses: Kentucky bluegrass, red fescue, ryegrass, and sometimes bentgrass.
Tolerant Grasses: Many improved cultivars of Kentucky bluegrass and hard fescue.
Cultural Control: Increase nitrogen.
Chemical Control: Apply anilazine, chlorothalonil, iprodione, mancozeb, or triadimefon.

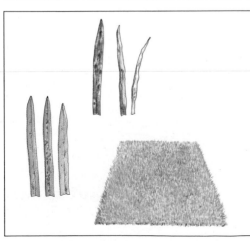

Rust
July to November

Description: This disease is appropriately named. The affected lawn has a rust-colored cast that is noticeable from a distance. The dustlike rust spores form in circular or long groups on grass blades. Rust rarely causes severe damage to home lawns, but is a serious disease where grasses are grown for seed.
Favorable Climatic Conditions: Moderately warm, moist weather. Dew that lasts for 10 to 12 hours is enough to promote germination of the fungus spores. Any stress conditions that restrict lawn growth favor the development of rust.
Susceptible Grasses: Rust affects almost all commonly grown grasses. Kentucky bluegrass and ryegrass are damaged the most frequently.
Resistant Grasses: Fine fescues, new cultivars of Kentucky bluegrass, and perennial ryegrass.
Cultural Control: Make the lawn grow rapidly by fertilizing with nitrogen and watering frequently. Then, mow every four or five days.
Chemical Control: Apply anilazine, chlorothalonil, cycloheximide, maneb, or triadimefon. Chemicals are necessary only in severe cases.

St. Augustine Grass Decline (SAD)
Anytime

Description: SAD is a virus that causes mottling of the leaf blades, overall yellowing, and a general decline in vigor. A St. Augustine grass lawn attacked by SAD is cusually invaded by Bermudagrass and weeds, which are not affected.
Favorable Climatic Conditions: Known to occur only in Texas and Louisiana.
Susceptible Grasses: St. Augustine grass.
Resistant Grasses: 'Floralawn', 'Floratam', 'Raleigh', 'Seville', and 'Tamlawn' St. Augustine grass.
Cultural Control: The only control is to plant plugs of resistant grasses into the middle of the infested areas, which eventually replace the diseased grass.
Chemical Control: None known.

Stripe Smut
April to November

Description: Plants that are diseased by stripe smut are usually pale green and stunted. Long, black stripes of spores are visible on grass blades. Affected blades curl, die, and become shredded by the advancing disease.
Favorable Climatic Conditions: The moderate temperatures of spring and fall. Hot, dry weather often halts the disease.
Susceptible Grasses: Bentgrass and Kentucky bluegrass are commonly attacked.
Resistant Grasses: 'Adelphi', 'A-34', and 'Sydsport' are a few of the many Kentucky bluegrasses that are resistant.
Cultural Control: Keep thatch to a minimum and avoid overwatering.
Chemical Control: PCNB, thiophanates, or triadimefon provide some control. Chemicals are best applied in late fall.

Summer Patch
June to August

Description: Formerly called fusarium blight, summer patch begins as scattered light green patches, ½ to 8 inches in diameter, that turn dull tan to reddish brown. Of the larger diseased patches in the lawn, the easiest to recognize is the "frog-eye" pattern—an apparently healthy green patch of grass that is partially or completely surrounded by a ring of dead grass.
Favorable Climatic Conditions: Hot, dry, and windy weather is especially favorable. It occurs most commonly in areas that have suffered water stress.
Susceptible Grasses: 'Fylking' and 'Park' Kentucky bluegrass, new cultivars of tall fescue, and perennial ryegrass.
Resistant Grasses: 'Adelphi', 'Columbia', 'Enmundi', 'Glade', 'Parade', and 'Sydsport' Kentucky bluegrass.
Cultural Control: Avoid fertilizing heavily. Follow correct watering and mowing practices. Light, frequent watering helps during drought. Planting a mixture of Kentucky bluegrass and perennial ryegrass reduces its occurrence.
Chemical Control: Apply benomyl, fenarimol, iprodione, thiophanates, or triadimefon. Water the night before, thoroughly drenching the fungicide into the turf.

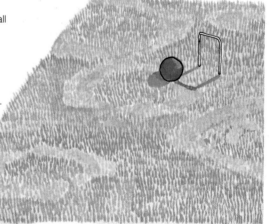

Necrotic Ring Spot
April to November

Description: This disease is a variation of summer patch that usually occurs where temperatures are cool.
Favorable Climatic Conditions: Symptoms appear under a range of temperatures and precipitation.
Susceptible Grasses: 'Arboretum', 'Fylking', 'Park', and 'Pennstar' Kentucky bluegrass.
Resistant Grasses: Not yet determined.
Cultural Control: The same as summer patch.
Chemical Control: Benomyl or fenarimol.

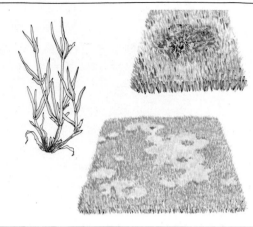

Take-All Patch
May to June, August to September

Description: Sometimes called ophiobolus patch, this disease thrives only in the cool, moist coastal regions of the Pacific Northwest. It first appears as small, brown spots that enlarge quickly in a favorable climate.
Favorable Climatic Conditions: Maritime climate.
Susceptible Grasses: Bentgrass is the most commonly damaged grass, but Kentucky bluegrass and ryegrass may also be bothered.
Resistant Grasses: All fescues.
Cultural Control: The best cultural control is to use slightly acid soil. Apply 2 pounds of sulfur per 1,000 square feet when the problem becomes severe.
Chemical Control: Try an acid-forming fertilizer, such as ammonium sulfate. Controlling with fungicides is difficult.

Typhula Blight
In Snow

Description: This disease, also known as gray snow mold, first appears as straw-colored or tan circular areas, a few inches to a few feet in diameter. The dead grass may be covered with a grayish fungal growth. It occurs primarily in the northern United States and Canada, not reaching as far south as fusarium patch (pink snow mold).
Favorable Climatic Conditions: A deep snow cover that is slow to melt.
Susceptible Grasses: Attacks almost all cool-season grasses.
Resistant Grasses: None.
Cultural Control: Be sure the lawn is not lush (overfertilized with nitrogen) before the first snowfall. Avoid excessive use of lime. Keep the thatch layer to a minimum.
Chemical Control: Apply anilazine, fenarimol, iprodione, or triadimefon in the fall before the first snowfall. Since typhula blight is found primarily in areas where snow lies on the ground for a long time, such as against a house or garage, these areas may be the only ones that need treatment.

Chemical Burn

Many lawns are damaged by spilled fertilizer, herbicide, gasoline, or dog urination. Chemical burn is characterized by distinct and abrupt patches of dead grass. Bright green grass surrounding a patch of dead grass is typical of burns from fertilizer and dog urination; both are caused by an abundance of nitrogen. The solutions to these problems vary. For water-soluble material (most herbicides, fertilizers, or urine), thoroughly drench the soil with water. For water-insoluble material (gasoline or oil), first drench the soil with soapy water (about the consistency of dishwater), then water thoroughly. There is no cure for persistent herbicides (the kind used on driveways). In all cases, once the symptoms appear it is too late to save the grass. Replace the soil under dead spots and patch damaged areas. See page 82 for instructions on patching.

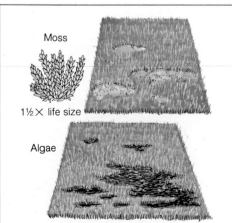

Moss

1½ × life size

Algae

Moss and Algae

Moss and algae in lawns usually result from cultural conditions such as improper amounts of fertilizer, poor drainage or air circulation, and too much shade. Moss is a green, velvety, low-growing collection of tiny plants that covers bare soil in shaded lawn areas. Algae appear as green to black, slimy scum that cover both bare soil and green lawn areas.

If you cannot control moss by raking, treat it with 3 tablespoons of copper sulfate for every 1,000 square feet or with 10 pounds of ammonium sulfate for every 1,000 square feet. This amount of ammonium sulfate may furnish too much nitrogen for cool-season grasses if applied in late spring. Treat algae with maneb, mancozeb, or wettable sulfur; apply two times, one month apart, in early spring. These suggested cures are only temporary for both problems. For permanent solutions, look for and eliminate the conditions causing them.

Mushrooms

After prolonged periods of wet weather, you may notice mushrooms coming up in the lawn. This often indicates the underground presence of decaying organic matter, such as construction debris or old tree roots and stumps.

Most mushrooms cause no damage to the lawn. If they grow in circles of dark green grass, called fairy rings (see page 74), they may injure the grass by making it impervious to water.

There is no effective chemical control for mushrooms. However, if you feel they are unsightly and poisonous, remove them with a rake or lawn mower.

Nitrogen or Iron Deficiency

Nitrogen is the nutrient needed by lawns in the greatest quantity. The actual amount varies with the type of grass, but most grasses need some lawn fertilizer every year. If you have not been applying fertilizer, your lawn is probably slightly yellow and not growing as well as it should.

If you have fertilized adequately and the lawn is still yellow and growing slowly, the problem could be a lack of iron or an improper pH level. Some grasses, such as centipedegrass, are especially sensitive to the lack of iron. Applying a typical lawn fertilizer to a lawn that needs iron may actually increase the yellowish look. Apply iron either as a liquid spray or in combination with nitrogen and sulfur.

Scalping and Dull Mower Injury

Lawn scalping occurs whenever too much grass is cut off at one time. Reducing the height of the lawn by more than one third creates a severe shock, but the results may not be immediately visible. When the mower blades dip down, suddenly removing most of the green part of the lawn, the browning effect is obvious and should not be confused with insect or disease damage.

Mowing your lawn with with dull blades gives the lawn a grayish cast a day or so later. This happens because the leaf tips are shredded instead of cut, and turn brown. The effect is especially noticeable in dry weather. Besides being unsightly, shredded tips make an easy entry point for many disease organisms.

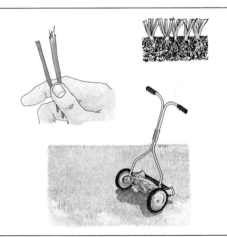

Summer Dryness

Dry soil affects all grasses and can do considerable damage. While dry parts of a lawn are easy to detect, they are often mistaken for insect or disease damage. Dried-out portions may be the result of compacted soil or spots that the sprinkler has missed.

The first indication of insufficient water is when areas of the lawn change color from bright to dull green. Water stress is confirmed if your footprints do not spring back in a reasonable length of time.

If your lawn is a cool-season grass, raise the cutting height at least ½ inch and water deeply. Check the moisture of the soil occasionally with a soil probe or moisture meter. If one area begins to show signs of drought, use a portable sprinkler or a hand-held hose to soak the area.

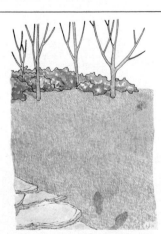

Trees in the Lawn

Establishing and caring for a lawn near trees is a headache for many people. It need not be. Many beautiful lawns are landscaped to grow around spreading trees. One way to success is understanding the relationship between a tree and the grass underneath.

Shade

There are many types of shade: light, half, dappled, full, heavy. Few grasses grow in full or heavy shade. Too much shade causes grass to become thin and spotty or gradually to die out. A lawn underneath a tree needs to receive about half of the sunlight that filters through the tree leaves.

Your job is to supply the requirements of the grass without harming the trees. Of course, you may decide to remove any tree that is not a functional part of the landscape, in favor of the grass.

Shade-Tolerant Grasses: One of the best steps toward growing a successful lawn in the shade is to plant a shade-tolerant grass. Grasses are listed according to their shade tolerance on page 19. Even within a grass type, certain cultivars are more shade tolerant than others. Check the cultivar charts from pages 14 to 18 for this strength.

In areas where turf is already established, you may want to renovate on a small scale by reseeding around trees with a better-adapted grass. Some people reseed every year with a turf-type ryegrass to keep fresh new grass under their trees.

The choice of grass may require some forethought. If you have recently planted young trees, shade probably is not a problem now, but may be in the future. If you choose a tall fescue for your lawn, do not plant the cultivar 'Alta' if there are young trees in the lawn; it is poisonous to them.

Proper Maintenance: If a suitable grass is already growing under your trees, good maintenance practices help a shaded lawn. Slight modifications of normal practices benefit your lawn even more.

Mow the lawn at a higher level—at the highest cut suggested on page 49. The longer the blade, the greater the ability to trap light. If your trees need to be fertilized, consider soil injections rather than applying fertilizer on the lawn underneath. Overfertilizing is a major problem of grass grown in the shade.

Watering deeply (but not overwatering) is especially important where trees are growing in the lawn. Shallow watering forces tree roots to the lawn surface. These exposed roots deprive the lawn of its needed nutrients and may damage your mower.

Too Much Shade: To bring more light to a shaded lawn, simply prune the tree. Cut off as many of the low branches as possible so that light can penetrate to the lawn. By using proper thinning methods, you can remove as much as 40 percent of the leaf surface without drastically changing the appearance of the tree. In fact, thinning usually enhances it.

Sometimes a lawn has too many trees growing in it. Removing a few not only helps the lawn, but also the trees that remain.

If you are considering planting trees in your lawn, plan ahead. Choose trees that cast filtered shade.

If your shaded lawn does not react favorably to your maintenance efforts, plant a ground cover that does well in low light. The Ortho book *All About Ground Covers* describes many of these. Other alternatives include covering the area with an attractive stone or a bark mulch.

Leaves on the Lawn

Some leaves easily blow away; others seem determined to stay on your lawn. Some trees drop their leaves in a short time, while others appear never to stop. Regardless of when and how they fall, rake up the leaves on your lawn and add them to the compost pile. They decay faster if you shred them. Leaves deprive the grass of light and increase the chances of insect and disease problems.

Damage to Trees

The main cause of damage to trees in a lawn is from lawn mowers bumping the trunk. Any wound in the bark is an invitation to insects and disease. Protect a young tree by placing three wooden stakes around it, about 1 foot away from the trunk.

Growing grass against the trunk of a young tree can severely retard its growth, even if you apply additional water and fertilizer. Applying a ring of mulch, 30-inches in diameter, around the tree gives the tree a good start. Keep mulch away from the trunk, also.

Changes in grade kill many trees. Piling soil around the trunk suffocates surface roots, whereas removing soil either damages roots or exposes them to drying. During the establishment of a lawn, make any changes in grade around trees gradual. Changing the grade more than a few inches requires the use of retaining walls or dry walls, which are best extended to the drip line of the tree.

Don't give up on growing grass in the shade. Proper maintenance practices and adapted cultivars make shade lawns possible in many situations.

Renovating

If your lawn deteriorates to the extent that routine cultural practices, such as mowing, fertilizing, watering, and controlling weeds, insects and disease, do not give the desired response, it is probably time to renovate. By renovating, it is possible to renew your lawn without going to the trouble of completely rebuilding it.

Renovation may involve the use of heavy equipment, which is available from a rental company (see page 83). If you need help, many gardening services specialize in lawn renovation. Regardless of who does the work, renovation is a way of improving the overall quality of your lawn.

Dethatching

If you need to renovate your lawn because of thatch buildup, you have lots of company. Thatch is a layer of slowly decomposing grass stems, dead roots, and debris that accumulates above the soil and below grass blades. The name thatch is well deserved. Like the thatched roof on a tropical hut, it stops water and fertilizer from reaching the soil. A lawn with a buildup of thatch feels spongy when you walk on it.

Thatch is only a problem when it becomes too thick. A thin layer of thatch—¼ to ½ inch—may actually be beneficial to the lawn. It buffers soil temperatures and adds to the resilience of the lawn, thereby reducing the compaction of soil that can result from heavy use.

When thick, however, thatch is water repellent or hydrophobic. A conscientious waterer may think he or she is watering enough when in fact the water never reaches the soil. Grass roots that grow in the thatch layer instead of in the soil are less drought resistant, since the moisture in the thatch evaporates faster than the moisture that penetrates the soil.

Although all lawn grasses have the potential for developing thatch, it accumulates the fastest in lawns composed of creeping grasses. Notorious thatch builders include warm-season grasses such as Bermudagrass, St. Augustine grass, and zoysiagrass, and cool-season grasses such as bentgrass and Kentucky bluegrass.

Insects and diseases find thatch a particularly suitable place to inhabit. Since water does not penetrate it readily, neither do pest- and disease-control products.

Finally, because the thickness and density of thatch varies, scalping by mowers is inevitable.

What to Do About Thatch: Several remedies for heavy thatch—some better than others—are available. Soil penetrants, or wetting agents, counteract the hydrophobic character of thatch, but only for a short while. Bacterial agents that supposedly break down thatch have also proven to be ineffective. Thatch hand rakes that have knifelike blades instead of the usual hard-steel teeth are useful for small lawns. Certain attachments for rotary mowers may be helpful. Fixed, flail, and spring-tooth mowers are also available for dethatching.

The most accepted way to dethatch a home lawn is by vertical cutting. A vertical cutter has a series of revolving vertical knives that cut through the thatch and bring it to the surface of the lawn. You then sweep, rake, or vacuum this material from the lawn.

For dethatching to be effective, adjust the depth and width of the vertical cutter blades for your type of grass. Generally, the blades should completely penetrate the thatch layer, and the top inch of soil underneath the thatch. Exceptions are grasses that are slow to recover, such as bahiagrass, centipedegrass, and St. Augustine grass, which need the blades adjusted at 1 inch from the ground and 2 to 3 inches apart. Bermudagrass and zoysiagrass

A heavy layer of thatch prevents nutrients and water from getting to the soil.

can stand heavy thinning—space the blades of the cutter about 1 inch apart, and cut close to the soil level in several directions. For other types of grasses, make only one pass with a vertical cutter.

While these adjustments are valuable given the recuperative powers of different grasses, it is often difficult to adjust the blades on a vertical cutter. If you rent one, before you bring it home, ask the rental company if they can adjust the blades for you.

As a last resort for grasses that have stolons, use a sod cutter to remove especially thick thatch or entire sections of turf. For thatch, adjust the sod cutter to cut just above the soil level instead of below it.

Lawns need to be renovated periodically to encourage vigorous growth. If your lawn is basically healthy with some bare spots, some minor renovating can make it look like new.

Aerating a lawn eliminates compaction, and allows air, water, and fertilizer to get to the root zone. A manual model works well for small lawns; use a power model for large lawns.

When to Dethatch: The best time to dethatch is just before a lawn has its most vigorous growth of the season. Dethatch warm-season grasses with the beginning of warm weather in late spring. The prime time to dethatch cool-season grasses is in the fall; the second·best time is in early spring.

Aerating

Roots need air as well as water and nutrients for growth. Many lawns, especially those lawns that receive heavy use, have restricted movement of air and water in the soil. This causes the soil to compact. A foot path worn into a lawn is a visible example of compaction. To correct compacted soil, lawn professionals have developed specialized tools and techniques with which to aerate the soil.

Aeration, also known as hole punching, coring, and aerification, is based on the following principle: Hollow metal tubes, ¼ to ¾ inch in diameter, are pushed into the soil by foot or machine, to an average depth of 2 to 3 inches. The soil should be moist during the aeration process—not too wet and not too dry. Take a look at the photographs at the top of page 85.

Aerating the soil regularly can help prevent thatch. By improving the air-water-soil relationship, thatch decomposes faster. If the soil cores caused by aeration are crumbled and returned to the lawn, the microorganisms in the microorganisms in the cores help to decompose the upper surface of thatch as well. Aerate lawns requiring high maintenance about once a year.

Keeping Lawns Green the Year Around

The only disadvantage of warm-season grasses is their winter dormancy. It is caused by low temperatures. Since most lawn owners prefer year-round green color, lawns can either be overseeded or colored green.

Overseeding: Dropping temperatures favor the germination and development of cool-season grasses and discourage further growth of established warm-season grasses. This is the reason why overseeding your Bermudagrass lawn with a cool-season grass works to give you a fresh, green lawn during the winter.

For successful overseeding, proceed when temperatures begin to drop, from October to November in most areas. Do not seed while temperatures are still warm or when they have gotten too cold—warm weather causes competition from the still active Bermudagrass and cold weather inhibits germination of the seeds.

The first step is to either vertical cut or mow close to the soil line with a heavy, reel or rotary mower. Rake up the clippings. Then mow and rake up clippings again. If possible, dethatch and aerate the lawn. These steps help to ensure the close contact of seed and soil. Seed four to eight times as much as you would for a new lawn, and finish by adding topsoil. Water frequently until the new grass is firmly rooted into the soil. Once the cool-season grass is established, mow extra high—about 2 inches.

The following spring, encourage the growth of the permanent lawn grass at the expense of the winter cover. Just before the late spring growth, vertical cut again or mow closely and fertilize. This will be enough of a shock to the winter cover and enough of a boost to the main lawn grass to reestablish it.

Although annual ryegrass is popular for overseeding, other types of grass provide a lawn of higher quality. For example, turf-type perennial ryegrass is excellent for overseeding. It is dark green and it has a slower growth rate than that of annual ryegrass, resulting in less mowing. Fine fescue is also good for overseeding. Use it alone or in combination with turf-type perennial ryegrass.

Lawn Colorants: Special green dyes or latex paints made especially for coloring lawns are an alternative to overseeding with a cool-season grass. Dying or painting can be used in summer on lawns browned from summer heat or lack of water, or in winter on browned Bermudagrass or zoysiagrass. Quality colorants do not rub off, walk off, or wash off. They are fade proof, nontoxic, and long wearing.

In the winter, make the first application of colorant immediately following the first killing frost. To prepare the turf, summer or winter, mow the grass to approximately 1 inch, depending on the type, then mow at right angles to the first pass to make the turf as even as possible. Remove all clippings, litter, and debris before applying the colorant. Mix the colorant according to the directions on the label. Use a pressure sprayer rather than a hose sprayer to apply a fine mist. Color the turf twice, making the second application at right angles to the first to assure uniform color. Allow the colorant to dry for several hours before watering.

Patching

Patching involves removing a weedy, dead, or damaged section of the lawn and replacing it either with a piece of sod or by reseeding, resprigging, or replugging. Always patch with the same type of grass as the present lawn. Many nurseries normally stock a small amount of sod just for this purpose.

Dig out the damaged area and loosen the soil underneath. If spilled gasoline or herbicide is the cause of the dead spot, remove several inches of the soil and replace it. (For more information on spills, see page 78.) Bring the underlying soil to proper grade and cut a piece of sod to fit.

If you are patching with seed, sprigs, or plugs, follow the same process as for any new planting. Regardless of the planting method you use, treat patched areas like you would treat a new lawn. Follow the watering guidelines for new lawns on page 44.

Changing the Grade

Even after a lawn is established, you may want to change the grade to correct water runoff or to level high and low areas. Changing a grade is simpler if you go at it gradually, adding or subtracting a little fill at a time. You can encourage new grass to grow by adding small amounts of sand, organic matter, and top soil.

Lawn Equipment

Do not worry about not having enough heavy-duty lawn equipment to take care of your lawn properly. Rental companies and some nurseries have lawn equipment to loan. You will find many different items to rent.

Lawn mowers for everyday use come in rotary and reel, and power and manual models. For special jobs there are such types as riding, flail, sickle-bar, heavy-reel, and high-wheel rotary models. If you have not invested in a lawn mower, rent the kind you are thinking of buying before you buy it. For more information on lawn mowers, see page 50.

Vertical cutters go by at least two other names: dethatchers and lawn combs. This piece of equipment cuts perpendicular to the surface of the lawn, slicing deep into thatch. After one pass it is easy to rake up the thatch debris.

Sod cutters are useful in two ways: you can strip off old turf and you can remove thatch.

Lawn aerators remove cores of soil, providing air to the root zone. The more soil becomes compacted, the less the amount of air space in the soil.

Edgers come in two basic styles, manual and power. Manual or hand edgers are fine for most trimming needs. Power edgers are an advantage for large lawns.

Lawn rollers are used for different purposes. The barrel type is filled with water; it reduces the fluffiness of freshly tilled soil and provides good contact between seed or sod and the soil. A mesh-type roller spreads bulky, organic top-dressing materials, such as peat moss, manure, or composted bark.

The easiest way to repair a damaged section of lawn is to patch it with a piece of sod that is custom cut to fit the area.

A Renovating Experience

The following two pages show the steps that were taken to completely renovate a particular lawn. Although this lawn was replanted with seed, you can adapt the instructions to planting sod, sprigs, or plugs. Maintain your new lawn by proper cultural practices.

Using heavy-duty lawn equipment need not be overwhelming to a beginner. Just read about the basics of the piece of equipment you need to complete your project, and pick up the appropriate piece at a rental yard. If you are not sure about its operation, ask the store clerk to show you.

How to Renovate a Lawn

1 Remove Undesirable Weeds and Grasses

The lawn at the right contained unwanted Bermudagrass and broadleaf weeds, requiring the most drastic kind of renovation. The entire lawn was killed with the systemic herbicide glyphosate. Always read labels carefully when using herbicides. Be sure chemicals are safe to use around trees and shrubs. Unless specifically recommended, do not use preemergence weed controls prior to reseeding. Make sure the chemical leaves no residue that may harm young grasses. For more information, see page 58.

2 Vertical Cut the Existing Lawn

To maximize contact between seed and soil, remove as much thatch as possible. Vertical cutters remove thatch like mechanical rakes, slicing vertically into the sod with knives or tines. Notice the grooves that the vertical cutter leaves in the soil. Use a vertical cutter on a moist (not too dry or wet) lawn. It is best to go over the lawn twice in opposite directions.

Low mowing and vigorous raking with a steel rake may be sufficient to remove thatch from small lawns. However, this process is strenuous and is less efficient than using a vertical cutter. Dethatching attachments are also available for rotary mowers, but are not as thorough.

3 Rake Up Debris

Thoroughly rake up the loose debris left by vertical cutting—there can be quite a lot. This guarantees the all-important contact between seed and soil.

Since this fibrous thatch decomposes quite slowly, do not add it to a compost pile. Discard the debris if you used herbicides or other chemicals previously.

4 Aerate the Soil

An aerator removes small cores of soil from the lawn, allowing air, water, and nutrients to pass freely to the roots. Aeration is best done on a moist lawn. Remove the soil cores by raking. After shredding them with a vertical cutter, you can use the cores to level any uneven spots.

This lawn had several low spots that made mowing difficult. If the new seedbed has high and low spots, add a good topsoil or peat moss and sand, then level with a rake. You may need to flatten high spots with a steel rake. If crushed soil cores left over from aeration are used for leveling, it may be desirable to blend them with additional organic matter.

5 Test Soil, Add Nutrients, and Sow Seed

This is the time to test the soil. See page 22 for information on soil testing. The results will show whether you need to balance the soil pH with lime or sulfur before planting. This is also the time to apply a complete, balanced fertilizer, such as formula 10-10-10.

If a high percentage of desirable grasses is present, it may not be necessary to reseed; just fertilize and water heavily. If you do seed or use vegetative methods to reestablish the lawn, follow a good watering program.

The most critical time in the reestablishment of healthy grass is right after planting. It may be necessary to water several times a day in hot weather to keep the new plantings moist.

6 The End Result: A Renovated Lawn

This photograph was taken just six weeks after the renovation process was completed. It is important to stress, however, that lawn care does not end here. To keep problems from recurring and to keep the lawn looking its best, follow an efficient program of watering, mowing, fertilizing, dethatching, and disease, insect, and weed control.

Lawns in Your Area

Lawns in every part of the country are different, with different needs and different possibilities. This chapter provides specific recommendations for growing a beautiful lawn in your area.

Whether you already have a lawn or are thinking about installing one, this chapter is for you. The guidelines throughout the book have been the basics of lawn growing. This chapter provides the specifics for your area.

The basis of this chapter is climate, and the effects of climate on lawn growing. Regional characteristics, such as summer highs or winter lows, play an important role in which type of grass to grow and how to care for it. The length of a growing season determines how much fertilizer your lawn needs each year. Summer rainfall patterns determine which lawns need more watering. These characteristics vary widely across North America.

Even though you may have the same type of lawn as someone in another part of the country, because of the different climate conditions, the specific requirements to take care of your lawn may be quite different. Bermudagrass lawns, for example, are grown in the Everglades of Florida, the delta of Mississippi, the plains of Texas, the deserts of Arizona, and the valleys of California. Because the country is so large and the climatic conditions so varied, this section is arranged by individual states or regions of the country. Check the index at the right to find your region.

Regional Recommendations

Each state or region contains specific information on the soil, climate, and lawn grasses in your area. The recommended grasses that are listed were compiled from extension bulletins from each state. These compilations are the result of years of research and experience and are one of the best guides to a beautiful lawn in your area.

At the end of each state or region are at least two addresses. One address is a state-run publication office you can write to for additional information. Most of these offices produce booklets that describe lawn growing. The other address listed is a state-provided soil-testing facility. (For information on soil testing, see page 22.) In many cases the test is free, but some laboratories charge a nominal fee.

Your local county extension agent can provide further up-to-date information on lawns in your area. Check your telephone directory for the number.

◀ *It is worth it: In any part of the country, everything looks better with a well-kept lawn.*

Index to Regions

Region	Page	Region	Page
Alabama	88	Montana	94
Alaska	88	Nebraska	95
Arizona	88	Nevada	95
Arkansas	89	New Hampshire	95
California	90	(*See* New England States)	
Canada	100	New Jersey	89
Colorado	90	(*See* Atlantic and	
Connecticut	95	Transitional States)	
(*See* New England States)		New Mexico	96
Delaware	89	New York	96
(*See* Atlantic and		North Carolina	96
Transitional States)		North Dakota	97
Florida	91	Ohio	97
Georgia	91	Oklahoma	97
Hawaii	91	Oregon	97
Idaho	92	Pennsylvania	98
Illinois	92	Rhode Island	95
Indiana	92	(*See* New England States)	
Iowa	92	South Carolina	98
Kansas	93	South Dakota	97
Kentucky	89	(*See* North Dakota and	
(*See* Atlantic and		South Dakota)	
Transitional States)		Tennessee	98
Louisiana	93	Texas	99
Maine	95	Utah	99
(*See* New England States)		Vermont	95
Maryland	89	(*See* New England States)	
(*See* Atlantic and		Virginia	99
Transitional States)		Washington	100
Massachusetts	95	West Virginia	89
(*See* New England States)		(*See* Atlantic and	
Michigan	93	Transitional States)	
Minnesota	93	Wisconsin	100
Mississippi	94	Wyoming	94
Missouri	94	(*See* Montana and Wyoming)	

ALABAMA

Soil and Climate: Northeastern Alabama is part of the Appalachian and Cumberland-Allegheny Plateau. Huntsville and Gadsden are cities in this area. The 200-day growing season is long compared with the United States average, but is among the shortest in Alabama. Most of the soil here is a type of loam—either stony, sandy, silty, or clay.

Lime is usually but not always needed. Through Coosa Valley and the Black Belts, the soil pH may naturally be close to ideal, but have the soil tested to be certain.

Central Alabama is a rolling to hilly region. The growing season is as long as 240 days. The Piedmont soil is mostly clay or clay loam.

Southern Alabama is highly influenced by the Gulf of Mexico. Around Mobile, the growing season is 265 days. This climate extends as far north as Chatom in Washington County. In the southern counties, heavy frosts are irregular due to the flow of cold air into low areas and down river valleys. In certain areas, this effect shortens the growing season.

Recommended Grasses: North of Goodwater, Mantevallo, and Panda, some cool-season grasses, such as Kentucky bluegrass and tall fescue, are grown, especially at higher elevations.

Most lawns in the state, particularly south of Jackson, Frisco City, Evergreen, and Ozark, are warm-season grasses, especially Bermudagrass and centipedegrass.

Soil Testing:
Soil Testing Laboratory
Auburn University
Auburn University, AL 36849

Publications Office:
Head, Administrative Services
Alabama Cooperative Extension Service
Auburn University
Auburn, AL 36380

ALASKA

Soil: If you live in a low, swampy area, your future lawn will benefit if you haul in soil to improve drainage. Afterwards, incorporate organic material into the soil before making the seedbed.

Soil in interior Alaska is generally low in nitrogen, phosphorus, and potassium. A complete fertilizer, such as 10-20-20, should be added to the soil before seeding. About 12 pounds of this formula fertilizer for 1,000 square feet is usually adequate.

Lime may be necessary. Check conditions with a soil test.

Recommended Grasses: Kentucky bluegrass and red fescue do quite well in Alaska. Certain cultivars of Kentucky bluegrass, such as 'Adelphi', 'Nugget', and 'Park' have good winter hardiness. Consider other cultivars too, as components of blends.

Snow mold is a serious disease of bluegrass in Alaska, so it is important to use cultivars that are resistant to it whenever possible, such as 'Nugget'.

'Aurora' and 'Reliant' hard fescues are superior to the other cultivars of fine fescue. They have good resistance to a variety of diseases and good tolerance to drought, shade, and low fertility. 'Boreal' is all right where little or no snow accumulates, but it is prone to snow-mold damage.

Perennial ryegrass is recommended for areas such as steep slopes where a quick temporary cover is needed but where winter survival is poor.

Lawns can be planted anytime after spring break-up until about August 1. Plantings between July 1 and August 1 usually have fewer weed problems and are healthier.

Soil Testing:
Palmer Plant & Soils Analysis Laboratory
Agricultural & Forestry Experiment Station
University of Alaska
533 East Fireweed
Palmer, AK 99645

Publications Office:
School of Agriculture & Land Resources
  Management
Agricultural Experiment Station
University of Alaska
Fairbanks, AK 99701

ARIZONA

Soil: May either be heavy clay or sandy. It is usually alkaline (pH 7.5 or higher). The high pH causes problems with the nutrient iron (see pages 53 to 57). Iron-containing fertilizers are often necessary. Lime is seldom needed, but might be of some benefit in mountain areas.

Recommended Grasses: Warm-season grasses, such as Bermudagrass and zoysiagrass, are best for southern Arizona. Common Bermudagrass is relatively pest free and makes an attractive lawn. Plant by seed from April through August. Overseed with ryegrass in winter if you do not like the straw color of dormant Bermudagrass.

Zoysiagrass can tolerate shade, but is even more susceptible to chlorosis in caliche soil. It tends to have more pest problems than Bermudagrass. Overseeding zoysiagrass does not work well. Dethatch about every two years. Plant sprigs or plugs from May through June. It is slow to establish.

Dichondra is a good lawn grass substitute, but does not stand up too well to foot traffic. It requires some shade. Plant plugs or seeds from mid-April through mid-July. Flea beetles are a serious pest—see page 72.

Lippia is another grass substitute. It is tough and takes either sun or shade, but one liability is that bees love the flowers. Plant sprigs from April through July.

Soil Testing:
Soil, Water & Plant Testing Laboratory
University of Arizona
Agricultural Science Building, Room 431
Tucson, AZ 85721

Publications Office:
Cooperative Extension Service
University of Arizona
Tucson, AZ 85721

ARKANSAS

Soil and Climate: If you draw an imaginary dividing line from the southwest to the northeast, you will notice that most of the west is mountainous while the east is lowlands. The soil of the lowlands is fertile and holds water well. Here, droughts rarely cause damage. The soil of the uplands is in many cases severely eroded, and has low fertility. Lawns in the uplands suffer during the hot and dry summers unless they are watered.

Rain is evenly distributed throughout the year. Spring rain is usually the heaviest. On the average, May is the wettest month and October is the driest month.

Lime usually needs to be added to the soil.

Recommended Grasses: Common Bermudagrass is the most widely used lawn grass in Arkansas. Mowed and fertilized on a regular basis, it makes an attractive lawn. Improved Bermudagrass is preferred by those who desire a fine-textured, high-quality lawn.

Use zoysiagrass in areas with 30 to 40 percent shade. It requires less mowing and forms a dense, weed-free lawn.

Centipedegrass is slow to form a lawn, but can make an attractive turf. 'Oklawn' is winter hardy throughout Arkansas.

Soil Testing:
Soil Testing Laboratory
Cooperative Extension Service
1201 McAlmont
Box 391
Little Rock, AR 72203

Publications Office:
Cooperative Extension Service
Extension Publications Specialist
University of Arkansas
1201 McAlmont
Box 391
Little Rock, AR 72203

ATLANTIC and TRANSITIONAL STATES

Soil and Climate: This is a large, diverse area that is complex because it is transitional. It includes Delaware, Kentucky, Maryland, New Jersey, and West Virginia, and stretches over 600 miles east to west, from coastal Atlantic City, New Jersey to Louisville, Kentucky.

In the western foothills of the Appalachian Mountains, Elkins and Beckley, West Virginia, have cool summers. Baltimore, Maryland, and Washington, D.C., typify the hot summer areas. Rainfall is plentiful. It averages about 45 inches on the coast, decreasing toward the west and north.

Soil types vary; many are good. Before planting, make sure the soil texture is adequate. Add organic matter, if necessary, then check the pH level. Some soil within this area is acidic (pH of 4.5 or more), while some is alkaline. Lime is necessary in some areas. Use according to soil test recommendations.

Recommended Grasses: The cool-season grasses are by far the most common. Some of the hardy, warm-season grasses are also quite common.

Kentucky bluegrass or a mixture of Kentucky bluegrass, fine fescues, and turf-type perennial ryegrass are good cool-season lawns for this region. Proportions vary, depending on local conditions and soil types.

If you are growing Kentucky bluegrass in a transition area where it is not well adapted, here is what to do: (1) Set your mower as high as possible during the summer. Do not mow lower than 2 inches. (2) Fertilize in early spring and again in fall as the weather cools—but never in summer. Stimulating new, succulent growth during hot weather invites disease. (3) Water in the morning, making sure the soil gets wet to at least 6 inches. Proper watering helps avoid many problems. (4) Use disease-resistant cultivars, such as 'Adelphi' and 'Majestic', in mixtures with other bluegrasses, fine fescues, and turf-type perennial ryegrass. The other grasses slow the spread of disease. Good mixtures are available as seed or sod. (5) Dethatch every two or three years. A thick layer of thatch prevents air and water from reaching the roots and generally weakens the lawn. If attention to detail is not your style, consider another kind of grass.

Where high summer temperatures and disease problems make growing the perfect lawn a full-time job, consider tall fescue. 'Kentucky 31', one of the most popular cultivars, originated from seed collected from William Suiter's farm in Menifee County, Kentucky. It makes an attractive and tough, though coarse-textured lawn. Many improved cultivars are available, however. New turf-type tall fescues that perform well include 'Apache', 'Bonanza', 'Falcon', 'Jaguar', 'Olympic', and 'Rebel'.

Bermudagrass is sometimes used in southern and central New Jersey, southern Maryland, and Delaware. 'Emerald' zoysiagrass can be grown throughout the region. It is used in Baltimore, Maryland and parts of Sussex County, Delaware, and is widely used along the south shore of New Jersey. Zoysiagrass is seen less across the Appalachians; the growing season is often too short.

Soil Testing:
Soil Testing Laboratory
Plant Science Department, Room 150-E TNS
University of Delaware
Newark, DE 19717-1303

Soil Testing Laboratory
Division of Regulatory Services
Scovell Hall
Lexington, KY 40546
(eastern Kentucky residents)

Soil Testing Laboratory
Division of Regulatory Services
West Kentucky Research & Education Center
Box 469
Princeton, KY 42445
(western Kentucky residents)

Soil Testing Laboratory
University of Maryland
College Park, MD 20742

United States Department of Agriculture
Beltsville, MD 20705
(Washington, D.C., residents)

Soil Testing Laboratory
Lipman Hall Annex
Box 231, Cook College
Rutgers University
New Brunswick, NJ 08903

Soil Testing Laboratory
Box 6108
Morgantown, WV 26506-6108

Publications Offices:
Agricultural Communications
Townsend Hall
University of Delaware
Newark, DE 19717-1303

Bulletin Room
Experiment Station Building
University of Kentucky
Lexington, KY 40506

Agricultural Duplication Services
University of Maryland
College Park, MD 20742

United States Department of Agriculture
Beltsville, MD 20705
(Washington, D.C., residents)

Publications Distribution Center
Cook College, Dudley Road
Rutgers University
New Brunswick, NJ 08903

Mailing Room
Communications Building
Evansdale Campus
West Virginia University
Morgantown, WV 26506

CALIFORNIA

Soil: The soil in California is as variable as the climate.

Lime is necessary in the far northwest. Much of the rest of the state has alkaline soil. Incorporate organic matter before planting. Gypsum, a mineral that contains sulfur, is useful in soil with excess sodium salts. A soil test will show the specific needs of your soil.

Recommended Grasses: Within this large state virtually all of the grass climates are represented. There are the cool and humid northern coast, the cold mountain areas, the hot central valleys, the southern coast, and the southern interior valleys.

Kentucky bluegrass is grown throughout much of the state. It is well adapted in the north and does well in the higher elevations of the south. Do not try to grow it in the San Joaquin or Imperial Valleys, unless you are prepared for a summer-long battle against disease. Along southern coastal and slightly inland areas stretching from Ventura to San Diego, Kentucky bluegrass is severely stressed during the summer; disease can wipe it out quickly.

If you are growing Kentucky bluegrass in a transition area where it is not well adapted, here is what to do: (1) Set your mower as high as possible during the summer. Do not mow lower than 2 inches. (2) Fertilize in early spring and again in fall as the weather cools—but never in summer. Stimulating new, succulent growth during hot weather invites disease. (3) Water in the morning, making sure the soil gets wet to at least 6 inches. Proper watering helps avoid many problems. (4) Use disease-resistant cultivars, such as 'Adelphi', 'Columbia', 'Majestic', and 'Parade', in mixtures with other bluegrasses, fine fescues, and turf-type perennial ryegrass. The other grasses slow the spread of any disease. Good mixtures are available as seed or sod. (5) Dethatch every two or three years. A thick layer of thatch prevents air and water from reaching the roots and generally weakens the lawn. If attention to detail is not your style, consider another kind of grass.

Turf-type perennial ryegrass is used in the northern and central coastal regions of California where moderate winters prevail. Because the seeds germinate faster than other cool-season grasses, it is popular in mixtures. Combine with Kentucky bluegrass to have a fast-growing "Kentucky bluegrass" lawn. The perennial ryegrass also provides resistance to certain diseases that attack bluegrass lawns.

Tall fescue grows well in California, and is more heat tolerant than most cool-season grasses. It should be 100 percent tall fescue or as close as possible. A small amount of tall fescue in a bluegrass lawn looks like weedy clumps after a few seasons. Tall fescue has received attention lately because of its tolerance to drought. It is an upright-growing grass, so mow it high, to about 3 inches. Tall fescue cultivars have dramatically improved over the years. While 'Alta', 'Fawn', and 'Kentucky 31' are still popular, new cultivars that perform better include 'Falcon', 'Jaguar', 'Olympic', and 'Rebel'.

Common Bermudagrass is a heat-loving grass that, if not chosen in the first place, often winds up in the lawn anyway. It spreads aggressively by seed, and by rhizomes and stolons. Where it is not wanted, it earns the name "devilgrass." Fertilized and mowed frequently to about 1 inch, it makes a handsome and hardy summer lawn. After it browns in the fall, it can be overseeded with ryegrass. You can keep two lawns at once: a cool-season mix on "top" and the common Bermudagrass "below." To ensure that the Bermudagrass does not take over completely, manage the lawn to favor the cool-season grasses and discourage the Bermudagrass. Most important, during summer, mow as high as possible and do not fertilize.

Improved Bermudagrass cultivars provide other alternatives. 'Tifgreen', 'Tifway', and 'Santa Ana' are favorites for home lawns. Beautiful when at their best, the improved Bermudagrasses are premium grasses that require extra care.

St. Augustine grass is another warm-season grass used occasionally in California. It is coarse bladed and has rounded leaf tips. Kikuyugrass, a common southern California weed, is similar in appearance, but its leaves taper to distinct points. Unlike Bermudagrass, St. Augustine grass tolerates some shade, but is not as tough otherwise. Start it with sprigs, plugs, or sod.

Dichondra is not a grass but is sometimes used as a lawn substitute along the southern coast and in the San Joaquin Valley. The heat of the Imperial Valley is too severe unless it is filtered by some shade. Dichondra may need less mowing, but weeds are harder to get out once they are established.

Residents of Bakersfield, Fresno, Modesto, Sacramento, Stockton, Redding, and others in the San Joaquin Valley should consider a Bermudagrass first. The same is true for the Imperial Valley—El Centro, Brawley, and Indio. Most of the rest of the state is transitional, so you can choose between cool- or warm-season grasses or any combination of both.

Soil Testing:
Soil testing is not provided by the state, but there are many commercial soil laboratories. Check your telephone directory or your county extension agent.

Publications Office:
ANR Publications
University of California
6701 San Pablo Avenue
Oakland, CA 94608-1239

COLORADO

Soil: Most Colorado soil, such as around Denver, Pueblo, and Grand Junction, is alkaline with low levels of available iron. Lawns grown in these areas benefit from iron-containing fertilizers.

In the mountains, soil is usually nearly neutral in pH, and is shallow and droughty. For a healthy, good-looking lawn, fertilize every 6 to 8 weeks during the growing season, applying about 1 pound of actual nitrogen per 1,000 square feet.

Recommended Grasses: Kentucky bluegrass is the most frequently planted lawn grass in Colorado. Its main drawback is a susceptibility to leaf spot. Good cultivars for the state include 'Adelphi', 'Baron', 'Bensum', 'Columbia', 'Eclipse', 'Midnight', 'Ram I', and 'Sydsport'. Plant a blend of three or more cultivars to combine their strengths.

Problems may result from planting seed or sod on heavy, poorly drained soil. Working in organic soil amendments before planting will reduce future maintenance problems.

Thatch is common in many lawns and can be corrected by vertical cutting and aerating. For information on these methods, see pages 81 to 82.

Inadequate watering causes or is related to many lawn problems in Colorado. If you have unanswered questions about watering your lawn, see pages 42 to 48.

Soil Testing:
Soil Testing Laboratory
Colorado State University
Fort Collins, CO 80523

Publications Office:
Extension-Experiment Station
Publications Office
Office of University Communications
Colorado State University
Fort Collins, CO 80523

FLORIDA

Soil and Climate: The entire state of Florida is included within the Coastal Plain. The climate is dominated by the surrounding water—no point in the state is more than 60 miles from the coast. Florida is flat. The highest point in the state is 325 feet above sea level; the average elevation in the state is somewhat less.

The soil is variable. The coast tends to have sandy pinelands and marshes. Darker, more fertile soil occurs toward the interior. Muck soil reclaimed from the Everglades is among the most fertile. A few areas have clay-like soil.

Lime is often necessary, but some soil is too alkaline. Check soil pH with a soil test.

Recommended Grasses: The grasses of Florida include bahiagrass, Bermudagrass, carpetgrass, centipedegrass, St. Augustine grass, and zoysiagrass. Bahiagrass, a native to Brazil, is better adapted to central Florida than anywhere else in the South. Improved cultivars of bahiagrass are available. 'Argentine' is the most popular cultivar for lawns. 'Pensacola' is used along highways. Common bahiagrass is used infrequently. Mole crickets are a major problem for bahiagrass.

Bermudagrass, especially improved types like 'Tifgreen', make a most attractive lawn, but require high maintenance.

Centipedegrass makes a good, low-maintenance lawn, but can be seriously damaged by nematodes—especially in sandy soil. For this reason, it is rarely recommended for planting south of Orlando, where sandy soil is commonplace. Ground pearls also present a problem.

St. Augustine grass often makes a beautiful lawn, especially in shady areas. It is the most popular lawn grass in the state. A good insect and disease program is necessary to keep it in good shape. The cultivar 'Bitter Blue', which is low growing and dense, was developed on the lower East Coast. It has an attractive color but does not tolerate heavy traffic. 'Floratine' is similar to 'Bitter Blue' in many respects, but is even more dense. It can be mowed as close as ½ inch. 'Floratam' has shown resistance to both chinch bugs and SAD disease (see page 77), but does not tolerate much shade.

Carpetgrass, another warm-season grass, makes a coarse-textured lawn similar to that of St. Augustine grass. It does not perform well in shade, however.

'Emerald' zoysiagrass is often recommended for Florida gardeners. It tolerates a great deal of shade, but coverage is slower than other grasses.

Overseeding is commonly done with a creeping bentgrass and perennial ryegrass mixture.

Soil Testing:
Soil Testing Laboratory
University of Florida
Gainesville, FL 32601

Publications Office:
Bulletin Room
Cooperative Extension Service
University of Florida
Gainesville, FL 32601

GEORGIA

Soil and Climate: The climate in Georgia is controlled by the altitude, latitude, and proximity to the ocean. The state essentially has a warm, humid climate, modified considerably by the height of the mountains in the northern parts of the state (from Atlanta to the Tennessee border).

More than half the state is included in the Coastal Plain. The soil is sandy and the land is fairly level. Piedmont soil is mostly clay and clay loam, but some has sand in the top few inches. All the soil is acid and not terribly fertile, though it is capable of good production.

Lime is usually necessary, especially for new lawns.

Recommended Grasses: Common Bermudagrass is by far the most prevalent lawn grass in Georgia. Dr. Glen Burton of the Georgia Coastal Plains Experiment Station developed several of the most-used improved Bermudagrasses, such as 'Tifgreen', 'Tifdwarf', 'Tiflawn', and 'Tifway'.

Carpetgrass is useful in wet soils; it is freqently found in the central and southern parts of the state.

Centipedegrass is another warm-season grass used in Georgia. Depending on the cultivar you choose, it can be started from seeds, sprigs, or plugs.

St. Augustine grass is the best shade-tolerant grass for most parts of Georgia.

Tall fescue is the most popular grass in the mountain and upper-Piedmont areas.

'Emerald' zoysiagrass is highly recommended for Georgia. It is attractive and well adapted to the area.

Soil Testing:
Soil Testing & Plant Analysis Laboratory
2400 College Station Road
Athens, GA 30601

Publications Office:
Extension Editor—Publications
University of Georgia
Athens, GA 30602

HAWAII

Soil: Most Hawaiian soil does not have ideal characteristics for lawn grasses. They need to be amended with organic matter, such as manure, leaves, grass clippings, compost, bagasse, peat moss, or hapuu.

Recommended Grasses: Bermudagrass, known locally as *manienie* or *mahiki*, is commonly planted. But do not try to grow it in the shade. Bermudagrass is tough and tolerates heavy traffic. 'Sunturf', an improved Bermudagrass, is endorsed by the Hawaii Cooperative Extension.

'Emerald' zoysiagrass is slow to establish—it may take two or three years to form a good lawn. Once it has filled in, it makes a dense, weed-choking turf. 'Emerald' also tolerates some shade.

Templegrass or Koreangrass is another kind of zoysiagrass. It is more of a ground cover than a lawn grass, though. When mature it makes a bumpy, wavy surface.

St. Augustine grass is known as buffalograss to some Hawaiians, although it is not the same buffalograss that is native to the continental Great Plains. The true St. Augustine grass that grows well in Hawaii is coarse bladed and shade tolerant.

Some lawn substitutes are popular in Hawaii as well.

Although it is also considered a lawn invader that kills Bermudagrass lawns, hilograss is well liked in Makiki, Lihue, Wahiawa, Kaneohe, and other cities that receive about 150 inches of rain each year. It is yellow to green in color, has wide blades, and grows rapidly except in shade.

McCoygrass, another lawn substitute, makes a beautiful lawn. Actually it is a sedge, not a grass. Roll it between your fingers and you can feel the three distinct sides characteristic of all sedges. Originally imported from Australia, the blades are delicate and dark green in color. It does poorly in areas of heavy traffic. It thrives at any elevation, in sun or shade.

Soil Testing:
Agricultural Diagnostic Service Center
University of Hawaii at Manoa
1910 East-West Road, Sherman Lab 134
Honolulu, HI 96822

Publications Office:
Cooperative Extension Service
College of Tropical Agriculture
University of Hawaii
Honolulu, HI 96822

IDAHO

Soil: Idaho soil is generally high in clay and has a fairly moderate pH. In some areas, the soil is rocky and must be cleaned before planting. Also before planting, plenty of organic material needs to be worked into the soil to a 6- to 8-inch depth.

Recommended Grasses: Kentucky bluegrass is by far the most common lawn grass in Idaho. Use the fine fescues mixed with a shade-tolerant Kentucky bluegrass for a shaded lawn area.

Turf-type perennial ryegrass has found favor in Idaho, particularly in the more southern regions where winter cold is not too intense.

Native grasses, such as buffalograss, blue grama, and wheatgrass, can be considered low-maintenance lawn grasses for areas that do not receive extra water.

Begin fertilizing about May 1 in Boise and a month later in Sandpoint. Applying no more than 1 to 1½ pounds at any single application, use 5 pounds of actual nitrogen for every 1,000 square feet of lawn over the course of the Idaho growing season. Fertilizing is also a good method of stopping weed invasion.

The bluegrass billbug has caused extensive damage in Idaho, particularly in the Boise Valley. This pest is illustrated and described on page 67.

Powdery mildew, gray snow mold, and pink snow mold are troublesome diseases. See pages 74 to 79.

Do not try to grow a more high-quality lawn than there is available water to support.

Soil Testing:
Analytical Services Lab
College of Agriculture
University of Idaho
Moscow, ID 83843

Publications Office:
Extension Bulletins
Agricultural Science Building
University of Idaho
Moscow, ID 83843

ILLINOIS

Soil and Climate: The range of climates in Illinois is wide due to the state's north to south length. Climatologists have divided the state into three regions, all with a continental climate. The northern third has the coldest winters with warm summers; it extends as far south as Kankakee. The middle third stretches from Kankakee to Effingham. There, winters and summers become progressively warmer toward the southern latitudes. The lowest third includes the rest of the state, from Effingham to Cairo. Milder winters and hotter, more humid summers are the norm in this region.

In the north, the growing season averages 150 days, whereas in Cairo, the frost-free growing season is 200 days or more. The northern two-thirds of Illinois soil is prairie. Prairie soil usually has a dark brown or dark grayish brown surface. It is deep and fertile, developed primarily from native grass vegetation.

Lime is often needed, especially in the southern part of the state, where it should be applied frequently. Before establishing a lawn, check the pH and add necessary limestone.

Recommended Grasses: Kentucky bluegrass is the best lawn grass for most of Illinois. (Check the cultivar list on page 14.) Mixing it with red fescue or turf-type perennial ryegrass enhances its establishment.

Planted alone, tall fescue is a good, tough, play lawn for central and southern Illinois, although severe winter weather may injure it.

Soil Testing:
Soil testing is not offered by any public agency in Illinois. Check the telephone directory for private laboratories.

Publications Office:
Agricultural Publications
47 Mumford Hall
1301 West Gregory Drive
Urbana, IL 61801

INDIANA

Soil and Climate: Indiana's climate is largely continental with no large bodies of water (except in the extreme northwest) to moderate it. The northern half of the state is mostly level prairie, while the southern portion has many hills that contribute to a varying climate, even within short distances.

Generally, both temperatures and rainfall increase toward the south. The longest season is in the Evansville area. The shortest season in the west is in the Kankakee Valley area. Angola, Auburn, and Garrett have the shortest season in the northeast.

About a third of the new lawns in Indiana need lime. Do not apply it unless the pH has been checked and found to be lower than 6.0.

Recommended Grasses: Indiana is prime Kentucky bluegrass country, except for areas in the extreme south. Some of the newest improved cultivars for Indiana are 'Adelphi', 'Baron', 'Columbia', 'Glade', 'Merit', 'Midnight', 'Ram I', 'Sydsport', and 'Victa'. Use a blend for an all-Kentucky bluegrass lawn or a mixture that contains fine fescues and turf-type perennial ryegrasses.

In the south, around Evansville, homeowners can plant tall fescue or even Bermudagrass or zoysiagrass.

Soil Testing:
Plant & Soil Analysis Laboratory
Life Science Building
Purdue University
West Lafayette, IN 47907

Publications Office:
Publications Mailing Room
301 South Second Street
Lafayette, IN 47905

IOWA

Soil and Climate: Iowa has a continental climate; most rain falls during the warm period of April to September. During the summer, periods of drought accompanied by hot winds will damage a lawn unless it is watered frequently. Northwood, near the Minnesota border, usually receives the heaviest snowfall; Bonapart, at the Missouri border, receives the least.

Lime is often lacking, especially in soil in which a lawn has not been grown before.

Recommended Grasses: Kentucky bluegrass is the dominant lawn grass of Iowa, as it is elsewhere in this climate. Kentucky bluegrass is acceptable in some situations; the improved types not only provide greater beauty and utility, but also improved disease resistance. Turf-type perennial ryegrass may be a mix component.

Tall fescue is coarse bladed and makes a tough play lawn in this state.

Soil Testing:
Soil Testing Laboratory
Cooperative Extension Service
Iowa State University
Ames, IA 50010

Publications Office:
Publications Distribution
Iowa State University
Ames, IA 50011

KANSAS

Soil and Climate: Kansas is in the center of the United States. The slope of the land is gradual from the northwest to the southeast. This slope is also apparent in measures of climate. The southeast—Independence, Parsonsville, Pittsburgh, Chanute—receives about twice the rain, has a longer growing season (by 40 or more days), and has warmer winters and summers compared with northwestern Kansas. The soil also varies. Kansas City soil is frequently acidic, as is soil in the cities of southeastern Kansas.

Western Kansas is a part of the Great Plains. Here, wind erosion is a problem, and blowing soil may make new lawn establishment difficult. The climate is quite variable, month to month and year to year. Humidity is low and evaporation is fast.

The soil is either sandy or fairly heavy (called ''hard lands''). Both types are fairly high in nutrients.

Lime may be necessary in the east, especially the southeast. Western Kansas rarely needs lime.

Recommended Grasses: Cool-season grasses are generally planted, but in the southern and western sections of the state, zoysiagrass, Bermudagrass, and some native grasses, such as buffalograss or blue grama, are useful. Buffalograss forms a ''lawn'' on less than 15 inches of rain a year. Buy treated buffalograss seed or else establishment may be slow and erratic.

Soil Testing:
Soil Testing Lab
Throckmorton Hall
Agronomy Department
Kansas State University
Manhattan, KS 66506

Publications Office:
Distribution Center
Umberger Hall
Kansas State University
Manhattan, KS 66506

LOUISIANA

Soil and Climate: Louisiana's climate is determined by its subtropical latitude and nearness to the Gulf of Mexico.

Rainfall is evenly distributed, with the most falling in winter and midsummer. An average of between 45 and 60 inches of rain falls each year. As much as 86 inches fall on New Orleans.

The western two-thirds of Louisiana is part of the Coastal Plain. It is mostly level country with sandy soil. The highest elevation in the northwest section is 400 to 500 feet above sea level.

Most Louisiana soil is acidic and needs regular lime applications. To be sure, check with a soil test.

Recommended Grasses: Centipedegrass is increasing in popularity in the Gulf Coast area. It produces a lawn in almost any type of soil (even poor) in the lower South.

Bermudagrass is adapted to well-drained, fertile soils with full exposure to the sun. It

persists, however, in both acid and overlimed soils. A tip: Buy hulled Bermudagrass seed.

St. Augustine grass is another option in this state for a warm-season grass.

Soil Testing:
Soil Testing Laboratory
Department of Agronomy
Louisiana State University
Baton Rouge, LA 70803

Publications Office:
Publications Librarian
Room 192
Knapp Hall
Louisiana State University
Baton Rouge, LA 70803

MICHIGAN

Soil and Climate: Along the shorelines, climate is dominated by the lakes. Both spring and fall arrive later than in the interior. The inland climate can be either continental or semimarine, depending on the direction the wind is blowing.

Most Michigan soil is inherently acidic and somewhat low in fertility. However, it is quite productive when the pH is adjusted upward and fertilizer is added.

Lime is not necessary unless a soil test indicates a pH of 5.7 or less. Most of the irrigation water used in Michigan contains enough lime to compensate for the naturally acidic soil.

Recommended Grasses: Mixtures of Kentucky bluegrass and fine fescues are the best for most parts of Michigan. Several cultivars of Kentucky bluegrass have been tested under Michigan conditions and found to be quite good. They include 'Adelphi', 'Baron', 'Fylking', 'Midnight', and 'Sydsport'. A blend of three or more bluegrass cultivars is preferable.

'Aurora', 'Flyer', 'Highlight', 'Jamestown', 'Reliant', and 'Shadow' are among the cultivars of fine fescue grown in Michigan.

The preferred time to seed is from August 15 to September 10 in southern Michigan, and from August 10 to September 1 in the northern part of the state.

Soil Testing:
Soil Testing Laboratory
Crop & Soil Sciences Department
Michigan State University
East Lansing, MI 48824

Publications Office:
MSU Bulletin Office
Box 231
East Lansing, MI 48824

MINNESOTA

Soil and Climate: Minnesota's climate is continental. Temperatures can swing widely within a short time and summer rain is often abundant. In general, there is a tendency toward climatic extremes. Rainfall is usually plentiful, moving south and east.

Minnesota soil varies from sandy and sandy loam to heavy clay. Tests have shown that most lawn soil in the Twin Cities area is high in phosphorus.

Lime should usually be applied every 6 to 10 years at rates of 50 to 150 pounds for every 1,000 square feet. The eastern half of the state commonly needs less liming. Make sure by conducting a soil test.

Recommended Grasses: Most Minnesota lawns are either Kentucky bluegrass, red fescue, or a combination of the two.

Turf-type perennial ryegrass also does well. Choose one of the more cold tolerant cultivars, such as 'Blazer', 'Manhattan II', 'Omega', and 'Palmer'.

Tall fescue makes a good lawn in transitional climates but lacks a tolerance of Minnesota's winters.

Bentgrass is difficult to maintain.

Soil Testing:
Soil Testing Laboratory
University of Minnesota
St. Paul, MN 55108

Publications Office:
Communication Resources/Distribution
3 Coffey Hall
University of Minnesota
1420 Eckles Avenue
St. Paul, MN 55108

MISSISSIPPI

Soil and Climate: The two most important factors controlling Mississippi's climate are the North American continent itself, to the north and west, and the Gulf of Mexico. Because the land is fairly level, topography has little influence on the climate. The highest land in the state, near the northern border, is less than 800 feet above sea level. The northeastern prairie belt and the delta section (between the Tallahatchie-Yazoo Basin and the Mississippi River) are fertile. Much of the state receives more than 50 inches of rain each year, producing an acid soil.

Lime should be added to most Mississippi soil before fertilizing. About nine tenths of the sandy soil in southern Mississippi needs lime, and more than two thirds of the delta soil needs it.

Recommended Grasses: Bermudagrass is the most common choice. Common Bermudagrass can be seeded, but the improved 'Tif' Bermudagrass cultivars produce a finer-textured lawn.

Zoysiagrass is slow to establish, but is attractive and relatively problem free once it covers. 'Emerald' and 'Meyer' zoysiagrass, and manilagrass (*Zoysia matrella*) are used, and perform well in moderate shade.

St. Augustine grass is best for shady lawns, but lacks much cold tolerance.

Soil Testing:
Soil Testing
Box 5405
Mississippi State University
Oxford, MS 39762

Publications Office:
Information Department
Box 5405
Mississippi State University
Mississippi State, MS 39762

MISSOURI

Soil and Climate: Missouri can be divided into three separate regions. The northwest is the prairie, which extends into neighboring Kansas, Nebraska, and Iowa. Cities such as St. Joseph and Independence in the northwest are often dry and have cold winters. Soil in these cities may be slightly alkaline.

Extending through the center of the state from the northeast to the southwest is the Ozark Plateau. Springfield and Rolla are located here. The Ozarks have less severe winters than the prairies and cooler summers compared to the southeast.

Cape Girardeau, Sikeston, and Poplar Bluff are cities in the southeast lowlands. The growing season is about 200 days long and rain is plentiful—about 45 inches a year. Soil here is acidic. Most areas are well drained, but some are swampy.

Lime is usually needed, especially in the southeast. Check by testing the soil.

Recommended Grasses: Kentucky bluegrass, fine fescues, tall fescue, and turf-type perennial ryegrass are the predominant cool-season grasses. Lawns of the highest quality are usually a mixture of improved cultivars of these three grasses. Improved tall fescue cultivars, such as 'Adventure',

'Apache', 'Bonanza', 'Falcon', 'Jaguar', 'Olympic', and 'Rebel' have become widely used in recent years.

'Meyer' zoysiagrass grows well in the southern areas of the state. It requires plenty of heat and a long growing season for best results.

Bermudagrass is also often grown in the southern areas.

Soil Testing:
Soil Testing Laboratory
University of Missouri
27 Mumford Hall
Columbia, MO 65211

Publications Office:
Extension Publications
222 South Fifth Street
University of Missouri
Columbia, MO 65211

MONTANA and WYOMING

Soil: Little of the soil in Montana and Wyoming is ideal, well-drained loam. Before planting, mix 2 or more inches of organic matter into the soil to a depth of 6 to 8 inches. The pH is usually alkaline.

Recommended Grasses: Kentucky bluegrass is the most important lawn grass. It grows slowly during the midsummer heat and quickly in late summer. The late summer period is the best time to plant a new lawn. Apply 1 pound of actual nitrogen per 1,000 square feet once in early spring, six weeks after the spring flush of growth, and six weeks before cold weather begins. If grass yellows in the summer, treat with iron in the fertilizer or with a spray.

Fine fescues are also important lawn grasses. The blades are so fine textured they are almost needlelike. They have good shade and drought resistance, and, if seeded heavily, form a tough, wear-resistant sod. Fine fescues mix well with Kentucky bluegrass.

Turf-type perennial ryegrass is an alternative to Kentucky bluegrass or fescue, although it is not as cold tolerant.

Crested wheatgrass and buffalograss are useful, long-lived grasses that survive with no supplemental water. Fairway wheatgrass is sometimes used for home lawns. Mow it no shorter than 3 inches and only three or four times per season. Clip buffalograss about 1 inch high two or three times per season.

Soil Testing:
Soil Testing Laboratory
Plant Science Department
University of Wyoming
Laramie, WY 82071

Soil Testing Laboratory
Montana State University
824 Leon Johnson Hall
Bozeman, MT 59717

Publications Offices:
Bulletin Room
Box 3313, University Station
University of Wyoming
Laramie, WY 82071

Bulletin Room
Cooperative Extension Office
Montana State University
Bozeman, MT 59717

NEBRASKA

Soil and Climate: Nebraska varies from the Dakotas by having a more mild climate: Summers are longer and winters are less cold. But like the Dakotas, soil is on the average better toward the east.

Recommended Grasses: Kentucky bluegrass combined with fine fescues make a good all-around Nebraska lawn. Turf-type perennial ryegrass is sometimes used as well. It mixes well in a bluegrass-fescue lawn, but is not quite as cold tolerant as Kentucky bluegrass or fine fescues.

Tall fescue is a favorite in southern Nebraska; its winter hardiness is roughly comparable to ryegrass.

Zoysiagrass and Bermudagrass are often grown south of the Platte in such cities as Lincoln, Hastings, and McCook, even though they are at the northern limits of their range.

Soil Testing:
Soil Testing Laboratory
University of Nebraska
Department of Agronomy
Keim Hall, East Campus
Lincoln, NE 68503

Publications Office:
University of Nebraska
Department of Agricultural Communications
Lincoln, NE 68583

NEVADA

Soil: Nevada soil is typically alkaline and low in organic matter. Generous additions of organic matter before planting prevent potential lawn problems before they start.

Recommended Grasses: In northern Nevada, a Kentucky bluegrass-fine fescue mixture is the usual choice. Use 2 to 3 pounds of seed per 1,000 square feet and never mow below 1½ inches. Quality Kentucky bluegrass sod is also widely available.

Tall fescue makes a good lawn when planted alone. It is too weedy when planted with bluegrass, growing in coarse, random clumps. Use about 10 pounds of seed for every 1,000 square feet.

In Las Vegas and the surrounding communities of Pahrump, Henderson, Border City, and Moapa, no grass makes a finer lawn than Bermudagrass. Improved Bermudagrass makes a good home putting green, but more maintenance is required than for common Bermudagrass. All Bermudagrass lawns should be periodically dethatched.

Zoysiagrass is used to a limited extent. It makes a lush summer lawn, but browns early and cannot be overseeded.

Lippia, a lawn substitute, is grown occasionally in Las Vegas. In the sun it forms a dense mat about 1 to 2 inches high. It can make an attractive lawn, although bees attracted by its flowers can be a problem.

Soil Testing:
Nevada Soil & Water Testing Laboratory
College of Agriculture
University of Nevada
Reno, NV 89507

Publications Office:
Agricultural Information Office
College of Agriculture
University of Nevada
Reno, NV 89557

NEW ENGLAND STATES

Soil and Climate: Relatively moderate temperatures prevail throughout most of the region and make only occasional problems for lawn growing.

Although rainfall is plentiful—rarely less than 30 inches in a year—because of the generally shallow soil, summer watering of lawns is usually necessary if they are to be kept green.

Lime is a must. Usually 50 to 200 pounds of ground limestone is necessary for every 1,000 square feet. The results of a soil test will often indicate the appropriate quantity.

Recommended Grasses: New England is solid Kentucky-bluegrass territory. Fine fescues and a small percentage of turf-type perennial ryegrass are often included in mixtures. For low-fertility lawns, mixtures of fine fescues and colonial bentgrass are well adapted.

Soil Testing:
Agronomy Section
College of Agriculture & Natural Resources
The University of Connecticut
Storrs, CT 06268

Maine Soil Testing Service
25 Deering Hall
University of Maine
Orono, ME 04473

Suburban Experiment Station
240 Beaver Street
Waltham, MA 02154

University of New Hampshire
Analytical Services Department
Durham, NH 03824

Soil Testing Lab
Department of Natural Resources Science
University of Rhode Island
Woodward Hall
Kingston, RI 02881

University of Vermont
Agricultural Testing Laboratory
Soil Analysis
Morrill Hall
Burlington, VT 05405-0106

Publications Offices:
Agricultural Publications, U-35
The University of Connecticut
Storrs, CT 06268

Cooperative Extension Service
University of Maine
Orono, ME 04469

Cooperative Extension Service
Stockbridge Hall
University of Massachusetts
Amherst, MA 01003

Cooperative Extension Service
Plant Science Department
Nesmith Hall
University of New Hampshire
Durham, NH 03824

Resource Information Office
10 Woodward Hall
University of Rhode Island
Kingston, RI 02881-0804

The Extension Service
University of Vermont
Burlington, VT 05401

NEW MEXICO

Soil: The soil is generally alkaline and low in organic matter. Use generous quantities of amendments. Elemental sulfur lowers the pH. Occasional heavy watering (to 3 or 4 feet) flushes salts from the soil. Hard, impenetrable soils that are high in sodium salts may benefit from heavy applications of gypsum, a mineral that contains sulfur.

Recommended Grasses: Bermudagrass is a common choice, particularly at low elevations and in the southern part of the state where the growing season exceeds 200 days. Common Bermudagrass likes heat and has deep drought-tolerant root systems. Improved cultivars, such as 'Texturf 10' (see page 14 for others), are fine textured but are somewhat more prone to pests. At high altitudes, Bermudagrass may be considered objectionable due to its long dormant season. Fertilizing Bermudagrass in the fall can encourage later dormancy and earlier spring green-up. Plant common Bermudagrass seed from April through May in Albuquerque. Plant improved Bermudagrass stolons from June through July.

Kentucky bluegrass does well in the cooler New Mexico climates, such as around Santa Fe. Summer heat stress is a factor. Plant disease-resistant cultivars, such as 'Adelphi', 'Baron', 'Columbia', or 'Midnight', mixed with turf-type perennial ryegrass. Mow high in summer.

Tall fescue is sometimes used for lawns in cooler areas, but fine fescues are rarely used.

Native grasses such as buffalograss are useful where water is scarce.

Aside from watering regularly during warm weather, lawns should be watered during extended dry periods in cool times of the year.

Soil Testing:
New Mexico State University
Soil, Water, & Plant Testing Laboratory
Crop & Soil Sciences Department
Box 3Q
Las Cruces, NM 88003

Publications Office:
Bulletin Office
Department of Agricultural Information
Drawer 3 A1
New Mexico State University
Las Cruces, NM 88003

NEW YORK

Soil and Climate: New York's climate, like most of the New England states, is humid and temperate. The quantity of rain is usually around 40 inches a year, most of which comes in the summer. But it is not unusual for summer periods of high temperatures to coincide with short droughts. Lawns that are not watered during these times suffer.

Throughout most of New York, the quantity of available sunshine is enough for an excellent growth of grasses. During the summer, about 60 percent of the total possible sunlight is available. The length of the growing season varies from as few as 100 to as many as 180 days.

Most of the soil of the Northeast developed under a natural forest cover. Almost all of New York was also covered by glaciers. The topography is characterized by long ridges of low mountains and hills that extend in a northeasterly direction.

Lime is frequently necessary. If the pH tests below 6.0, use a soil test to determine exact needs. See page 22.

Recommended Grasses: Kentucky bluegrass blends are the best lawn grass for New York. Red fescue is often mixed with Kentucky bluegrass for dry regions. Turf-type perennial ryegrass is also frequently used in mixtures.

Zoysiagrass is occasionally grown in warm areas of the state.

The major lawn pests are white grubs, chinch bugs, and sod webworms. (See pages 65 to 72.) Leaf spot or melting-out disease, caused by the fungus helminthosporium, is the primary disease to watch for. It can be prevented by using the new improved cultivars of Kentucky bluegrass that are tolerant of it (see page 14). Dollar spot, summer patch, and stripe smut are disease problems in the southern part of the state.

Soil Testing:
Agronomy Department
804 Bradfield Hall
Cornell University
Ithaca, NY 14853

Publications Office:
Mailing Room
Building 7, Research Park
Cornell University
Ithaca, NY 14853

NORTH CAROLINA

Soil and Climate: North Carolina divides into geographic thirds: the Blue Ridge Mountains, the Piedmont, and the Coastal Plain.

The abundant rainfall the state receives, combined with the natural soil, makes the soil acidic. Lime, in the form of natural ground limestone, is almost always necessary.

Recommended Grasses: In the west around Asheville and the entire area west of the Blue Ridge Mountains, use Kentucky bluegrass at high elevations. Use Bermudagrass, Kentucky bluegrass, tall fescue, or zoysiagrass, at low elevations.

For the Piedmont around Winston-Salem, Shelby, Hickory, and Eden, use Bermudagrass, tall fescue, or zoysiagrass. Centipedegrass can be grown in the warmest sections, Kentucky bluegrass in the coldest.

Along the Coastal Plain, use Bermudagrass, centipedegrass, or zoysiagrass in well-drained soil, and either carpetgrass or tall fescue in moist soil. Zoysiagrass and centipedegrass are best in light shade. St. Augustine grass is all right near the coast.

Soil Testing:
Agronomic Division
North Carolina Department of Agriculture
Raleigh, NC 27611

Publications Office:
Publications Office
Box 7603
North Carolina State University
Raleigh, NC 27695-7603

NORTH DAKOTA and SOUTH DAKOTA

Soil and Climate: The climate is semiarid and given to wide and rapid temperature fluctuation. The average rainfall is about 30 inches a year, and may fall gently or in heavy cloudbursts. Some western areas receive no more than 10 to 15 inches of rain a year.

The eastern edge of the Dakotas has a generally fertile loam soil, though it may vary in depth. To the west, soils are far more variable, ranging from poor to excellent.

Lime applications are rarely needed. Check soil amendment needs with a soil test.

Recommended Grasses: The short, native grasses are the natural vegetation of the northern Great Plains. Blue grama, buffalograss, wheatgrass, and others are hardy and adapted to the dry, harsh climate.

Most home lawns, however, are Kentucky bluegrass and fine fescue mixtures or blends.

Soil Testing:
Soil Testing Laboratory
Waldron Hall
North Dakota State University
Fargo, ND 58102

Soil Testing Laboratory
South Dakota State University
Brookings, SD 57007

Publications Offices:
Agricultural Communication Bulletin Room
Morrill Hall
North Dakota State University
Fargo, ND 58105

Agricultural Communications Office
Ag. Communications Center
South Dakota State University
Box 2231
Brookings, SD 57007

OHIO

Soil and Climate: Ohio is the most eastern of the lake states. As such, its climate is similar to the neighboring states of Illinois and Indiana. Summer temperatures are high. Most climate variation is determined by latitude.

Topographically, northwestern Ohio is flat and the southeast is hilly. This is because the northwest was previously covered by a lake that was much higher than Lake Erie. Probably the best soil in the state is in this northwestern section.

More specifically, along the southeast through Portsmith, Wheeling, and as far north as Youngstown the soil tends to be stony and thin. North-central soil is also stony, but the depth is more variable. The average statewide pH is 6.3; around Toledo the pH averages 6.5. These are nearly ideal conditions for growing Kentucky bluegrass.

Lime may be necessary; apply it only if soil test indicates.

Recommended Grasses: The most used Ohio lawn grass is Kentucky bluegrass. Use a blend of improved cultivars, such as 'Adelphi', 'Baron', 'Fylking', or 'Sydsport'.

Use fine fescues only in shaded, low-maintenance areas or in a mixture with Kentucky bluegrass.

Soil Testing:
Ohio Agricultural Research
  & Development Center
Research Extension Analytical Laboratory
Wooster, OH 44691

Publications Office:
Cooperative Extension Service
Publications Office, Room 4
2120 Fyffe Road
Columbus, OH 43210

OKLAHOMA

Soil and Climate: The climate of Oklahoma is continental—it has wide seasonal and geographic ranges in both temperature and rainfall.

Vast open plains make up the central and western sections. The western parts of the state are relatively cool and dry, while the east is hilly and the air moist, with frequent showers.

Rain is fairly frequent throughout most of the state, though much less so in the panhandle.

The average length of the growing season varies from 180 days in the western part of Cimarron County to 240 days in the southeast.

Droughts and dust storms sometimes occur in the western parts of the state, but are rarely damaging to lawns outside the panhandle.

Soil in the lowlands is the most fertile and is used extensively for agriculture. Soil in the uplands is similar to the soil of the Plains States.

Lime is usually required. Determine need by testing the soil. Use finely ground limestone.

Recommended Grasses: Bermudagrass is the most commonly used lawn grass. The common seeded cultivar is the most versatile, but some improved Bermudagrasses are also available.

The native buffalograss is well adapted to much of western Oklahoma. Buy seed that has been treated to prevent germination from being slow and irregular.

Soil Testing:
Soil Testing Laboratory
Agronomy Department
Oklahoma State University
Stillwater, OK 74074

Publications Office:
Central Mailing Service
Oklahoma State University
Cooperative Extension Office
Stillwater, OK 74074

OREGON

Soil and Climate: The soil in Oregon is usually fertile. Oregon has two climates. One, west of the Cascade Range, includes much of coastal Oregon and the great Willamette Valley. Here, it is mild and humid. The other climate, east of the Cascade Range, is not as humid, has colder winters, and has a shorter growing season.

Lime is necessary west of the Cascade Range, but probably not east of the Cascades.

Recommended Grasses: Cool-season grasses, such as Kentucky bluegrass, fine fescues, perennial ryegrass, and sometimes bentgrass, are typical for home lawns in Oregon. Most of the seed for these grasses is produced in the lawn-seed center of the Willamette Valley, which reaches from the Portland-Vancouver area south to Roseburg.

In the western part of the state, improved perennial ryegrass, which is sensitive to extreme cold, is favored. Annual bluegrass is a serious weed west of the Cascades. The best control is proper maintenance of the desired grasses. Diseases such as rust and red thread are also common problems.

Kentucky bluegrass is popular for home lawns in eastern Oregon. Gray snow mold can be a problem (see page 75).

Soil Testing:
Soil Testing Laboratory
Oregon State University
Corvallis, OR 97331

Publications Office:
Bulletin Mailing Service
Industrial Building
Oregon State University
Corvallis, OR 97331

PENNSYLVANIA

Soil and Climate: The main geographic features of Pennsylvania are the Appalachian Mountains and the somewhat lower Allegheny Mountains. The elevation changes and microclimates created by them are responsible for most climate distinctions. Two of the consistently coldest cities of Pennsylvania are Erie on the shore of Lake Erie and Wilkes-Barre in the Pocono Mountains. Summer rain is heavier in cities such as Philadelphia and Allentown that are near the Atlantic Ocean.

Soil along the Allegheny Plateau is mostly stony and thin. This includes the cities of Clearfield, Greensburg, and Indiana. The soil in Harrisburg and Scranton is mostly clay. The pH level varies throughout the state and should be checked. Lime is usually necessary in quantity. If soil test indicates the need, apply ground limestone in the fall.

Recommended Grasses: Kentucky bluegrass is the best adapted and most widely used lawn grass in Pennsylvania. Cultivars tested in and recommended for the state are: 'Adelphi', 'Baron', 'Columbia', 'Glade', 'Midnight', 'Sydsport', and 'Victa'.

Red fescue is used in mixtures in the cooler regions of western and northern Pennsylvania, especially where excessive shade is a problem.

Tall fescue is a tough lawn grass for the transitional climates of Pittsburgh and Philadelphia.

Soil Testing:
College of Agriculture
Pennsylvania State University
201 Agricultural Administration Building
University Park, PA 16802

Publications Office:
Agricultural Mailing Room
Agricultural Administration Building
University Park, PA 16802

SOUTH CAROLINA

Soil and Climate: The general climatic pattern is similar to that of North Carolina. However, the western mountains are not nearly as extensive, and the more southern latitude means that the climate is warmer.

South Carolina is divided into the Piedmont and the Coastal Plain. The border of the two regions is roughly from the eastern boundary of Aiken County, through central Chesterfield County, to the North Carolina border. The western edge of the Coastal Plain is known as the Sandhills.

On the average, rainfall is the heaviest in July and the lightest in November. Thunderstorms are frequent in the summer.

The shortest growing season in South Carolina is just under 200 days. Along the southern coast of the state, the growing season averages 300 days.

The soil of the Piedmont and Coastal Plain is essentially the same as that described for North Carolina.

Recommended Grasses: Bahiagrass is well adapted in the Sandhills vicinity of the state,

as well as in most of the rest of the South Carolina Coastal Plain.

Common Bermudagrass is one of the most widely used grasses. Improved types of Bermudagrass, such as 'Tifgreen' and 'Tifway', are often planted (see page 14).

Carpetgrass is useful where the soil is too wet or infertile for Bermudagrass, even though it does not make the most handsome lawn.

Centipedegrass is frequently used in the Piedmont, Sandhills, and Coastal Plains areas.

In sun or some shade, St. Augustine grass is best confined to the Coastal Plain.

Of the zoysiagrasses, 'Meyer' is the easiest to maintain, 'Emerald' is the most attractive, and manilagrass (*Zoysia matrella*) is the most widely adapted.

Tall fescue is the most heat tolerant of all the cool-season grasses.

Use annual ryegrass or a premium cool-season mixture to overseed dormant Bermudagrass.

Soil Testing:
H.P. Cooper Agricultural Service Lab
Clemson University
Cherry Road
Clemson, SC 29631

Publications Office:
Department of Agricultural Communications
Clemson University
Clemson, SC 29631

TENNESSEE

Soil and Climate: Tennessee is in a region that receives abundant rainfall—an average of 50 inches a year. As much as 80 inches has

been measured in some of the mountain areas. Even with such rainfall, summer droughts are common.

Tennessee topography is varied. The east is mostly mountains but has broad fertile valleys. These eastern valleys are similar to Maryland's Cumberland Valley and the Shenandoah Valley in Virginia. The soil here is derived from limestone, sandstone, and shale, and is quite productive.

The Central Basin is a large section of central Tennessee that has rolling hills to 800 feet high. It is surrounded by hills several hundred feet higher, called the Highland Rim. The Central Basin has rich limestone soil, the same kind as in the Kentucky bluegrass region of north-central Kentucky.

Lime is often necessary. Check lime and other soil amendment needs with a soil test.

Recommended Grasses: Kentucky bluegrass is widely adapted in Tennessee. Try cultivars such as 'Adelphi', 'Baron', 'Columbia', 'Sydsport', or 'Victa'.

Zoysiagrass and tall fescue are gaining in popularity.

Bermudagrass is the most drought resistant. It browns in winter, but is easily overseeded with ryegrass or any other cool-season grass. Improved Bermudagrass may perform well in certain regions of Tennessee.

Soil Testing:
Soil Testing Laboratory
University of Tennessee
Box 110019
Nashville, TN 37222-0019

Publications Office:
Agricultural Extension Service
University of Tennessee
Box 1071
Knoxville, TN 37901

TEXAS

Soil and Climate: Texas is so large and diverse that it has been divided into four climatic regions. The southeast has the Coastal Plains. This region extends from the coast to the Balcones Escarpment.

The north-central plains extend from the blacklands westward to the Great Plains.

The Great Plains extend downward from the north and northwest into Texas on the high ridge between the headwaters of the Canadian, Red, Brazos, and Colorado rivers.

The last division is called the Trans-Pecos Mountain Area; it is a plateau lying west of Pecos Valley.

The growing season averages 185 days in the northern panhandle and 230 days along the eastern and southern borders of the north-central divisions. From there to the coast, most of the counties have growing seasons over 300 days in length.

Rainfall averages over 50 inches in the east, but in the extreme west it averages less than 10 inches.

The soil varies to a similar degree. Most areas require generous amounts of organic matter. Lime is necessary in the eastern counties of the state.

Recommended Grasses: Common Bermudagrass and St. Augustine grass are the most widely used and practical warm-season grasses for Texas. Common Bermudagrass is the easiest to plant and care for. Improved kinds, such as 'Texturf 10' and 'Tifdwarf', are available. Drought tolerance is good and the lawn is relatively trouble free.

St. Augustine grass is not as cold hardy or drought tolerant as Bermudagrass; it should not be planted west or north of Ft. Worth. It grows satisfactorily east of an imaginary line from Vernon to Brady to Del Rio. 'Floratam', selected through a combined effort of Florida and Texas agricultural scientists, has good pest resistance. St. Augustine grass is sometimes confused with carpetgrass, which is rarely grown in Texas.

'Emerald' zoysiagrass is widely recommended for Texas. It is fine textured, dense growing, and dark green. Although manilagrass (*Zoysia matrella*) is fine textured, it is only recommended for the southern parts of the state. 'Meyer' zoysiagrass accepts cold weather well.

Buffalograss is occasionally used in areas of the north and west where irrigation water is scarce.

Centipedegrass is adapted to sandy, well-drained soil in east, south, and central Texas.

Tall fescue is a good lawn grass for north and west Texas. It requires watering, but makes a green lawn the year around. 'Adventure', 'Apache', 'Bonanza', 'Falcon', 'Jaguar', 'Olympic', and 'Rebel' are improved cultivars.

Soil Testing:
Texas Agricultural Extension Service
Texas A&M University
Soil Testing Laboratory
College Station, TX 77843

Publications Office:
Department of Agricultural Communications
Texas Agricultural Extension Service
Room 229D, Reed McDonald Building (2112)
Texas A&M University
College Station, TX 77843

UTAH

Soil: Most Utah soil is naturally low in organic matter. Around the Salt Lake area, the soil is usually a heavy clay. If it is hard packed because of a high sodium content, incorporating gypsum before planting improves tilth.

If iron chlorosis (yellowing) is a problem in your lawn, and regular fertilizing has no effect, try using ferrous ammonium sulfate (FAS) or other fertilizers or products that contain available iron.

Recommended Grasses: Kentucky bluegrass is planted the most often. Look for improved, low-growing cultivars. In shady areas, use cultivars that have demonstrated some tolerance of shade, such as 'Adelphi', 'Bensun', 'Columbia', 'Glade', 'Midnight', and 'Sydsport'.

The best time to start a Kentucky bluegrass lawn is in early spring, from March through April. Lawns can be planted during midsummer, but require frequent watering to compensate for the drying heat. Early fall, from September through mid-October, is the other good time to plant lawns.

Fertilize three to four times per year with a high-nitrogen fertilizer. Use 1 pound of actual nitrogen per 1,000 square feet. Make the first application in April, the second around Labor Day. For infertile soil, fertilizing in late May or June encourages a deep green growth. Fertilize again in the fall.

Fine fescues are widely used in the shade, and are usually mixed with Kentucky bluegrass.

Turf-type perennial ryegrass is not generally as cold tolerant as either Kentucky bluegrass or fine fescues. Some, however, such as 'Manhattan II' or 'Citation II', can be used in mixtures.

Toward the Arizona border, in towns such as St. George, Bermudagrass and other warm-season grasses are sometimes planted.

Soil Testing:
Soil, Plant & Water Analysis Laboratory
UMC 48
Utah State University
Logan, UT 84322

Publications Office:
Publications
UMC 50-B
Utah State University
Logan, UT 84322

VIRGINIA

Soil and Climate: Much of Virginia is in a transition zone where some kinds of both cool-season and warm-season grasses grow but where neither type is especially well adapted.

Lime is normally needed if the soil has not previously been limed. Apply lime as indicated by soil test results. One application lasts for at least three years and frequently much longer.

Recommended Grasses: West of the Blue Ridge Mountains and in the northern Piedmont area, cool-season grasses should be planted. They include Kentucky bluegrass, tall fescue, fine fescues, and turf-type perennial ryegrass.

Warm-season grasses, such as Bermudagrass and zoysiagrass, are best adapted in the southern Piedmont and much of the tidewater area (Quantico through Farmville to Danville). Improved Bermudagrasses, such as 'Midiron' and 'Tufcote', are best adapted for lawns.

Tall fescue makes a tough lawn and is a good compromise in a transitional area. It is the most extensively used species for lawns in this area. Newly developed turf-type cultivars, such as 'Adventure', 'Apache', 'Bonanza', 'Falcon', 'Jaguar', 'Olympic', and 'Rebel', have improved qualities over that of the former favorite, 'Kentucky 31'.

Soil Testing:
Soil Testing Laboratory
Cooperative Extension Service
Virginia Polytechnic Institute & State University
Blacksburg, VA 24061

Publications Office:
Bulletin Room
Extension Division
Virginia Polytechnic Institute & State University
Blacksburg, VA 24061

WASHINGTON

Soil: All Washington soil benefits from the addition of generous quantities of organic matter before planting.

In western Washington, lime is usually necessary for a good lawn. Have soil tested before planting. If an established lawn does not respond to fertilizer, lack of lime may be the problem.

Sulfur improves color and controls certain lawn weeds and diseases. It is available as gypsum or as a component of common fertilizers.

Recommended Grasses: Kentucky bluegrass, bentgrass, and fine fescues are commonly planted in Washington. Turf-type perennial ryegrass is a component of many seed mixtures and is sometimes used alone, particularly in the west.

Kentucky bluegrass is better adapted to eastern rather than western Washington, but with proper liming, fertilizing, mowing, and adequate drainage, it too makes a good lawn in the west. Cultivars that have done well include 'Adelphi', 'Challenger', 'Columbia', 'Eclipse', and 'Sydsport'. Bentgrass is adapted to the cool, acid soil of western Washington. It needs close mowing and occasional thatch removal.

'Astoria', 'Exeter', and 'Highland' are recommended cultivars of colonial bentgrass. Do not use bentgrass in a mixture with Kentucky bluegrass.

Turf-type perennial ryegrass germinates quickly and blends well with Kentucky bluegrass and fine fescues. It has good performance records throughout the state.

Sod webworms, billbugs, cutworms, and wireworms are common insect pests. See pages 65 to 72. Rust and red thread are common diseases. See pages 73 to 79.

Soil Testing:
Contact your county extension office for a local soil testing service.

Publications Office:
Bulletin Office
Cooper Publications Building
Cooperative Extension
Washington State University
Pullman, WA 99164-5912

WISCONSIN

Soil and Climate: Wisconsin winters are cold; the temperature has reached −40°F around Eau Claire and west-central parts of the state. In Milwaukee, the winters are warmer and the summers cooler due to the moderating influence of Lake Michigan. Summer thunderstorms are common. The wettest time of the year is from May through September.

Much of the soil in Wisconsin developed under an evergreen forest. Such soil is acidic and generally low in nutrients. It must be adequately limed and fertilized for proper lawn growth.

Recommended Grasses: Blends of three or more Kentucky bluegrass cultivars (see page 14) make a handsome, hardy Wisconsin lawn.

Use fine fescues in sandy, dry soil or in shady locations. Colonial bentgrass sometimes makes a good lawn (unmixed), especially along the lake shore.

Soil Testing:
Soil & Plant Analysis Laboratory
5711 Mineral Point Road
Madison, WI 53705

UWEX Soil & Forage Lab
8396 Yellowstone Drive
Marshfield, WI 54449

Publications Office:
University of Wisconsin
Department of Agricultural Journalism
Agricultural Bulletin Building
1535 Observatory Drive
Madison, WI 53706

EASTERN CANADA

Soil and Climate: This region includes the provinces of Manitoba, Nova Scotia, Ontario, and Quebec. Soil and climate specifics are essentially the same as the most northern states of the United States.

Lime is necessary in Nova Scotia and most of eastern Quebec, less so traveling westward. Use a soil test to be sure.

Recommended Grasses: A mixture of Kentucky bluegrass and creeping red fescue makes a good home lawn throughout most of eastern Canada.

Soil Testing:
Department of Soil Science
University of Manitoba
Winnipeg, Manitoba
Canada R3T 2N2

Soils & Crops Branch
Nova Scotia Agricultural College
Truro, Nova Scotia
Canada B2N 5E3

Agri-Food Laboratories
503 Imperial Road, Unit 1
Guelph, Ontario
Canada N1H 6T9

Publications Office:
Contact a research branch office of Agriculture Canada, a provincial agricultural representative, or a university plant science department for publications about lawns.

WESTERN CANADA

Soil: The soil is usually quite fertile. Lime is often a necessary additive to the soil along the coast of British Columbia. Check soil test results for appropriate amounts.

Recommended Grasses: Of the many grasses tested at the Sidney and Agassiz research stations, bentgrass, fine fescues, Kentucky bluegrass, and turf-type perennial ryegrass are the ones most often recommended for residents of coastal British Columbia.

Colonial bentgrass makes a lovely, fine-textured lawn. It thrives in cool, wet climates and is adapted to the heavy, moist soil found in Canada. It requires attention to certain maintenance practices, such as periodic dethatching and close mowing to remove thatch accumulation.

Fine fescues are also well adapted to coastal conditions. They tolerate shade and poor soil.

The new turf-type perennial ryegrasses, such as 'Citation II', 'Manhattan II', and 'Omega II', also grow well along the coast. Inland, they do not have the necessary winter hardiness.

Kentucky bluegrass is the primary lawn grass of interior parts of Canada. Generally, it does not do as well as bentgrass and fescue under coastal conditions. Seed or sod of red fescue and Kentucky bluegrass mixtures do best throughout central British Columbia and Alberta. Fertilizing in the late fall to stimulate new succulent growth tends to promote snow mold in most areas.

Soil Testing:
Soil Testing Unit
British Columbia Department of Agriculture
1873 Small Road
Kelowna, British Columbia
Canada V1Y 4R2

Soil & Feed Testing Laboratory
Room 905, O.S. Longman Building
6909 116th Street
Edmonton, Alberta
Canada T6H 4P2

Publications Offices:
Publications Office
Ministry of Agriculture & Food
Parliament Buildings
Victoria, British Columbia
Canada V8W 2Z7

Lawn Calendars

Temperatures, rather than strict calendar months, control the timetable of your lawn. Growth and maintenance depend largely on average monthly high and low temperatures. Other influencing factors are the average number of days in the growing season, average occurrences of first and last frosts, and average amounts of monthly rainfall. In checking the calendar for your region, keep in mind that conditions may vary slightly in your area.

The pages that follow contain lawn calendars for three large regions: the West, the Midwest/Northeast, and the South. Besides the growing season charts for each region, we have provided a monthly checklist for lawn maintenance chores. Check the illustrated map for the designated region for your state. Then, turn to the appropriate calendar to find out what to do each month for your lawn.

Lawn Calendar Map

| If you live in the West, check the lawn calendar on pages 102 to 103. | If you live in the Midwest or Northeast, check the lawn calendar on pages 104 to 105. | If you live in the South, check the lawn calendar on pages 105 to 106. |

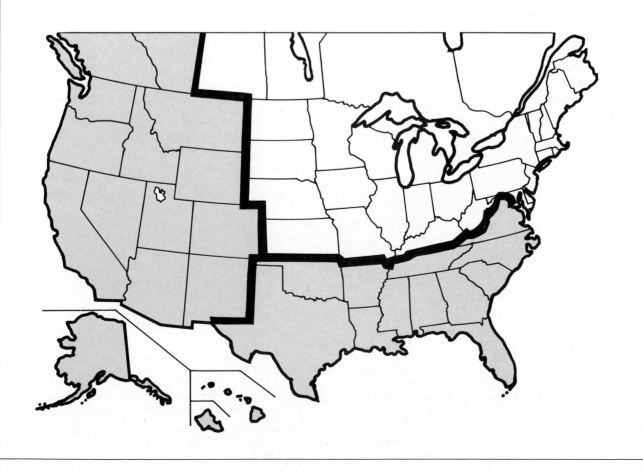

WESTERN REGION

January–February

Planting and Fertilizing: Where temperatures are favorable (Southern California and parts of Arizona), begin planting and fertilizing. See discussions for planting and fertilizing under the March–April section.

Weeding: Stop crabgrass before it starts. Timing is the critical factor in its control. A month before temperatures reach 65° F to 70° F, apply preemergence controls containing benefin, bensulide, or DCPA for four to five consecutive days. The time to do this is January to February in Southern California, late February or March in Northern California.

March–April

Fertilizing: Cool-season grasses are now growing in Southern California and are about to begin growing in the cool northern areas. Cool-season grasses begin to grow when temperatures are between 60° F and 90° F; their favorite range is 70° F to 75° F. Fertilizing a cool-season grass now gets it off to a good start, especially if you missed the important feeding last fall. Along with all that green top growth, your lawn is also sending out tillers, rhizomes, and stolons. The best growing months are just ahead.

Warm-season grasses now begin to stir from winter dormancy. Exactly when this happens depends on where you live. The first sign of new, green growth is the signal to fertilize and to start mowing. Fertilizing now helps a lawn to break winter dormancy earlier and gives it a head start on combatting vigorous weeds.

Do not fertilize an overseeded lawn for several weeks. It encourages the temporary cool-season grass to grow instead of your permanent warm-season grass.

Planting: Now is the second best time of year to plant a cool-season lawn (fall is best). Sow seed as soon as possible; the lawn will be established before hot weather arrives.

Dethatching: If thatch is a problem, now is a good time to do something about it. Bentgrass in particular tends to accumulate too much thatch. Rent a power rake or vertical cutter for medium to large lawns.

Mowing: If you overseeded your Bermudagrass lawn in the fall with annual ryegrass or another cool-season grass, start mowing low (less than 1 inch). This discourages the winter grass and lets in more light and warmth to the permanent lawn below.

Weeding: May is crabgrass time in many parts of the interior Northwest and in Rocky Mountain cities, so apply preemergence controls in April.

Look for broadleaf weeds. Blooming dandelions are the easiest to spot. Others that are just as troublesome, such as clover, chickweed, plantain, and spotted spurge, aren't far behind. Now is the time to control them. They are more vulnerable while they are young, and the weed killers formulated for their control work well in the cool weather of spring and fall.

Disease Control: Cool, damp weather increases the chances of leaf spot—a common disease of Kentucky bluegrass. Brown-gray spots appear on the grass blades and there is a general thinning of the lawn. Warm weather usually chases leaf spot away, but applying a fungicide prevents the chance of it getting worse.

May

Fertilizing: Fertilize cool-season grass again to keep the lawn green and vigorous. Generally, fertilizing a few times in the spring suffices. If heavy rains wash nutrients away, consider an extra application. Rocky Mountain cities still have plenty of spring planting weather left.

Planting: Warm weather and the hot summer ahead combine to make this the best time of year to plant dichondra, Bermudagrass, and other warm-season grasses in areas of the Southwest. These grasses are going strong when temperatures are 80° F to 90° F, while the cool-season types grow less. If Bermudagrass or young stages of annual bluegrass and crabgrass are in your dichondra lawn, you can apply dalapon, a selective grass killer, or apply a weed and fertilizer product designed for use on dichondra.

Dethatching: Thatch accumulation slows water and air penetration, harbors pests and diseases, and encourages shallow rooting of grasses. To dethatch, rent a vertical cutter or rake hard with a heavy steel rake. For warm-season grasses except dichondra, this

Growing Seasons

City	Days in Growing Season	Avg. Last Frost	Avg. First Frost
Albuquerque, NM	198	4/13	10/28
Anchorage, AK	118	5/18	9/13
Bakersfield, CA	277	2/21	11/25
Billings, MT	133	5/15	9/25
Boise, ID	177	4/23	10/17
Casper, WY	133	5/19	9/29
Centralia, WA	173	4/27	10/17
Denver, CO	171	4/26	10/14
Eugene, OR	205	4/14	11/4
Eureka, CA	328	1/26	12/20
Honolulu, HI	365	—	—
Las Vegas, NV	239	3/16	11/10
Medford, OR	161	5/3	11/14
Phoenix, AZ	295	2/14	12/6
Pasadena, CA	313	2/3	12/13
Pocatello, ID	161	4/28	10/6
Portland, OR	263	3/6	11/24
Provo, UT	171	4/26	10/14
Pueblo, CO	174	4/23	10/14
Reno, NV	155	5/8	10/10
Sacramento, CA	307	3/8	11/20
Salt Lake City, UT	192	4/13	10/22
San Diego, CA	365	—	—
San Jose, CA	299	2/10	12/6
Santa Barbara, CA	331	1/22	12/19
Spokane, WA	184	4/12	10/13
Tacoma, WA	250	3/13	11/18
Vancouver, WA	226	3/30	11/11

is best done during this month, just before the grass begins its most vigorous growth.

Disease Control: In all but the warmest areas, leaf spot may begin damaging your lawn this month.

Weeding: Weeds are now making an appearance in the Northwest and the Rocky Mountains. The yellow flowers of dandelions are the easiest to spot, but others are present that aren't as obvious (see March–April). Control spurge and other hard-to-kill weeds with 2,4-D or MCPP-dicamba combinations.

June

Fertilizing: Fertilize cool-season grass once more, especially if you live in the Rocky Mountains. During the summer, Kentucky bluegrass and other cool-season grasses make use of stored nutrients as heat arrives. If the lawn stays yellow in spite of fertilizing, there may be a shortage of iron.

Mowing: Set your mower ½ to 1 inch higher as temperatures increase. This is especially important with Kentucky bluegrass.

Weeding: If your lawn has crabgrass, you will begin to notice it this month. Various products are available for controlling it. Apply one of them as soon as you see the weed, when the soil is moist. For more information on crabgrass, see page 60.

Annual bluegrass may also show up this month. The unsightly seed stalks form no matter how low you mow. The whole plant may die out in hot weather, but the seeds remain to sprout when the weather cools. East of the Cascade Range in the Northwest, annual bluegrass isn't much of a problem, but west of the mountains to the Puget Sound area it is a real annoyance and is often a major component of a lawn. It is so well adapted to this area that it sometimes lives as a perennial. There is nothing preventive you can do at this time of year—wait until September.

Insect Control: Cutworms appear during late spring and early summer in dichondra lawns. These caterpillars thrive in hot weather and are most destructive in late summer and early fall. If you have had trouble with cutworms before, treat the lawn for them before they build up.

Sod webworms may become evident in cool northern and Rocky Mountain climates. The adult moths fly low across the lawn at dusk. Use a flashlight to check for night-feeding caterpillars—they hide deep in the grass during the day. You may have to repeat spraying monthly throughout hot weather as later generations move in.

July–August
Watering: Kentucky bluegrass and other cool-season grasses become semidormant in hot weather. In some hot areas, fertilizing won't help, but proper mowing and watering keep them attractive. Bermudagrass and dichondra are at their prime this month.

Insect Control: Flea beetles are one of the few insect problems you will have with dichondra, one other being cutworms. This beetle kills in patches as it tunnels through the grass. There

are even fewer problems with Bermudagrass; two possible pests are mites and billbugs.

Sod webworms may be a problem in California and Arizona. See June for a description of damage and control.

Grub damage is not restricted to one type of lawn. Because grubs chew off the roots, you can lift out dead patches of lawn, as you would a piece of sod. Control grubs now, not next spring when they are more mature. It may take three weeks to control mature grubs. Water thoroughly so that the chemicals filter down to the roots.

Disease Control: In the Northwest, watch out for the most common summer disease: brown patch. It favors hot, humid weather (60° F to 80° F). Suspect brown patch when brown circles, from several inches to several feet wide in diameter, appear in your lawn. A light case only injures top growth; a healthy lawn recovers in a few weeks. But if disease-favoring weather continues, so will brown patch, unless it is treated.

The relatively cool, dry weather of the mountain states keeps diseases to a minimum, though spells of humid weather may cause periodic problems. The best way to prevent disease is to maintain the lawn properly.

September
Planting and Fertilizing: This is the best season for planting and fertilizing cool-season grasses. In Arizona and California, wait for the cool nights of mid-September or soon afterward. A lawn that is fertilized at this time spends more energy on strengthening roots and less on top growth. The grass will be sturdier during the winter and get off to a better start in the spring. Although it is too late in the season to start a new lawn of dichondra or Bermudagrass, September is the time to fertilize established lawns.

Dethatching: September is a good month for vertical cutting. Besides removing thatch, you benefit your lawn by reducing conditions that favor moss. Your cool-season lawn will recover quickly during the months of good growing weather to come.

To prolong the growing season and green color of Bermudagrass, remove the thatch that has built up over the summer. Rake thatch out by hand or with a power machine. Afterward, be sure to fertilize and water well to aid recovery.

Weeding: Do something about the annual bluegrass that made your lawn unsightly in spring and summer. This year's crop of seeds will soon sprout. Before they do, lay down a seed barrier by using the same preemergence chemicals as you did for crabgrass in the spring. (See pages 58 to 64.)

October
Planting and Fertilizing: The good weather for planting and fertilizing cool-season grasses continues during this month.

Overseeding: In inland climates, where Bermudagrass stays dormant for three or more months, it makes good sense to overseed with annual ryegrass, fescue, or other cool-season grasses. First, rake out old thatch, mow extra low, and remove the grass clippings. Then sow the seed and keep the soil moist until the seed comes up. Fertilize any cool-season grass monthly and mow extra high (2 inches).

Weeding: Broadleaf weeds may come up in cool weather. Many kinds get started after fall rains in the Northwest and Rocky Mountain regions. As in the spring, herbicidal controls are most effective against young, vigorously-growing weeds.

November
Planting: Good planting weather continues in the Southwest for cool-season grasses, but plant soon to beat the rainy season.

Fertilizing: In most climates of the West there is still plenty of time left to fertilize one more time. Exceptions are areas with high altitudes and cold weather. Include lime now if a soil test indicates the need.

Disease Control: If snow mold attacked some areas of your lawn last spring in the Northwest and Rocky Mountain states, the disease organisms are probably still present and snow provides the necessary conditions to activate them. Grass infected with snow mold becomes white to pink or gray to black. Control it after the first frost, again during a midwinter thaw, and finally in the spring after the snow melts.

Red thread and fusarium patch are problems of cool, humid winters, even where there is no snow. Treat them while the weather is still wet.

MIDWEST AND NORTHEAST REGIONS

January–February

Disease Control: If you did not treat your lawn for disease the past fall, take advantage of the midwinter thaw to treat a lawn that showed damage from snow mold last spring.

March–April

Planting and Fertilizing: Second only to fall, spring is the best time to start a lawn. Cool-season grasses—Kentucky bluegrass, fescue, bentgrass, and ryegrass—find temperatures of 70° F to 75° F ideal for growth. If seeding is done when temperatures are favorable, lawns become established quickly, overcoming much of the competition from weeds and avoiding erosion from heavy spring rains. Begin planting and fertilizing now where temperatures are favorable for lawn growth, such as in Kentucky, West Virginia, and Maryland.

Sodding can be done any time during the growing season, though spring and fall are ideal for quick establishment.

If you missed the chance to fertilize your lawn last fall, make sure you do it this spring as soon as temperatures reach about 60° F.

Rolling: If you live in an area where the ground is still frozen or covered with light snow, seeds that are already planted will begin to sprout as soon as temperatures rise. After the spring thaw, roll fall-seeded lawns and areas raised by frost with a roller half filled with water.

Dethatching: Thatch slows air and water penetration, harbors pests and diseases, and slows growth by insulating the grass roots and crowns against warming spring temperatures. Your lawn will recover in a short time from dethatching when temperatures are above 70° F and the grass is growing vigorously. For adequate absorption, dethatch before applying preemergence herbicides. For more information, see pages 81 to 82.

Aerating: Early spring is a fine time to perform this chore. Aerating opens up the soil, providing roots with more water and air. If done prior to fertilizing, nutrients will reach the root zone quickly for spring green-up.

Weeding: You can do your lawn a big favor if it was bothered by crabgrass last summer. Crabgrass seeds left over from last year will start to sprout when temperatures reach 65° F to 70° F for four to five consecutive days. You can stop these seeds from coming up by applying a preemergence barrier *before* seeds germinate. Timing is important. If you plan to do any spring seeding, use a product containing siduron. This herbicide will not harm germinating grass seed.

Blooming dandelions are a sure sign of weeds, but other broadleaf weeds that aren't as obvious can be just as troublesome, plantain and knotweed among others. There are two good reasons to control them now. First, they are most susceptible to herbicides when young and actively growing. And second, the weed killers developed for their control work efficiently in warm weather.

Insect Control: As the soil warms up, grubs move up to the root zone from deep winter burrows. Treat them with an insecticide such as diazinon. Be patient; insecticides move slowly through the root zone. Follow label directions carefully.

Disease Control: The cool, moist weather of spring favors the development of several diseases. Leaf spot is a problem for bluegrass. Look for it in fall as well as spring. A healthy lawn will usually make a strong comeback as the weather warms.

Stripe-smut symptoms are the most pronounced during early to late spring, and again during similar fall weather. Symptoms are almost nonexistent during midsummer. Dollar spot can occur anytime from now until late summer, especially when temperatures go into the 80s and humidity is high.

May

Fertilizing: If you think heavy rains have washed out nutrients, now is the time for a second application of fertilizer. If you applied fertilizer heavily in the fall, May is the time to apply fertilizer again. Fertilize zoysiagrass and Bermudagrass as they begin to green. Their best growing period is just ahead, so fertilizing early speeds recovery from winter dormancy. This head start also helps to prevent weed growth.

Planting: When temperatures reach the mid-70s, sprigging and plugging weather has arrived in areas where

Growing Seasons

City	Days in Growing Season	Avg. Last Frost	Avg. First Frost
Albany, NY	169	4/27	10/13
Bismarck, ND	136	5/11	9/24
Boston, MA	192	4/16	10/25
Burlington, VT	148	5/8	10/3
Charleston, WV	193	4/18	10/28
Cincinnati, OH	192	4/15	10/25
Concord, NH	142	5/11	9/30
Detroit, MI	182	4/21	10/20
Duluth, MN	125	5/22	9/24
Evansville, IN	216	4/2	11/4
Grand Rapids, MI	190	4/23	10/30
Green Bay, WI	161	5/6	10/13
Hartford, CT	180	4/22	10/19
Louisville, KY	220	4/1	11/7
Marquette, ME	159	5/13	10/19
Minneapolis/ St. Paul, MN	166	4/30	10/13
North Platte, NE	160	4/30	10/7
Peoria, IL	181	4/22	10/20
Pittsburgh, PA	187	4/20	10/23
Providence, RI	197	4/13	10/27
Sioux City, IA	169	4/27	10/13
Sioux Falls, SD	152	5/5	10/3
Springfield, IL	186	4/20	10/23
Springfield, MO	201	4/12	10/30
Topeka, KS	200	4/9	10/26
Trenton, NJ	211	4/8	11/5
Washington, DC	200	4/10	10/28

Bermudagrass and zoysiagrass are adapted. The hot weather ahead makes this the best time of year to plant these grasses.

Overseeding: If you have overseeded your Bermudagrass lawn (zoysiagrass does not lend itself well to this practice), now is the time to discourage the winter grass. Start mowing low—less than 1 inch—to allow warmth and light to reach the Bermudagrass.

June

Fertilizing: Any fertilizing should be done early in the month, before your cool-season grass begins to go dormant. During dormancy, grasses live off of stored nutrients, manufacturing little. Continue fertilizing Bermudagrass and zoysiagrass throughout the growing season, until temperatures fall below 70° F and your lawn begins to grow slowly.

Weeding: If you did not treat your lawn with a preemergence herbicide in the spring, crabgrass should be evident in your lawn by now. Various sprays are available for the selective control of crabgrass. Apply one of them as soon as you notice any crabgrass in the lawn, keeping the soil sufficiently moist.

Insect Control: This month sod webworms may begin to cause irregular brown patches in the lawn. You will probably see the adult moths fluttering close to the lawn at dusk. Actually, it is the night-feeding larvae that do the damage. Armyworms also appear in the summer. They are about twice as large as webworms and feed on the grass in broad daylight.

Chinch bugs are especially bad in warm, dry weather in the Northeast. Discovering them is the first step toward controlling them (see page 67). Hunt near the damaged area. Hatching often occurs during the first weeks of June and August.

Disease Control: Leaf spot continues to be a problem in southern areas of the Midwest and Northeast. Brown patch is severe in hot weather. High humidity and temperatures between 60° F and 80° F are favorable for its development.

July–August
Watering: It is the nature of cool-season grasses to go dormant in the summer. Some people like it that way, but if you want to keep your lawn green, see page 82 for instructions.

Fertilizing: July and August are not the best months to fertilize cool-season grasses. Warm-season Bermudagrass and zoysiagrass, however, are growing most vigorously and may require additional nutrients.

Planting: From the middle of August to the middle of September is one of the best times to reseed an old lawn or plant a new one. The summer heat quickens sprouting time, and the cool weather that is soon to follow relieves you of frequent watering.

Disease Control: A light case of brown patch can injure top growth, but the lawn should recover in a few weeks if temperatures drop. If hot, disease-favoring weather continues, so will brown patch, and chemical control may be necessary.

Insect Control: In the Northeast, the small, black-and-red chinch bug may have hatched a second generation, so be on the lookout.

In midsummer, adult beetles lay their eggs in the lawn. The tiny, white grubs that hatch from these eggs feed near the surface until the first cold spell arrives. Then they burrow more than a foot deep into the ground for overwintering. Control is most effective on surface-feeding, young grubs.

Weeding: Continue to treat crabgrass as it appears.

September
Cool nights bring few problems with lawn care. Cool-season grasses take on new life after the hard times of summer.

Weeding: Now is a good time to begin controlling vigorously growing broadleaf weeds. Young weeds are the most susceptible to chemical control. Chemicals designed for weed control work best in warm, not hot, weather.

Planting and Dethatching: The year's best planting weather continues into this month. As established grasses perk up, consider the chore of removing thatch, especially since the favorable weather ensures quick recovery.

Overseeding: Overseed Bermudagrass this month; the cooling weather favors germination and development of winter grass and discourages further growth of the Bermudagrass.

Mow first, then rake and mow again, removing the clippings. Rake seeds into the lawn and keep moist until they come up.

Fertilizing and Liming: Discover the results of applying fertilizer in the fall. A lawn fed now spends less effort on top growth, more on building up roots. The result is a lawn that is sturdier for winter and that makes a stronger start next spring.

Lime applied in the fall is washed by rains down into the soil, where it is needed. Winter freezing and thawing further help the process.

Disease Control: Look for leaf spot on Kentucky bluegrass. As in the spring, it is the cool, moist weather that favors its development. See page 75 for control.

October–November
Planting and Fertilizing: Where weather permits, the opportunities of last month—planting, fertilizing, and killing weeds—carry over into at least the first half of October.

Disease Control: If snow mold gave you trouble last spring, take precautions in November so that it won't return. The disease organisms are still present; snow supplies the moisture to activate them. Crusted patches of mold form on infected grass that appear white to pink or gray to black. Control once after the first frost (sometime in midwinter) when there is no snow on the ground, and again after the snow melts next spring.

Lawns in the Midwest and Northeast usually receive abundant rainfall. Watch for lawn problems from poor drainage and too much shade, such as mushrooms, moss, and algae.

January–February

Weeding: In areas of the South where weather warms up early, apply pre-emergence controls for crabgrass, spurweed, and annual bluegrass about one month before seeds germinate (see more information on crabgrass control under the March–April section). You can also spot-treat wild garlic as it emerges with 2,4-D or other recommended chemicals.

Fertilizing: In the warmest areas of the South, where a lawn may stay green all year long, grasses such as Bermudagrass, bahiagrass, St. Augustine grass, and zoysiagrass can benefit from the boost they will get from fertilizing early.

Insect Control: If it is warm enough to apply fertilizer where you live, then grubs that overwintered in the soil should be approaching the surface of the soil, where they can be controlled. Get rid of them now if you missed the chance last fall.

March–April

Watch for the first signs of green growth as Bermudagrass, St. Augustine grass, centipedegrass, carpetgrass, or bahiagrass begin to grow faster. Grass can begin to appear as early as January or February in the mildest climates, but may not show until April in the upper areas of the South. When spring does arrive, a temperature of about 70° F signals the opening of the lawn season.

Mowing: Set your mower to cut just above the new grass blades to expose new growth to more light and to warm the soil. If you had a temporary winter lawn of ryegrass or fescue, low mowing discourages its growth and gives your permanent warm-season lawn a chance to take over. For more information on mowing, see pages 49 to 52.

Fertilizing: Some but not all warm-season grasses require fertilizer at this time. Fertilize a lawn of Bermudagrass or St. Augustine grass if you did not feed it last month. During April, fertilize both carpetgrass and centipedegrass. Cool-season grasses such as Kentucky bluegrass, fescue, and ryegrass require fertilizing in the spring if you did not apply fertilizer heavily in the fall.

Along with the green top growth, tillers, stolons, and rhizomes develop rapidly in the rush of spring growth.

Patching: Repair winter damage with pieces of sod, sprigs, or plugs. You may want to use seed if your lawn is bahiagrass or a cool-season grass.

Sodding: Sodding is a practice that can be done anytime during the growing season, although it is normally done in spring and fall.

Weeding: Do your lawn a favor if crabgrass or annual bluegrass was a problem last summer. Seeds left over from last year will sprout when temperatures reach 65° F to 70° F continually for four to five days. To stop their germination, use a preemergence barrier a month before seeds are due to germinate. This should be in February in the mildest areas, in mid-March in the Coastal Plain, and the end of March in the upper South. Use a pre-emergence chemical such as siduron if you plan to do any spring seeding. It kills crabgrass but not most lawn seeds. Read the label to be sure.

Disease Control: The cool, moist weather of spring favors the development of several fungus diseases. Cottony blight on ryegrass and leaf spot are among those present now and again in the fall. Dollar spot can occur anytime until late summer, especially with high humidity and temperatures that exceed 80° F. (See diseases, beginning on page 73.)

May

Planting: Warming weather makes May and June prime months for planting a warm-season grass lawn. You can plant as late as July, but later plantings may not have time to establish before cooler weather begins. It is all right to start common Bermudagrass lawns from seed, but improved Bermudagrass, St. Augustine grass, and most of the other warm-season grasses should be started vegetatively. Be sure to control weeds, so that the lawn can establish quickly without competition for light, water, and nutrients.

Dethatching: Scrutinize established lawns for the build up of thatch—particularly in Bermudagrass and St. Augustine grass. Thatch blocks out air and water, and fosters pests and diseases. Thin it out with a heavy rake if

Growing Seasons

City	Days in Growing Season	Avg. Last Frost	Avg. First Frost
Atlanta, GA	244	3/15	11/14
Augusta, GA	260	3/8	11/17
Baltimore, MD	234	3/20	11/12
Birmingham, AL	241	3/15	11/13
Charleston, SC	294	3/1	11/10
Corpus Christi, TX	335	1/12	12/20
Dallas, TX	249	3/17	11/22
Jackson, MS	248	3/10	11/13
Knoxville, TN	220	3/30	11/8
Little Rock, AR	244	3/10	11/11
Lubbock, TX	205	4/10	10/30
Memphis, TN	237	3/15	11/7
Miami, FL	365	—	—
New Orleans, LA	302	2/10	12/10
Norfolk, VA	254	3/15	11/24
Raleigh, NC	237	3/17	11/12
Roanoke, VA	187	4/15	10/15
Savannah, GA	291	2/24	12/6
Shreveport, LA	272	3/1	12/3
Tulsa, OK	216	3/30	10/30

the area is small, rent a power rake (renovator), or hire a lawn service company for large lawns.

Fertilizing: This month fertilize warm-season grasses, except carpetgrass and centipedegrass. If a lawn stays yellow in spite of fertilizer applications, it may be short of iron. This condition, common to centipedegrass and other southern grasses, such as bluegrass, fescue, or ryegrass, can be corrected by spraying with a solution containing extra iron. Warm-season grasses will grow well before the hot weather of summer slows them down.

Weeding: Blooming dandelions are a sure sign of weeds, but plantain, sheep sorrel, and many others are less obvious and just as troublesome. Most weeds grow well at 70° F and are vulnerable to herbicides while still young. In addition, weed killers are the most effective in warm, but not hot, weather. If tough-to-kill weeds, such as oxalis and spotted spurge, are pestering your lawn, see pages 58 to 64 for directions on their control.

June

Watering: Lawns that have received the right care should be masterpieces this month, though cool-season lawns begin to slump with the onset of hot weather (proper watering will help keep them looking their best).

Fertilizing: Bermudagrass and zoysiagrass need fertilizer this month. Bluegrass, fescue, and ryegrass remain slow growing until fall brings cooling weather.

Insect Control: Chinch bugs are a fact of life with St. Augustine grass. The bugs thrive in the sunniest, driest spots of the lawn. Infested patches turn yellow, then brown. Make this test to be sure that the problem is caused by chinch bugs: Starting near the edge of the damaged area, push a bottomless can down into the lawn; keep it filled with water for about five minutes. If chinch bugs are there, they will float to the surface. Treat the whole lawn; chinch bugs spread rapidly.

Another likely June pest is the sod webworm. You will probably notice the adult moths first—fluttering close to the lawn at dusk and laying their eggs. Two weeks later, the worms hatch and start feeding on grass blades at night. To confirm their presence, examine dead patches for larvae. Look for them during the day; they curl up in the thatch of the turf.

Armyworms also feed on lawns. They are twice as big as webworms and feed in broad daylight. Control is the same as for sod webworms. It is best to apply any of these insecticides in the late afternoon or evening.

Weeding: If you have crabgrass in your lawn, it has grown enough to be noticeable by now. You can stop adolescent and mature growth with post-emergence annual grass controls.

Other grassy weeds become prominent this month. Dallisgrass and nutsedge are hard to get rid of and may require monthly applications for control. In June, you may also notice annual bluegrass. It is light green and pretty enough in spring, but when hot weather comes it goes to seed and dies in unsightly patches. There is not much you can do about it now. Wait until August and September.

July–August

Hot weather calls for some changes in your lawn maintenance routine as detailed below.

Fertilizing: Continue fertilizing as needed for your type of lawn. Bermudagrass and zoysiagrass favor being

With the long growing season in most southern states, warm-season lawns may stay green all year long. Give your lawn enough water, nutrients, and care to keep it at its best.

fertilized in both July and August. Bahiagrass, carpetgrass, centipedegrass, and St. Augustine grass can skip the August application. Beware: Overfertilizing favors sod webworms and armyworms.

Insect Control: Keep watching for sod webworms and chinch bugs. (See description in June.)

Mowing: Raise mowing height to provide more shade for roots. This is important if you want to keep a cool-season grass from going dormant.

Watering: Watering is the most important job during these hot months. How much watering you do depends on soil type and climate, but the general rules of watering deeply and infrequently hold true under most conditions.

Disease Control: The most likely summer lawn disease is brown patch. Warm, humid weather favors its development. To keep it from spreading, especially if the warmth and humidity continue, mow, rake, fertilize and water the lawn thoroughly. Good maintenance is usually an adequate safeguard against brown patch.

During warm, rainy periods, gray leaf spot may appear on St. Augustine grass. (See page 75.)

September

Continue summer routines, even as the weather cools—fertilizing, controlling chinch bugs and sod webworms, and preventing disease.

Fertilizing: It is particularly important to continue regular fertilizing—the last feeding of the year (except in the Deep South) is an important one for bahiagrass, carpetgrass, centipedegrass, and St. Augustine grass. Bermudagrass can also take another dose. For Kentucky bluegrass, fescue, and ryegrass, the months ahead are

the most important times of the year to fertilize—these grasses are building up root systems and storing reserves, while producing less top growth than they did in the spring.

Planting: September is the best time of year to start a cool-season lawn. Warm temperatures germinate seeds and, with the coming of cool weather and fall rains, you will have to do less watering and the lawn will establish quickly.

Weeding: Now is the chance to begin a campaign against annual bluegrass by preventing seeds from sprouting this fall. Early this month, apply a pre-emergence herbicide labeled for this purpose. Apply it again next spring.

Disease Control: You may have a continuing battle with brown patch on St. Augustine grass. Treat appropriately. (See July–August.)

October–November

Fertilizing: In early fall, fertilize bahiagrass, Bermudagrass, St. Augustine grass, and zoysiagrass one last time to build strength for the winter, to develop a vigorous root system, and to help get it off to a fast start early in the spring. This is the most important feeding of the year for a cool-season lawn.

Overseeding: If your Bermudagrass lawn becomes dormant in the upper South, you may want to overseed with ryegrass or fescue. Rake the lawn and mow closely before seeding. Sow seeds and keep moist until germination. An alternative is to color the lawn (see page 82).

Weeding: The return of cool weather gives you another try at eradicating broadleaf weeds. Many kinds start out in the fall and are at their most vulnerable stage. Herbicides for broadleaf weeds work best in warm weather.

Appendix

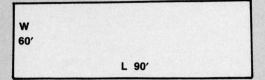

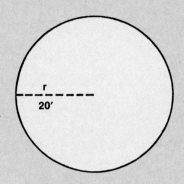

Square or Rectangle
Area = LW
L = Length
W = Width
A = 90′ × 60′
A = 5,400 square feet

Circle
Area = πr^2
π = 3.14
r = Radius
A = 3.14 × 20′ × 20′
A = 1,256 square feet

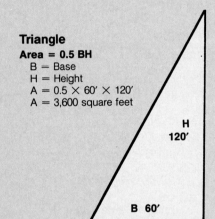

Triangle
Area = 0.5 BH
B = Base
H = Height
A = 0.5 × 60′ × 120′
A = 3,600 square feet

Unusual Shapes
Make calculations by sections and total them.

In this example, calculate these areas and add figures together:

Area of triangle
Area of rectangle
One-half area of circle
TOTAL = square feet in area

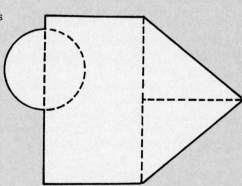

Irregular Shapes
(within 5% accuracy)
Measure a long (L) axis of the area. Every 10 feet along the length line, measure the width at right angles to the length line. Total widths and multiply by 10.

Area = (A_1A_2 + B_1B_2 + C_1C_2 etc.) × 10

A = (40′ + 60′ + 32′) × 10
A = 132′ × 10′
A = 1,320 square feet

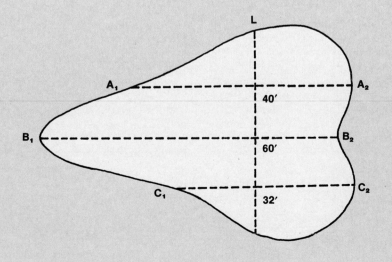

Some Common Lawn Chemicals

Chemical Name	Trade Name*	Herbicide	Insecticide	Fungicide
Acephate	Orthene®		•	
Anilazine	Dyrene®			•
Atrazine	AAtrex®	•		
Benefin	Balan®	•		
Benomyl	Benlate®			•
Bensulide	Betasan®	•		
Cacodylic Acid	Phytar® 560	•		
CAMA		•		
Captan	Orthocide®			•
Carbaryl	Sevin®		•	
Chloroneb	Terraneb® SP			•
Chlorothalonil	Daconil® 2787			•
Chlorpyrifos	Dursban®		•	
Cycloheximide	Acti-dione®			•
Dalapon	Dowpon®	•		
DCPA	Dacthal®	•		
Diazinon	Spectracide®		•	
Dicamba	Banvel®	•		
Dicofol	Kelthane®		•	
Etridiazole	Koban®			•
Fenarimol	Rubigan®			•
Glyphosate	Kleenup®; Roundup®	•		
Iprodione	Chipco® 26019			•
Isofenphos	Oftanol®		•	
MAMA		•		
Mancozeb	Dithane® M-45			•
Maneb	Dithane® M-22			•
MCPP	Mecoprop	•		
Metalaxyl	Subdue®			•
Metaldehyde	Halizan™		•	
Metam	Vapam®	•		
Methiocarb	Mesurol®		•	
Methoxyclor	Marlate®		•	
MSMA	Ansar® 170	•		
NPD	Aspon®		•	
Oxadiazon	Ronstar®	•		
PCNB	Terraclor®			•
Pendimenthalin	Prowl®	•		
Propamocarb	Banol®			•
Propoxur	Baygon®		•	
Siduron	Tupersan®	•		
Thiophanates	Topsin®			•
Thiram	Spotrete™			•
Triadimefon	Bayleton®			•
Trichlorfon	Dylox®		•	
2,4-D	Weed-B-Gon®	•		
2,4-DP		•		

*This is only a partial list. Chemicals are available in many combinations under several trade names.

KLEENUP, ORTHENE, ORTHOCIDE, WEED-B-GON—Reg.TMs of Chevron Chemical Co. DYRENE—Reg. TM of Mobay Chemical Corp. ASPON, BETASAN, VAPAM—Reg. TMs of Stauffer Chemical Co. AATREX, SPECTRACIDE, SUBDUE—Reg. TMs of Ciba-Geigy Corp. BALAN, RUBIGAN—Reg. TMs of Eli Lilly & Co. BENLATE, MARLATE, SPOTRETE, TUPERSAN—TMs of E.I. DuPont de Nemours & Co. ANSAR, PHYTAR—Reg. TM of Ansul Co. SEVIN—Reg. TM of Union Carbide Corp. TERRANEB—Reg. TM of Kincaid Enterprises, Inc. DACONIL, DACTHAL—Reg. TMs of Diamond Shamrock Corp. DOWPON, DURSBAN—Reg. TMs of Dow Chemical Co. ACTI-DIONE, BANOL—Reg. TMs of Upjohn Co. KOBAN—Reg. TM of Mallinckrodt Chemical Works. CHIPCO, RONSTAR—Reg. TM of Rhone-Poulenc Inc. BAYGON, BAYLETON, DYLOX, OFTANOL—Reg. TMs of Bayer AG. DITHANE, KELTHANE—Reg. TM of Rohm & Haas Co. PROWL—Reg. TM of American Cyanamid. TOPSIN—Reg. TM of Nippon Soda Co., Ltd. ROUNDUP—Reg. TM of Monsanto Co. BANVEL—Reg. TM of Velsicol Chemical Corp. HALIZAN—TM of Tamogan Ltd. TERRACLOR—Reg. TM of Olin Mathieson Chem. Corp.

Index

Page numbers in *italics* refer to illustrations.

A

Acephate, 65, 109
Agropyron cristatum. See Fairway wheatgrass
Agrostis palustris. See Bentgrass, creeping
Algae, 78, *78*
Ammophila brevilgulata. See Beachgrass, American
Anilazine, 73, 109
Annual weeds, defined, 58
Ants, 71, *71*
Armyworms, 65, 66, *66*, 105, 107
Atrazine, 58, 109

B

Bacillus thuringensis, 65
Bahiagrass (*Paspalum notatum*), 11, *11*
 dethatching, 81
 fertilizing, 11, 56, 105, 107
 mowing height, 11, 49
 pests of, 11, 65, 69
 planting method, 33
 seed facts, 28
 as warm-season grass, 7, 11
Barnyardgrass, preemergence herbicide for, 59
Beachgrass, American (*Ammophila brevilgulata*), 18
Beggarweed, postemergence herbicide for, 59
Benefin, 58, 102, 109
Benomyl, 73, 109
Bensulide, 58, 102, 109
Bentgrass, creeping (*Agrostis palustris*), 8, *8*
 as cool-season grass, 7, 8
 diseases of, 8, 74–78
 fertilizing, 8, 56
 as fine textured, 26
 herbicide cautions, 58, 59
 mower type for, 50
 mowing height, 8, 49
 pests of, 66, 67
 planting, 32, 104
 seed facts, 28
 as weed, 77
 in western region, 102–3
Bermudagrass, common (*Cynodon dactylon*), 12, *12*
 coloring, 82
 dethatching, 81
 diseases of, 74, 75, 76
 fertilizing, 12, 56, 104, 105, 106, 107
 as fine textured, 26
 germination, 28, *29*
 mowing, 12, 49, 50
 overseeding, 82, 102, 104, 105, 107
 for paving-block lawn, 34
 pest control, 103
 pests of, 66, 67, 69, 71, 72
 planting methods, 32, 33, 106
 planting times, 102, 104, 106
 plugging, 33
 popularity of, 25
 seed facts, 28

 southern region calendar, 106–7
 sprigging, 32, 35
 as warm-season grass, 7, 12
 weed control, 59
Bermudagrass, common (*Cynodon dactylon*), as weed, 27, 59, *59*, 77, 84
 in dichondra, 102
 timing control, 106
Bermudagrass, improved (*Cynodon* species), 12, *12*
 cultivars, 14
 fertilizing, 12, 56
 mowing, 12, 49
 pests of, 66, 72
 planting, 32, 106
Bermudagrass mites, 71, *71*
Billbugs, 67, *67*, 103
Bindweed (*Convovulus arvensis*), 27
Biological controls, 65
Blood meal, 53
Blue grama (*Bouteloua gracilis*), 7, 18, 28
Bluegrass, annual (*Poa annua*), as weed, 27, 59, *59*, 77
 timing controls, 102, 103, 106, 107
Bluegrass, Kentucky (*Poa pratensis*), 9, *9*
 'Adelphi', 14, 75, 77
 'Arboretum', 77
 'A-34', 14, 77
 'Birka', 14, 76
 'Challenger', 15, 75
 'Columbia', 15, 77
 as cool-season grass, 7, 9
 cultivars, 8, 14–15
 'Delta', 75
 diseases of, 74–78, 102, 105
 'Eclipse', 15, 75
 'Enmundi', 77
 fertilizing, 9, 56, 106, 107
 as fine textured, 26
 'Fylking', 15, 77
 germination, 28, *29*
 'Glade', 15, 76, 77
 Improved, 49, 74, 75, 76
 'Kenblue', 15, 75
 'Merion', 8, *29*
 'Midnight', 15, 75
 mowing, 9, 49, 103
 'Nugget', 15, 76
 'Parade', 15, 77
 'Park', 15, 75, 77
 'Pennstar', 77
 pests of, 67, 68
 planting times, 104
 popularity of, 25
 seed facts, 25, 28
 in seed mixtures, 27
 'Sydsport', 15, 77
Bluegrass, rough (*Poa trivialis*), 9, *9*
 as fine textured, 26
 mowing height, 49
 nitrogen requirements, 56
Bouteloua gracilis. See Blue grama
Brown patch, 74, *74*
 fungicides for, 73
 preventing, 107
 susceptible times, 103, 105, 107
Buffalograss (*Buchloe dactyloides*), 18
 climate for, 7
 mowing height, 49
 seed facts, 28
Bunch grasses, described, 6
Burclover (*Medicago hispida*), 60, *60*

C

Cacodylic acid, 59, 109
Calcium requirements, 53
CAMA, 59, 109
Canada thistle (*Cirsium arvense*), 27
Captan, 73, 109
Carbaryl, 65, 109
Carpetgrass
 fertilizing, 106, 107
 mowing height, 49
 planting methods, 33
 seed facts, 28
Caterpillars, 65
Centipedegrass (*Eremochloa ophiuroides*), 12, *12*
 brown patch attacks, 74
 dethatching, 81
 fertilizing, 12, 56, 106, 107
 iron deficiency in, 79
 mowing height, 49
 pests of, 65, 69, 72
 planting methods, 33
 plugging, 33
 preemergence herbicide for, 58
 seed facts, 28
 as warm-season grass, 7, 12
Centipedes, 72, *72*
Cheeseweed (*Malva* species), 62, *62*
Chemical burn, 54, 78, *78*
Chemicals, lawn, 109
 See also Fungicides; Herbicides; Insecticides
Chickweed, 58, 59
Chiggers, 71, *71*
Chinch bugs, 65, 67, *67*, 105, 107
Chloroneb, 73, 109
Chlorothalonil, 73, 109
Chlorpyrifos, 65, 109
Choosing a lawn grass, 5–19
 buying seed, 25–28
 climate factors, 7, 19
 comparisons, 19
 insect problems, 65
 regional recommendations, 87–100
 shade tolerance, 19, 80
Clay soil, 22, 23, 42
Climate
 comparisons, 19
 lawn calendars by, 101–7
 regional variations, 87–107
 turfgrass climate map, 7
 watering frequency and, 42
Clover, white (*Trifolium repens*), 64, *64*
 postemergence herbicide for, 59
Clover mites, 67, *67*
Cold tolerance, compared, 19
Colorants, 82
Compost, 23, 24. *See also* Organic matter
Concrete paving blocks, 34, *34*
Cool-season grasses, 7
 clippings, 50
 dethatching, 82
 fertilizing, 53, 55–56, 73, 105, 106
 mowing frequency, 49
 overseeding with, 82, 102, 103, 104, 105, 107
 planting times, 102, 103, 104, 105, 107
 preventing summer dryness damage, 79
 thatch builders, 81
 types, 8–11

 typhula blight attacks, 78
 in western region, 102–3
Cottony blight. *See* Pythium blight
Crabgrass (*Digitaria* species), 58, 60, *60*
 herbicides for, 59
 timing controls, 102–7
Crane flies, 68, *68*
Creeping grasses, 6
 thatch builders, 81
Crickets, 71, *71*
Cultural problems. *See* Diseases and cultural problems
Cutworms, 66, *66*, 103
Cycloheximide, 73, 109
Cynodon species. *See* Bermudagrass entries

D

Dalapon, 59, 102, 109
Dallisgrass (*Paspalum dilatatum*), 60, *60*, 107
Damping off, 73, 74, *74*
Dandelion (*Taraxacum officinale*), 58, 60, *60*, 104, 106
DCPA, 58, 102, 109
Dethatching, 81–82
 before renovation, 84
 timing, 102–6
 watering efficiency and, 44
Devilgrass. *See* Bermudagrass, common, as weed
Diazinon, 65, 109
Dicamba, 59, 102, 109
Dichondra (*Dichondra micrantha*), 13, *13*
 DCPA warning, 58
 diseases of, 13, 58
 mowing height, 13, 49
 nitrogen requirements, 56
 pest control, 103
 pests of, 13, 65, 72
 planting, 102
 seed facts, 28
 weed control, 59, 102
Dichondra flea beetles, 72, *72*
Dicofol, 67, 109
Diethyltoluamide, 71
Diseases and cultural problems, 41, 73–79
 preventing, 73
 thatch and, 81
 timing controls, 102–7
Dock (*Rumex* species), 61, *61*
Dodder (*Cuscuta* species), 27
Dog urine, chemical burn from, 78
Dollar spot, 73, 74, *74*, 104, 106
Dolomitic limestone, 24
Drainage problems, 23, 73, 78
Drought
 damage, 79, *79*
 tolerance, compared, 19
 watering during, 44

E

Earthworms, 68, *68*
Earwigs, 65, 71, *71*
Edgers, 83
English daisy (*Bellis perennis*), 61, *61*
Etridiazole, 73, 109

F

Fairway wheatgrass (*Agropyron cristatum*), 18
Fairy ring, 74, *74*
Fenarimol, 73, 109

Fertilizer, 53–55
 burn from, 54, 78
 combined with pesticides, 54–55
Fertilizing, 41, 53–57
 amounts, 19, 55
 importance of, 53
 insects and, 65
 before installing lawn, 24, 36
 methods, 56–57
 mowing frequency and, 49
 nutrient requirements, 53, 56
 after overseeding, 102
 as problem cause, 54, 73, 74, 78, 107
 before renovation, 85
 requirements compared, 19
 timing, 53, 54, 55–56, 73, 102–7
 trees in lawns, 80
 watering efficiency and, 44
 for weed control, 58
 worksheet, 56
Fescue, chewings (*Festuca rubra* var. *commutata*), 9, *9*
 See also Fescue, fine
 cultivars, 15, 16
 fertilizing, 9, 56
 mowing height, 9, 49
 'Shadow', 16, 76
Fescue, fine
 See also Fescue, chewings; Fescue, hard; Fescue, red or creeping red
 cultivars, 15–16
 disease resistance, 10, 76, 78
 disease susceptibility, 74, 75
 fertilizing, 106, 107
 as fine textured, 26
 germination, 28, *29*
 for overseeding, 82
 oxadiazon warning, 59
 planting times, 104
 popularity of, 25
 seed facts, 25, 28
 in seed mixtures, 27
Fescue, hard (*Festuca ovina* var. *duriuscula*), 10, *10*
 See also Fescue, fine
 'Aurora', 15, 76
 cultivars, 15, 16
 disease resistance, 10, 76
 fertilizing, 10, 56
 mowing height, 10, 49
 'Reliant', 16, 76
Fescue, red or creeping red (*Festuca rubra rubra*), 10, *10*
 See also Fescue, fine
 cultivars, 15, 16
 fertilizing, 10, 56
 'Flyer', 16, 76
 'Fortress', 16, *29*, 76
 germination, *29*
 mowing height, 10, 49
 red thread attacks, 76
Fescue, tall (*Festuca arundinacea*), 10, *10*
 'Alta', 16, 80
 brown patch attacks, 74
 cultivar chart, 16–17
 cultivars, 8, 16–17
 disease resistance, 78
 disease susceptibility, 74, 75, 76, 77
 fertilizing, 10, 56, 106, 107
 lawn tree caution, 80
 mowing height, 10, 49
 for paving-block lawn, 34
 planting times, 104

popularity of, 25
seed facts, 28
Fescue, tall (*Festuca elatior*), as weed, 59, 63, *63*
Fiery skippers, 66, *66*
Flea beetles, 72, *72*, 103
Fleas, 71, *71*
Fluorescence, 28
Foxtail, 59
Fungicides, 73, 109
in fertilizers, 54–55
Fusarium patch, 73, 75, *75*, 103
fungicides for, 73
timing control, 103

G
Gasoline spills, 78, 83
Germination, 26–27, 28
Glyphosate, 23, 59, 109
Gnats, 71, *71*
Goosegrass, herbicide for, 59
Gophers, 70, *70*
Grading
changing grade, 83
final grade, 24
before installing lawn, 23, 24
before renovation, 85
before sodding, 35, 36
around trees, 80
Grass clippings, 50
Grasses, 6, 7, 18. *See also* Choosing a lawn grass; Cool-season grasses; Warm-season grasses
Grasshoppers, 72, *72*
Gray leaf spot, 73, 75, *75*, 107
Gray snow mold. *See* Typhula blight
Grease spot. *See* Pythium blight
Greenbugs, 65, 68, *68*
Ground bark, 23, 24. *See also* Organic matter
Ground covers, 18, 80. *See also* Dichondra
Ground limestone, 24
Ground pearl, 72, *72*
Growing seasons, 102, 104, 106
Growth regulators, 49
Grubs, 65, 69, *69*
insecticides for, 65
moles or gophers and, 70
timing controls, 103, 104, 105

H
Henbit (*Lamium amplexicaule*), 61, *61*
Herbicides, 58–59, 109
chemical burn from, 78
for existing weeds, 59
in fertilizers, 54–55
grass clippings caution, 50
before installing lawn, 23, 58–59
postemergence, 58, 59
preemergence, 58–59, 102
before reseeding, 84
timing application, 106
Herbicide spills, 78, 83
Hole punching (aeration), 82
Hose repair, *43*
Hoses, 43
Hydroseeding, 21, *21*

I
Insecticides, 65, 109
Insects. *See* Pests; Pest control
Installing a lawn, 21–39
border, 23, *23*

establishment time, 35
measuring area, 23
preparation steps, 21–24, 30
seed, 25–31
sod, 35–39
sprigs or plugs, 32–34
timing, 102–7
around trees, 80
weed control, 23, 58–59
Iprodione, 73, 109
Iron deficiency, 79, *79*
correcting, 106
as problem cause, 53, 55, 73
Isofenphos, 65, 109

J
Japanese beetles, 65
Johnsongrass (*Sorghum halepense*), 27

K
Knotweed (*Polygonum aviculare*), 59, 61, *61*, 104

L
Lawn calendars, 101–7
Lawn colorants, 82
Lawn equipment, 83
aerator, 82, *82*, 83, 85
edgers, 83
renovator, 106
rollers, 83
sod cutters, 83
vertical cutters, 81, 82, 83, 84
Lawn mowers. *See* Mowers
Lawn seed. *See* Seed
Lawn stripes, *54*
Leafhoppers, 65, 69, *69*
Leaf spot, 75, *75*
fungicides for, 73
susceptible time, 104, 105, 106
western region calendar, 102
Leafy spurge (*Euphorbia esula*), 27
Leveling the seedbed, 30
Liming soil, 24, 105
Loam soil, 22, 42
Lolium species. *See Ryegrass entries*

M
Magnesium requirements, 53
Mallow (*Malva* species), 62, *62*
MAMA, 59, 109
Mancozeb, 73, 109
Maneb, 73, 109
Manganese deficiency, 53
Manure, 23, 24, 53. *See also* Organic matter
MCPP, 59, 102, 109
Measuring a lawn, 23, 108
Melting out. *See* Leaf spot
Metalaxyl, 73, 109
Metaldehyde, 65, 109
Metam, 23, 58, 109
Methiocarb, 65, 109
Methoxyclor, 65, 109
Methyl bromide, 23, 58
Micronutrient requirements, 53
Milky spore disease, 65
Millipedes, 72, *72*
Mites
Bermudagrass, 71, *71*
clover, 67, *67*
timing control, 103
Mole crickets, 65, 69, *69*
Moles, 70, *70*
Moss and algae, 78, *78*

Mouse-ear chickweed (*Cerastium vulgatum*), 62, *62*
Mowers, 50–52, 83
for dethatching, 81
dull, lawn injury from, 79
safety tips, 52
Mowing, 41, 49–52
frequency, 49
height, 19, 44, 49
hints, 52
new lawns, 49–50
as problem cause, 73
after sodding, 35
timing, 102–7
for weed control, 58
MSMA, 59, 109
Mugwort, herbicide for, 59
Mulching
with grass clippings as, 50
under lawn trees, 80
after seeding, 31
Mushrooms, 79, *79*

N
Native grasses, 18
Necrotic ring spot, 73, 77, *77*
Nematodes, 70, *70*
Nitrogen
fertilizer types and, 54, 55
from grass clippings, 50
requirements, 56
role of, 53
Nitrogen deficiency, 53, 79, *79*
from fresh organic matter, 23
red thread from, 76
"Nitrogen draft," 23
Nitrogen excess, 53, 78
Northern native grasses, 18
Noxious weeds, listed, 27
NPD, 65, 109
Nuisance pests, 71
Nursegrass, 27
Nutsedge, 107

O
Oil spills, 78
Ophiobolus patch. *See* Take-all patch
Organic arsenicals, 59
Organic fertilizers, 53–54
Organic matter
fairy ring from, 74
importance of, 22
before installing lawn, 23–24
mushrooms from, 79, *79*
roller for, 83
Overfertilizing, 73, 74, 78, 107
Overseeding, 82, 102, 103, 104, 105, 107
Overwatering, 53, 74
Oxadiazon, 59, 109
Oxalis (*Oxalis* species), 59, 62, *62*

P
Patching lawns, 82–83, 106
Paving-block lawns, 34, *34*
PCNB, 73, 109
Pearl scale, 72, *72*
Peat moss, 23, 24. *See also* Organic matter
Pendimenthalin, 59, 109
Perennial sowthistle (*Sonchus arvensis*), 27
Perennial weeds, defined, 58
Periodical cicadas, 72, *72*
Pest control, 65–72
See also specific pests
chemicals, 65
while fertilizing, 54–55
methods, 66
timing, 103–7

Pests
diagnosing, 65, 66–72
nuisance, 71
occasional, 71–72
thatch and, 81
Phosphorus, 24, 53, 54
Pillbugs, 72, *72*
Pink patch. *See* Red thread
Pink snow mold. *See* Fusarium patch
Plantain (*Plantago* species), 62, *62*, 104, 106
Planting methods
paving-block lawns, 34
plugs, 32, 33–34
seed, 25–31
sod, 35–39
sprigs, 32–33
Plugging patches, 82–83
Plug lawns, 32, *33*
establishment time, 35
first mowings, 49–50
installing, 33–34, *34*
Poa pratensis. See Bluegrass, Kentucky
Poa trivialis. See Bluegrass, rough
Postemergence herbicides, 58
Potassium, 53, 54, 55
Powdery mildew, 73, 76, *76*
Preemergence herbicides, 58–59
timing applications, 102, 103, 104, 106, 107
Propamocarb, 73, 109
Propoxur, 65, 109
Purslane (*Portulaca oleracea*), 58, 63, *63*
Pythium blight (Cottony blight), 73, 76, *76*, 106

Q
Quackgrass (*Agropyron repens*), 27, 63, *63*

R
Raking
after aerating, 85
after dethatching, 84
after mowing, 50
before seeding, 30
thatch, 81
Red sorrel, herbicide for, 59
Red thread, 73, 76, *76*, 103
Regional lawn calendars, 102–7
Renovating lawns, 81–85
buying seed, 25
timing, 105
under trees, 80
weed control before, 59, 84
Renovator, 106
Rollers, 83
Rolling the lawn
before installation, 24
after seeding, 30, 104
after sodding, 39
after plugging, 33
after sprigging, 32, 33
Rough grading, 23
Russian knapweed (*Centaurea picris*), 27
Rust, 73, 76, *76*
Ryegrass
See also Ryegrass, annual or Italian; Ryegrass, turf-type perennial
as cool-season grass, 7, 11
cottony blight susceptibility, 106
popularity of, 25
Ryegrass, annual or Italian (*Lolium multiflorum*), 11, *11*

See also Ryegrass
diseases of, 74, 75, 76, 78
fertilizing, 11, 106, 107
fluorescence, 28
mowing height, 11, 49
nitrogen requirements, 56
for overseeding, 82
planting times, 104
seed facts, 28
Ryegrass, turf-type perennial (*Lolium perenne*), 11, *11*
See also Ryegrass
as "crisis grass," 8
cultivars, 8, 17–18
disease resistance, 74, 76
disease susceptibility, 74, 75, 76, 77
fertilizing, 11, 56, 106, 107
as fine textured, 26
germination, 28, *29*
'Manhattan', 17, *29*
mowing height, 11, 49
nitrogen requirements, 56
for overseeding, 82
planting times, 104
seed facts, 28
in seed mixtures, 8, 27
for under trees, 80

S
SAD (St. Augustine Grass Decline), 77, *77*
St. Augustine grass (*Stenotaphrum secundatum*), 13, *13*
dethatching, 81
diseases of, 13, 74, 107
fertilizing, 13, 56, 106, 107
'Floralawn', 77
'Floratam', 13, 67, 77
mowing height, 13, 49
pests of, 65, 67, 69, 107
planting methods, 33, 106
planting times, 106
plug establishment time, 35
'Raleigh', 77
'Roselawn', 75
SAD virus, 13, 77, *77*
'Seville', 77
'Tamlawn', 75, 77
for under trees, 80
as warm-season grass, 7, 13
weed control, 58, 59
Sandy soil, 22, 42
Sawdust, 23, 24, 31. *See also* Organic matter
Scalping, 52, 79
Sedges, 58
Seed, 25–28
blends, 28
mixtures, 26, 27–28
ratings, 28
sowing, 30
straights, 27
watering, 28, 30
Seeding, 31
See also Seed; Seed lawns
drop spreaders for, 57
hydroseeding, 21, *21*
overseeding, 82
patches, 82–83
reseeding, 83–85
Seed lawns
See also Seed; Seeding
damping off, 74, *74*
establishment times, 19, 35
first mowings, 49–50
germination percentages, 26–27, 28
germination times, 28
installing, 25–31
postseeding care, 28
Seed meals, 53

Sewage sludge, 53
Shade-tolerant grasses, 19, 80
Sheep sorrel, 106
Shredding sprigs, 32–33
Siduron, 59, 104, 106, 109
Slopes
  laying sod on, 35
  mower types for, 50, 52
  mowing problems, 52
  seeding on, 31
Slow-release fertilizers, 54
Snails and slugs, 65, 70, *70*
Snow mold, 103, 104, 105. *See also* Fusarium patch; Typhula blight
Sod, described, 35
Sod cutters, 81, 83
Sodding, 35–39
  patches, 82–83, *83*
  timing, 104, 106
Sod lawns
  buying sod, 35
  establishment time, 35
  first mowings, 49–50
  soil importance for, 21–22
Sod webworms, 71, *71*
  diagnosing, 71, 107
  insecticides for, 65
  susceptible times, 107
  timing controls, 103, 105
Soil aeration, 82, *82*
  before renovation, 85
  for thatch control, 82
  timing, 104
  watering efficiency and, 44
Soil aerators, 83, 85
Soil amendments, 23–24
Soil compaction, 22, 73, 79, 82
Soil fumigation, 23, 58
Soil moisture testers, 42
Soil penetrants, 80
Soil pH, 24, 53
Soil preparation, 21–24
  before sodding, 35, 36
  weed control, 58–59
Soil sulfur, 24
Soil testing, 22, 85
  state soil-testing offices *See chart, page 87*
Soil types, 22
Sowbugs, 72, *72*
Sowthistle, perennial (*Sonchus arvensis*), 27
Speedwell. *See* Veronica
Spills, 78
  patching after, 82–83
Spittlebugs, 72, *72*
Sprayers, 56, *57*
Spreaders, 56–57, *57*
Sprig lawns, 32, *32*
  establishment time, 35
  first mowings, 49–50
  installing, 32–33, *33*
  patches, 82–83
Sprinkler systems, 44–48
  timing installation, 24
  types of sprinklers, 45, *45*, 46–47, *47*
Spurge, spotted (*Euphorbia maculata*), 63, *63*, 102
Spurweed, 106
Stenotaphrum secundatum. *See* St. Augustine grass
Stolonizing, 19, 32–33
Stolons, 6
Straw, 23, 24, 31
Stripe smut, 73, 77, *77*, 104
Sulfur, 24, 53
Summer dryness, 79, *79*
Summer patch, 73, 77, *77*
Syringing, 43

T

Take-all patch, 78, *78*
Thatch, 81, *81*
  from grass clippings, 50
  mowing height and, 49
  as problem cause, 71, 73, 74
  removing, 52, 81–82
  soil aeration and, 82
Thiophanates, 73, 109
Thiram, 73, 109
Thistle (*Cirsium* species), 27, 64, *64*
Ticks, 71, *71*
Trees, 23, 73, 80
Triadimefon, 73, 109
Trichlorfon, 65, 109
2,4-D, 59, 109
  on grass clippings, 50
  timing application, 102
2,4-DP, 59, 109
Typhula blight, 73, 78, *78*

V

Veronica (*Veronica filiformis*), 64, *64*
Vertical cutters, 81, 83, 84
  for overseeding, 82
  for shredding soil cores, 85

W

Warm-season grasses, 7
  clippings, 50
  dethatching time, 82
  fertilizing, 53, 56, 106
  mole crickets attack, 69
  mowing frequency, 49
  overcoming winter dormancy, 82
  planting, 33, 102, 106
  regional care calendars, 102–7
  temperature tolerance comparison, 19
  thatch builders, 81
  types, 11–13
Watering, 41, 42–48
  amount, 42–43
  compacted soil and, 44
  during drought, 44
  fertilizing and, 44
  frequency, 42
  for heat stress, 43
  hoses, 43
  increasing efficiency, 44
  insects and, 65
  measuring distribution, *44*, 44–45
  mowing height and, 44
  new lawns, 44
  as problem cause, 73, 79
  after reseeding, 85
  after seeding, 28, 31
  when sodding, 35, 36, 37, 39
  sprinkler systems, 44–48
  syringing, 43
  thatch and, 44, 81
  time of day for, 43
  under trees, 80
  for weed control, 58
Water-insoluble nitrogen (W.I.N.), 54
Wearability, lawn grasses compared, 19
Webworms. *See* Sod webworms
Weed control, 41, 58–64
  existing weeds, 59
  before installing lawn, 23
  before planting, 58–59
  postemergence herbicides, 59
  preemergence herbicides, 58–59
  before renovation, 84
  timing, 102–7
  weed-and-feed products, 54–55
Weeds, 58–64
  in grass clipping mulch, 50
  noxious, listed, 27
  types of, 58
  winter, fertilizing timing and, 56
Weed seeds, in lawn seed, 27
Wetting agents, 80
Wheatgrass, fairway (*Agropyron cristatum*), 18
White clover (*Trifolium repens*), 64, *64*
Whitetop, 27
Wild garlic, 64, *64*, 106
Wild onion, 64, *64*
Winter dormancy, overcoming, 82
Wireworms, 65, 72, *72*

Y

Yellowing, causes for, 53, 55, 79, 106

Z

Zoysiagrass (*Zoysia* species), 13, *13*
  coloring, 82
  dethatching, 81
  diseases of, 74, 75, 76
  fertilizing, 13, 56, 104, 105, 106, 107
  mowing, 13, 49, 50
  pests of, 13, 67, 69
  planting methods, 33
  planting times, 104
  plugging, 33
  preemergence herbicide for, 58
  sprigging, 32
  for under trees, 80
  as warm-season grass, 7, 13

U.S. MEASURE AND METRIC MEASURE CONVERSION CHART

	Symbol	Formulas for Exact Measures: When you know:	Multiply by	To find:	Rounded Measures for Quick Reference		
Mass (Weight)	oz	ounces	28.35	grams	1 oz		= 30 g
	lb	pounds	0.45	kilograms	4 oz		= 115 g
	g	grams	0.035	ounces	8 oz		= 225 g
	kg	kilograms	2.2	pounds	16 oz	= 1 lb	= 450 g
					32 oz	= 2 lb	= 900 g
					36 oz	= 2¼ lb	= 1,000 g (1 kg)
Volume	tsp	teaspoons	5.0	milliliters	¼ tsp	= 1/24 oz	= 1 ml
	tbsp	tablespoons	15.0	milliliters	½ tsp	= 1/12 oz	= 2 ml
	fl oz	fluid ounces	29.57	milliliters	1 tsp	= ⅙ oz	= 5 ml
	c	cups	0.24	liters	1 tbsp	= ½ oz	= 15 ml
	pt	pints	0.47	liters	1 c	= 8 oz	= 250 ml
	qt	quarts	0.95	liters	2 c (1 pt)	= 16 oz	= 500 ml
	gal	gallons	3.785	liters	4 c (1 qt)	= 32 oz	= 1 l.
	ml	milliters	0.034	fluid ounces	4 qt (1 gal)	= 128 oz	= 3¾ l.
Length	in.	inches	2.54	centimeters	⅜ in.	= 1 cm	
	ft	feet	30.48	centimeters	1 in.	= 2.5 cm	
	yd	yards	0.9144	meters	2 in.	= 5 cm	
	mi	miles	1.609	kilometers	2½ in.	= 6.5 cm	
	km	kilometers	0.621	miles	12 in. (1 ft)	= 30 cm	
	m	meters	1.094	yards	1 yd	= 90 cm	
	cm	centimeters	0.39	inches	100 ft	= 30 m	
					1 mi	= 1.6 km	
Temperature	° F	Fahrenheit	5/9 (after subtracting 32)	Celsius	32° F	= 0° C	
					68 °F	= 20° C	
	° C	Celsius	9/5 (then add 32)	Fahrenheit	212° F	= 100° C	
Area	in.^{2}	square inches	6.452	square centimeters	1 in.^{2}	= 6.5 cm^2	
	ft^2	square feet	929.0	square centimeters	1 ft^2	= 930 cm^2	
	yd^2	square yards	8,361.0	square centimeters	1 yd^2	= 8,360 cm^2	
	a	acres	0.4047	hectares	1 a	= 4,050 m^2	